THE DINNER PARTY COOK BOOK

A recipe collection for all occasions

THE DINNER PARTY COOK BOOK

*A recipe collection
for all occasions*

Edited by

HILAIRE WALDEN

THUNDER BAY
P·R·E·S·S

Published in the United States by
Thunder Bay Press
An imprint of the Advantage Publishers Group
5880 Oberlin Drive, San Diego, CA 92121-4794
www.advantagebooksonline.com

1 2 3 4 5   00 01 02 03 04

All correspondence concerning the content of this volume should be addressed to
Salamander Books Ltd.

ISBN 1-57145-285-0

Library of Congress Cataloging-in-Publication Data available.

CREDITS

Project managed by Stella Caldwell
Editorial Consultant: Hilaire Walden
Typeset by SX Composing DTP
Printed in Spain

CONTENTS

INTRODUCTION

AS ANY COOK KNOWS, preparing a meal that friends and family eat with relish brings great pleasure. Taking a little trouble to choose dishes that will suit the occasion and have specific appeal to your guests will make all the difference to any gathering. From stylish dinner parties and the cocktail 'do' to informal get-togethers, *The Dinner Party Cook Book* is a comprehensive and imaginative collection of recipes from around the world providing everything you need to put together the perfect menu.

The book is divided into six sections: Salads, Soups, Starters, Main Courses, Desserts and Baking, and Drinks and Cocktails. All levels of cooking expertise are catered for and an inventive range of recipes accommodates every taste and budget. If you're looking to create a theme around a meal such as Thai or Greek, the diverse cuisine range covered will provide plenty of ideas. Some of the dishes require a little time and skill, while others can be achieved with the minimum of effort. Recipes catering for special dietary requirements such as vegetarian, vegan or low fat are also included, making this book the ideal source for any cook.

The Dinner Party Cook Book is a fully accessible volume which removes the need to search through countless cookery books and old magazine clippings, and allows the host or hostess time to relax. With color photographs to accompany each dish, and illustrated step-by-step instructions demonstrating key techniques, this book will prove an inspiring addition to every kitchen.

SALADS

TROPICAL SALAD

3 pink grapefruit
1 large papaya
3 avocados
3 tablespoons olive oil
2 teaspoons pink peppercorns, lightly crushed
salt

Cut rind from pink grapefruit, removing white pith at the same time. Hold grapefruit over a bowl to catch juice and cut between membranes to remove segments.

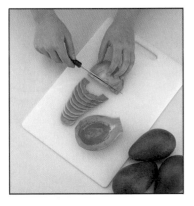

Peel papaya, cut in half and scoop out seeds with a teaspoon. Cut flesh into thin slices. Halve avocados lengthwise, remove pits and peel. Cut flesh into thin slices.

Arrange grapefruit segments, papaya slices and avocado slices on serving plates. Mix together 2 teaspoons reserved grapefruit juice, the olive oil, crushed peppercorns and salt. Drizzle over fruit and serve at once.

Serves 6.

TUNISIAN ORANGE SALAD

6 small oranges
1 fennel bulb
1 red onion
1 tablespoon cumin seeds
1 teaspoon coarsely ground black pepper
1 tablespoon chopped fresh mint
6 tablespoons olive oil
fresh mint sprigs and black olives, to serve

Cut the peel off the oranges, removing all the pith. Thinly slice the oranges, catching any juice

Cut the fennel in half and slice it thinly. Slice the onion thinly. Arrange the orange, fennel and onion slices in a dish, sprinkling each layer with cumin seeds, black pepper, mint and olive oil. Drizzle the reserved orange juice over.

Leave the salad to marinate in a cool place for 1-2 hours. Just before serving, scatter the salad with mint sprigs and black olives.

Serves 6.

Note: Leaving the salad to marinate for up to 2 hours allows the flavors to develop and the onion to soften. However, do not leave the salad for longer than this before serving.

EGGPLANT & OLIVE SALAD

GREEN PAPAYA SALAD

1 lb eggplant, diced
salt
10 tablespoons light olive oil
2 onions, chopped
1 clove garlic, chopped
4 sticks celery, sliced
2 small zucchini, sliced
1 tablespoon chopped fresh rosemary
14 oz can chopped plum tomatoes
1 tablespoon sun-dried tomato paste
2 teaspoons sugar
3 fl oz/⅓ cup red wine vinegar
6 oz pitted mixed olives, halved
2 tablespoons capers in wine vinegar, drained
salt and freshly ground black pepper
fresh Italian parsley sprigs to garnish

1 small unripe green papaya, peeled and thinly
  shredded
1 large or 2 small carrots, peeled and thinly
  shredded
salt and freshly ground black pepper
few lettuce leaves
1 tablespoon crushed roasted peanuts, to garnish
DRESSING:
1 clove garlic, chopped
1 shallot, chopped
2 small red or green chilies, seeded and chopped
1 tablespoon dried shrimps, soaked and rinsed
2 tablespoon sugar
3 tablespoons lime juice or vinegar
2 tablespoons fish sauce

Put eggplant in a colander; sprinkle with
plenty of salt and leave to drain for 30-40
minutes. Rinse thoroughly to remove salt,
drain and pat dry on absorbent kitchen
paper. Heat 4 tablespoons of the oil, in a skillet over a high heat. Add eggplant and fry for
4-5 minutes until evenly browned. Transfer
eggplants to absorbent kitchen paper. Heat
remaining oil in a large skillet. Sir in onions
and garlic and fry gently for 5 minutes to
soften.

Mix the shredded papaya and carrot with salt
and pepper. Arrange a bed of lettuce leaves
on a serving dish and pile the papaya and
carrot on top. Using a pestle and mortar,
pound the garlic, shallot, chilies, shrimps
and sugar to a fine paste. Blend with the lime
juice or vinegar and the fish sauce to make
the dressing.

Add celery, zucchini and rosemary and cook
for a further 5 minutes. Stir in tomatoes, sun-
dried tomato paste, sugar and vinegar and
cook, stirring frequently, for 10 minutes until
vinegar has evaporated. Transfer to a serving
dish. Set aside to cool, then add reserved
eggplant, olives and capers. Season with salt
and freshly ground black pepper and toss
well. Chill. Serve garnished with Italian
parsley sprigs.

Serves 4-6.

Garnish the salad with the crushed peanuts
and pour the dressing all over it. Do not toss
or mix the salad until at the table and ready
to serve.

Serves 4-6.

Note: This salad can be served either as a
starter or as a side dish with main courses.

SNOW PEA SALAD

1 lb snow peas
2 fl oz/¼ cup olive oil
juice ½ lemon
salt and freshly ground black pepper
1 clove garlic
1 tablespoon chopped fresh cilantro
1 tablespoon chopped fresh mint
lemon rind strips, to garnish

Top and tail snow peas. In a large saucepan, heat 1 tablespoon oil, add snow peas and stir to coat with oil.

Add enough water to cover snow peas. Bring to the boil, cover and cook for about 5 minutes until snow peas are just cooked and still have a slight crunch. Drain and return to pan.

Pour lemon juice and remaining oil over snow peas. Add salt and pepper and mix well. Turn into a serving dish and leave to cool. Before serving, chop garlic finely and scatter over snowpeas with cilantro and mint; garnish with lemon rind.

Serves 4-6.

ROAST VEGETABLE SALAD

1 large eggplant
4 zucchini
1 yellow and 2 red bell peppers
2 small fennel bulbs
12 cherry tomatoes
2 cloves garlic, crushed
2 teaspoons pesto
4 fl oz/½ cup olive oil
1 teaspoon coarse sea salt
1 tablespoon lemon juice
freshly ground black pepper
basil sprigs, to garnish

Preheat oven to 400F (200C). Slice eggplant and cut into chunks. Cut zucchini into chunks.

Quarter peppers and remove cores and seeds. Trim fennel, cut lengthwise into quarters and slice. Cut a cross in the bottom of each tomato. In a bowl, mix together garlic, pesto and olive oil. Arrange vegetables in a large, heavy roasting pan. Pour over pesto mixture and toss vegetables to coat. Sprinkle with sea salt.

Put in oven and roast for 45 minutes, or until vegetables are browned and tender. Drizzle over lemon juice and season with black pepper. Leave in pan until tepid or cold. Garnish with basil sprigs and serve.

Serves 6.

BELL PEPPER & ANCHOVY SALAD

SUMMER SALAD

3 large red and 3 large yellow bell peppers
2½ fl oz/⅓ cup olive oil or olive oil and sunflower oil mixed
1 tablespoon wine or balsamic vinegar
salt and freshly ground pepper
2 oz can anchovies, drained, rinsed and chopped
4 oz black olives, pitted
3-4 tablespoons chopped fresh parsley
2 hard-cooked eggs

Preheat oven to 475F (240C). Place peppers in a large roasting pan and roast in oven for 20-30 minutes until they begin to char, turning once.

Remove peppers from the oven and place in a polythene bag, closing tightly. Leave for 10 minutes, then remove them from the bag and scrape off the skins. Pull out the stalks and the seeds should come with them. Halve peppers, scrape out any remaining seeds then cut the flesh into wide strips. Put oil, vinegar, salt and pepper, anchovies, olives and parsley into a large bowl and mix well. Add peppers and toss to coat thoroughly.

Halve eggs and remove yolks. Roughly chop whites and scatter them over the peppers. Sieve the yolks and sprinkle them over the whites. Chill before serving.

Serves 6 (or more if served with other antipasti).

¾ cucumber
12 oz strawberries
1 teaspoon pink peppercorns
mint leaves, to garnish
DRESSING:
2 tablespoons balsamic vinegar
2 fl oz/¼ cup olive oil
salt

To make dressing, mix together vinegar, olive oil and salt in a large bowl. Slice cucumber very thinly, using a mandoline or slicing disc on a food processor.

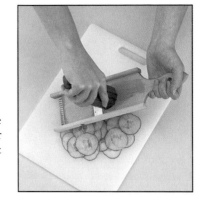

Put cucumber slices into bowl with dressing and mix gently to coat. Slice strawberries. Arrange a circle of overlapping slices of cucumber on serving plates.

Arrange strawberry slices in a circle inside cucumber, then arrange remaining cucumber slices inside strawberries. Place remaining strawberries in center. Lightly crush peppercorns and sprinkle over salads. Using scissors, snip mint leaves over salads and serve at once.

Serves 6.

CHILI CUCUMBER SALAD

1 lb cucumber
2 teaspoons salt
1 green bell pepper
2 tablespoons sesame seeds
strips of fresh red chili, to garnish
DRESSING:
2 shallots, finely chopped
1 fresh red chili, seeded and chopped
3 tablespoons white rice vinegar
1 tablespoon rice wine
2 teaspoons superfine sugar
2 teaspoons light soy sauce
1 teaspoon sesame oil

ZUCCHINI SALAD

2 tablespoons pine nuts
1 lb zucchini
2 tablespoons olive oil
1 clove garlic, crushed
2 tablespoons currants
2 teaspoons chopped fresh mint
juice ½ lemon
salt and freshly ground black pepper
2 scallions

Put pine nuts in a large skillet and cook, stirring, until just beginning to brown. Remove pine nuts and reserve. Top and tail zucchini and slice thinly.

Peel cucumber and slice very thinly. Place in a bowl, sprinkle with the salt and set aside for 15 minutes. Halve and seed the pepper and thinly slice lengthwise.

Heat oil in skillet, add zucchini, garlic, currants and pine nuts. Cook, stirring, until zucchini are just beginning to soften and brown slightly.

Mix together the dressing ingredients. Rinse the cucumber slices, drain well and pat dry with kitchen paper. Place in a bowl and carefully mix in the green pepper. Pour over the dressing, cover and chill for 1 hour. Mix well, sprinkle with sesame seeds, garnish with chili strips and serve.

Serves 4.

Stir in mint, lemon juice, salt and pepper. Transfer to a serving dish and leave until cold. Slice the scallions and scatter them over the top.

Serves 4.

LEEK SALAD

8 long, slim leeks
1 small red bell pepper, peeled, seeded and cut into
    strips
4 tablespoons white wine vinegar
4 fl oz/½ cup virgin olive oil
pinch superfine sugar
large pinch paprika
salt and freshly ground black pepper
chopped fresh parsley, capers (optional) and pitted
    oil-cured black olives, to garnish

Cook leeks in boiling salted water for about
6 minutes until just tender but still firm.

Meanwhile, in a bowl, mix together red pepper, vinegar, oil, sugar, paprika and salt and
pepper. Drain leeks well, briefly lay on
absorbent kitchen paper to absorb excess
moisture, then place in a warm, shallow dish.

Pour over vinegar mixture, turn leeks to coat
well, then cover and leave for a few hours in
a cool place, turning leeks occasionally.
Garnish with chopped parsley, capers, if
using, and black olives.

Serves 4.

ROQUETTE & PINE NUT SALAD

2 oz/½ cup pine nuts
3 oz roquette
4 scallions, thinly sliced
8 sprigs fresh chervil, roughly torn
2 thin slices Parma ham, cut into strips
DRESSING:
juice 1 lemon
3 tablespoons extra virgin olive oil
1 tablespoon walnut oil
½ teaspoon Dijon mustard
salt and freshly ground black pepper

In a small saucepan heat pine nuts, without
oil, over a medium heat, stirring continuously
for about three minutes until golden brown.

Remove nuts to a plate and set side to cool.
Place arugula, scallions, chervil and ham in a
serving bowl. Toss gently to mix.

To make dressing, mix ingredients together in
a small bowl until evenly blended or shake
together in a screw-top jar. Pour over salad
and toss. Sprinkle over reserved pine nuts.

Serves 4-6.

MIXED VEGETABLE SALAD

ASPARAGUS & EGG SALAD

3 large carrots, cut into thin 3 in long sticks
10 hard long beans, or 3 oz French beans, cut into
  2 in pieces
½ small cauliflower, divided into florets
1 cucumber, peeled, halved, seeded and cut into strips
8 oz wedge green cabbage, cored and shredded
2 cloves garlic, smashed
6 candlenuts or cashew nuts, chopped
2 fresh red chilies, cored, seeded and chopped
6 shallots, chopped
1½ teaspoon ground turmeric
4 tablespoons vegetable oil
3½ oz light brown sugar
4 fl oz/½ cup rice vinegar
salt
1½ oz roasted unsalted peanuts

2¼ lb asparagus
7 eggs, hard-cooked
6 tablespoons olive oil
2 tablespoons white wine vinegar
2 small pickled gherkins, finely chopped
salt and freshly ground black pepper
chopped fresh Italian parsley and sprigs to garnish

Snap off and discard woody ends of asparagus stems. Using a small, sharp knife, scrape stems, rinse then tie into small bundles using string.

Bring a large saucepan of water to a boil. Add carrots, beans and cauliflower. Simmer for 2-3 minutes until tender but still crisp. Add cucumber and cabbage and simmer 1 minute longer. Drain, rinse under cold running water and drain thoroughly. Put garlic, nuts, chilies, shallots and turmeric in a blender. Mix to a paste.

Stand bundles upright in a deep pan of boiling salted water so tips are above water. Cover, making a dome of foil, if necessary. Boil for 15 minutes until tips are just tender. Drain, refresh under cold running water, drain, untie bundles and leave to cool.

Heat oil in a wok or skillet over medium heat. Add spice paste and cook, stirring, for 3-5 minutes until slightly thickened and spices are fragrant. Add sugar, vinegar and salt to taste. Bring to a boil. Add vegetables to pan. Stir and toss to coat thoroughly. Transfer to a bowl. Cover tightly and leave at room temperature for about 1 hour. To serve, mound vegetables in a serving dish and sprinkle peanuts on top.

Serves 8-10.

Finely chop four hard-cooked eggs and place in a bowl. Using a wooden spoon stir in oil, vinegar and gherkins. Season with salt and ground black pepper. Set aside. Quarter remaining eggs and arrange with asparagus around edge of a serving plate. Pour egg sauce into center and sprinkle with chopped Italian parsley. Garnish with Italian parsley sprigs.

Serves 4-6.

CARROT/CELERY ROOT SALAD

1 large celery root
4 fl oz/⅔ cup mayonnaise
4 teaspoons Dijon mustard
2½ fl oz/⅓ cup olive oil
1 tablespoon tarragon vinegar
1 clove garlic, crushed
salt and freshly ground black pepper
1 lb carrots
2 tablespoons chopped fresh parsley
parsley sprigs, to garnish
ANCHOVY TOAST:
6 anchovies
2 oz/¼ cup butter
4 slices white bread, crusts removed

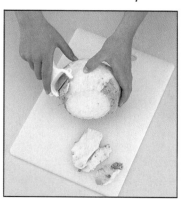

Trim and peel celery root. Coarsely grate.

Immediately mix celery root with mayonnaise and mustard. In a large bowl, whisk together olive oil, vinegar, garlic and salt and pepper. Finely grate carrot and mix into dressing. Stir in parsley. Arrange celery root and carrot mixtures on serving plates.

Preheat broiler. To make anchovy toast, mash together anchovies and butter. Toast bread on one side. Spread untoasted side with anchovy butter and broil until crisp. Cut toast into fingers. Garnish salads with parsley and serve with anchovy toast.

Serves 6.

EGG & WALNUT SALAD

1 head lettuce
6 tomatoes, roughly chopped
½ red onion, thinly sliced
16 pitted black olives, halved
1½ oz/⅓ cup walnut pieces
4 eggs, hard-cooked, quartered
1 tablespoon chopped fresh fennel
1 tablespoon snipped fresh chives
DRESSING:
3 tablespoons extra virgin olive oil
2 tablespoons walnut oil
2 tablespoons red wine vinegar
1 teaspoon wholegrain mustard
pinch granulated sugar
salt and freshly ground black pepper

Tear lettuce into bite-sized pieces and put in a salad bowl with tomatoes, onion, olives, walnuts, eggs and herbs. Toss gently to mix.

To make dressing, mix ingredients together in a small bowl until evenly blended or shake together in a screw-top jar. Pour over salad and serve at once.

Serves 4-6.

WARM SPINACH SALAD

1 lb young spinach leaves
6 slices thick-cut streaky bacon, cut into strips
2 slices bread, crusts removed
4 tablespoons olive oil
4 teaspoons red wine vinegar
1 teaspoon Dijon mustard
salt and freshly ground black pepper

Put spinach in a serving bowl. Heat a non-stick skillet, add bacon and dry-fry until crisp and brown. Remove with a slotted spoon and drain on kitchen paper.

Cut bread into cubes. Heat 1 tablespoon oil in skillet, add bread and fry over a moderately high heat until crisp and golden. Remove and drain on kitchen paper. Add to spinach with bacon.

Stir vinegar and mustard into skillet and bring to boil. Add remaining oil and salt and pepper. Heat through and pour over salad. Toss and serve immediately.

Serves 4.

WARM ANTIPASTI SALAD

mixed salad leaves, such as red leaf lettuce, escarole, radicchio and rocket, to serve
5 tablespoons olive oil
3 tablespoons red wine or balsamic vinegar
14 oz can artichoke hearts, rinsed and drained, cut in half if large
8 oz can cannellini beans, rinsed and drained
1 clove garlic, chopped
1 red onion, chopped
½ teaspoon dried basil
7 oz jar roasted sweet pimientos, drained and cut into ½ in strips
4 sun-dried tomatoes, drained and cut into thin strips
1 tablespoon capers, rinsed and drained
3 oz black olives
fresh basil leaves (optional)

In a large bowl, toss the salad leaves with 3 tablespoons olive oil and 2 tablespoons vinegar. Arrange the mixed salad leaves on a large, shallow serving dish. Heat the wok until hot. Add the remaining oil and swirl to coat. Add the artichoke hearts, cannellini beans, garlic, red onion and basil and stir-fry for 2-3 minutes until heated through. Carefully spoon the mixture onto the salad leaves.

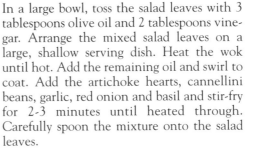

Add the pimientos and sun-dried tomatoes to wok and toss gently for 1-2 minutes to heat through. Arrange over the artichoke and bean mixture. Sprinkle with the capers, black olives and basil leaves, if wished, and serve warm with crusty bread.

Serves 4-6.

CARROT SALAD WITH PITTA

1 lb carrots, thickly sliced
2 cloves garlic, crushed
¼ teaspoon cayenne pepper
½ teaspoon ground cumin
½ teaspoon ground allspice
½ teaspoon sugar
juice of ½ lemon
salt and freshly ground black pepper
7 fl oz/scant 1 cup olive oil
4 pitta breads
fresh mint leaves, to garnish
ZAHTAR:
2 oz sesame seeds
1 oz ground sumac
1 oz ground dried thyme

Boil carrots for 5-10 minutes until soft. Drain, refresh in cold water and drain again. Place in a food processor or blender with garlic, cayenne pepper, cumin, allspice, sugar, lemon juice, salt and pepper. Process until smooth; continue to process while trickling in 4 tablespoons of the olive oil. Check seasoning and transfer to a serving bowl. Cover and chill for 2 hours. To make the zahtar, in a heavy skillet, dry roast sesame seeds over a medium heat, stirring, until lightly browned. Place in a bowl and leave to cool. Stir in sumac and thyme. Set aside.

Split the pitta breads in half. Drizzle the remaining olive oil over the cut sides of the bread and sprinkle 1 tablespoon of zahtar over each piece. Cook under a warm broiler until browned and crisp. When cool, break into rough pieces. Allow the carrot salad to come to room temperature. Garnish with mint leaves and serve with the pitta toasts.

Serves 6.

Note: Store the unused zahtar in a screw-top jar for up to 3 months.

HOT BAMBOO SHOOT SALAD

1 tablespoon fish sauce
2 tablespoons tamarind water
½ teaspoon crushed palm sugar
1 clove garlic, finely chopped
1 small fresh red chili, seeded and finely chopped
6 oz bamboo shoots, cut into fine strips
1 tablespoon coarsely ground browned rice
2 scallions, including some green parts, sliced
cilantro leaves, to garnish

In a saucepan, heat fish sauce, tamarind water, sugar, garlic, chili and 2 tablespoons water to the boil. Stir in bamboo shoots and heat for 1-2 minutes.

Stir in rice, then turn into a warmed dish, scatter over scallion and garnish with cilantro leaves.

Serves 2-3.

FRIED HALOUMI SALAD

a selection of salad leaves
8 oz haloumi cheese
1 egg, beaten
2 oz/1 cup breadcrumbs
oil for frying
marigold petals, to garnish
SALAD DRESSING:
2½ fl oz/⅓ cup olive oil
1 tablespoon balsamic vinegar
1 teaspoon lemon juice
1 teaspoon Dijon mustard
salt and freshly ground black pepper

WATERCRESS & CHEESE SALAD

3 oz/3 cups watercress
3 oz/3 cups rocket
1 ripe pear, quartered and sliced
½ oz/1 tablespoon pumpkin seeds, toasted
3 oz Gorgonzola cheese, crumbled
DRESSING:
3 tablespoons olive oil
½ teaspoon balsamic vinegar
1 teaspoon wholegrain mustard
1 tablespoon chopped fresh mint
salt and freshly ground black pepper

Wash and dry salad leaves. Arrange on 6 individual plates.

Trim and discard any thick stalks from the watercress. Wash and dry the watercress and rocket. Shake off excess water, transfer to a large bowl and stir in the sliced pear, pumpkin seeds and cheese.

To make dressing, in a screw-top jar, mix together oil, vinegar, lemon juice, mustard, salt and pepper. Screw on lid and shake vigorously. Cut cheese into ½ in. cubes. Put beaten egg in a bowl and breadcrumbs on a board or plate. Toss cheese in egg, then in breadcrumbs.

Heat oil in a deep skillet. Fry cheese until golden brown. Drain on absorbent paper. Pour the dressing over the salad. Arrange cubes of cheese on each plate. Scatter with marigold petals and serve immediately.

Serves 6.

Whisk all the dressing ingredients together until blended, pour over the salad, toss well and serve at once.

Serves 4.

ROQUEFORT SALAD

2 oz/½ cup walnut pieces
2 bunches watercress
4 oz Roquefort cheese
DRESSING:
1 tablespoon red wine vinegar
½-1 teaspoon Dijon mustard
4 tablespoons olive oil
salt and freshly ground black pepper

To make dressing, whisk together vinegar and mustard then slowly pour in oil, whisking constantly. Season with salt and pepper and set aside.

Preheat broiler. Spread walnut pieces on a baking sheet and broil turning occasionally, until crisp and evenly browned.

Put watercress in a serving bowl, crumble over Roquefort cheese and sprinkle with toasted walnuts. Whisk dressing, pour over salad, toss and serve.

Serves 4.

POTATO SALAD

1½ lb new potatoes
4-5 mint leaves, chopped
1 tablespoon chopped fresh chives
½ shallot, finely chopped
mint springs, to garnish
DRESSING:
1 tablespoon wine vinegar
2 teaspoons Dijon mustard
salt and freshly ground black pepper
3 tablespoons olive oil

Cook potatoes in a saucepan of boiling salted water for 15 minutes, until tender.

Meanwhile, make dressing. Whisk together vinegar, mustard and salt and pepper. Slowly pour in oil, whisking constantly.

Drain potatoes thoroughly, cut into halves or quarters, if necessary, then immediately toss with dressing, herbs and shallot. Leave to cool. Garnish with mint sprigs and serve.

Serves 4.

WATERMELON & FETA SALAD

½ small watermelon or a wedge weighing about 1⅓ lb
4½ oz feta cheese
freshly ground black pepper
12 pitted black olives
2 tablespoons roughly chopped fresh mint
2 tablespoons olive oil
2 teaspoons lime juice

Cut the rind off the watermelon and cut the melon into cubes, picking out and discarding the seeds.

Arrange the melon cubes on a serving dish. Roughly crumble the feta cheese over the melon. Sprinkle with freshly ground black pepper. Arrange the olives on top.

Scatter the chopped mint over. Mix together the olive oil and lime juice and drizzle over the salad.

Serves 4.

Variations: Sliced radishes or pomegranate seeds may be added to this traditional salad.

BULGAR WHEAT SALAD

8 oz/1 cup bulgar wheat
1 red bell pepper
1 bunch of scallions
2 large tomatoes
3 oz fresh parsley
1 oz fresh mint
juice of 1 lemon
2 fl oz/¼ cup olive oil
salt and freshly ground black pepper
6 large, cup-shaped radicchio leaves
mint leaves and flat-leaf parsley sprigs, to garnish

Put bulgar wheat into a bowl, cover with warm water and leave to soak for 30 minutes.

Turn bulgar wheat into a colander and leave to drain. Dice red pepper and blanch in boiling water for 1 minute. Drain, rinse in cold water and drain again. Slice scallions. Put tomatoes in a bowl, cover with boiling water and leave for 1 minute. Transfer to a bowl of cold water and leave for 1 minute. Peel and coarsely chop. Chop parsley and mint.

Put bulgar wheat, red pepper, scallions, tomatoes, parsley and mint into a large bowl. Add lemon juice, olive oil and salt and pepper and mix thoroughly. Let stand for 1 hour. Pile into radicchio 'cups', garnish with mint leaves and flat-leaf parsley sprigs and serve.

Serves 6.

Variation: The salad can also be used to fill hollowed-out tomatoes.

SUMMER NOODLE SALAD

6 oz egg noodles
1 teaspoon sesame oil
2 tablespoons crunchy peanut butter
2 tablespoons light soy sauce
2 teaspoons superfine sugar
pinch of chili powder
1 lb tomatoes, thinly sliced
4 oz scallions, finely chopped
4 oz bean sprouts
4 oz grated carrot
2 oz pitted dates, finely chopped

Cook the noodles in a pan of boiling water for 4-5 minutes. Drain well and rinse in cold water. Leave in cold water until required.

Mix together the oil, peanut butter, soy sauce, sugar and chili powder. Drain noodles well, place in a large bowl and mix in the peanut sauce. Arrange the tomato slices on a serving plate.

Using chopsticks or 2 forks, toss the scallions, bean sprouts, grated carrot and dates into the noodles and mix well. Pile on top of the sliced tomato and serve.

Serves 4.

GARBANZO BEAN SALAD

12 oz/1½ cups garbanzos, soaked overnight
1 tablespoon finely chopped fresh parsley
1½ teaspoons finely chopped fresh tarragon
4 scallions, finely chopped
sliced scallions and flat-leaf parsley, to garnish
DRESSING:
2 cloves garlic, finely chopped
1 tablespoon red wine vinegar
2-3 teaspoons Dijon mustard
salt and freshly ground black pepper
4 tablespoons olive oil

Drain and rinse garbanzos. Put in a saucepan and cover with cold water.

Bring to the boil. Cover pan and simmer for 1-1½ hours, until garbanzos are tender. Meanwhile, make dressing. Mix together garlic, vinegar, mustard and salt and pepper. Slowly pour in the oil, whisking constantly.

Drain garbanzos and immediately toss with dressing, parsley, tarragon and scallions. Garnish with scallion slices and flat-leaf parsley and serve warm.

Serves 4.

WILD & BROWN RICE SALAD

4 oz/1 cup wild rice
salt
6 oz/1¼ cups brown rice
2 oz/⅔ cup pecan nuts
6 scallions, trimmed
2 oz/⅓ cup dried cherries, cranberries or raisins
2 tablespoons chopped fresh cilantro
1 tablespoon chopped fresh parsley
DRESSING:
3½ fl oz/⅓ cup olive oil
2 teaspoons raspberry vinegar
¼ teaspoon clear honey or sugar
salt and freshly ground black pepper

TORTELLONI SALAD

12 oz green, cheese- or meat-filled tortelloni
4 fl oz/½ cup olive oil
2 cloves garlic, finely chopped
8 oz asparagus, cut into 2 in pieces
6 oz broccoli, cut into small flowerets
1 yellow bell pepper, thinly sliced
6 oz jar marinated artichoke hearts, drained
1 red onion, thinly sliced
2 tablespoons capers
3-4 tablespoons black olives
3 tablespoons red wine vinegar
1 tablespoon Dijon mustard
salt and freshly ground black pepper
3 tablespoons shredded fresh basil or parsley

Cook the wild rice in a pan of lightly salted boiling water for 35-40 minutes until just tender. Cook the brown rice in a pan of lightly salted boiling water for 25 minutes or until just tender. Drain well and place both rices in a large bowl. Meanwhile, preheat oven to 400F (220C).

In a large saucepan of boiling water, cook tortelloni according to packet directions. Drain and rinse. Drain again and toss with 1 tablespoon olive oil. Set aside. Heat wok until hot. Add 2 tablespoons olive oil to wok and swirl to coat. Add garlic, asparagus and broccoli and stir-fry for 4-5 minutes until vegetables are tender but still crisp. Add pepper and stir-fry for 1 minute. Remove vegetables to a large bowl and toss with reserved tortelloni, artichoke hearts, red onion, capers and olives. Allow to cool to room temperature.

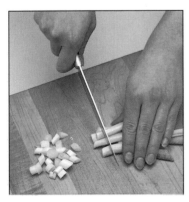

Roast the nuts in the oven for 5-6 minutes until browned; cool and coarsely chop. Set aside. Chop the scallions and add to the rice with the dried fruit and herbs and stir well. Blend the dressing ingredients well together and pour over the salad, stir once, cover and leave rice to cool. Just before serving, toss in the roasted nuts and season to taste.

Serves 4-6.

In a small bowl, whisk together the wine vinegar, mustard, and salt and pepper to taste. Slowly whisk in remaining olive oil until creamy. Pour the dressing over the tortelloni and vegetables. Add the shredded basil or parsley and toss gently to mix well. Serve at room temperature.

Serves 4-6.

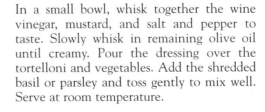

SALADE NIÇOISE

8 oz small green beans
1 crisp lettuce
4 ripe beef tomatoes, cut into wedges
1 red bell pepper, chopped
3 hard-cooked eggs, quartered
7 oz can tuna in olive oil, drained
leaves from small bunch of flat-leaf parsley, coarsely
 chopped
16 pitted black olives
6-8 anchovy fillets, halved lengthwise
DRESSING:
8 tablespoons olive oil
2 teaspoons wine vinegar
1-2 cloves garlic, crushed
salt and freshly ground black pepper

Halve beans and cook in a saucepan of boiling salted water for 10 minutes, until tender. Drain, rinse in cold water and drain again. Leave to cool. Tear lettuce leaves and arrange on a large serving plate with beans, tomatoes, pepper, eggs and tuna.

Scatter over parsley and olives. Arrange anchovies on top in a lattice pattern. To make dressing, whisk together olive oil, vinegar, garlic and salt and pepper. Pour over salad and serve.

Serves 4.

WARM PASTA SALAD

8 oz mixed mushrooms, wiped
1 oz/¼ cup drained sun-dried tomatoes in oil, sliced
4 fl oz/½ cup olive oil
2 cloves garlic, chopped
grated zest 1 lemon
1 tablespoon lemon juice
2 tablespoons chopped fresh mint
8 oz/2½ cups dried penne
2 ripe tomatoes, skinned, seeded and chopped
salt and freshly ground black pepper

Thinly slice the mushrooms and place in a large bowl with the sun-dried tomatoes.

Heat 1 tablespoon oil and sauté the garlic for 1 minute until starting to turn golden. Remove the pan from the heat and stir in the remaining oil, lemon zest, juice and mint, pour half over the mushrooms and reserve the rest. Stir mushrooms until well coated, cover and set aside to soften for several hours.

Cook the pasta in lightly salted, boiling water for 10 minutes until *al dente* (just cooked). Drain well, toss with the remaining dressing and stir into the marinated mushrooms with the fresh tomatoes. Season with salt and pepper.

Serves 4.

Note: Use a selection of button, field, oyster and shiitake mushrooms.

CRAB & AVOCADO SALAD

12 oz dressed crab
1 tablespoon lime juice
grated rind of 1 lime
1 tablespoon chopped fresh cilantro
salt and freshly ground black pepper
2 ripe avocados
9 oz mixed salad leaves
lime slices and cilantro leaves, to garnish
LIME DRESSING:
1 tablespoon lime juice
2½ fl oz/⅓ cup olive oil
1 tablespoon chopped fresh cilantro
½ teaspoon superfine sugar

Mix together crab, lime juice, lime rind, cilantro and salt and pepper. Halve avocados lengthwise, remove pits and peel. Cut flesh into ½ in cubes.

To make lime dressing, in a large bowl, mix together lime juice, olive oil, cilantro, sugar and salt and pepper. Put salad leaves into bowl and toss to coat thoroughly. Arrange salad leaves on serving plates. Put a spoonful of crab mixture in center of each plate. Arrange diced avocado around crab mixture. Garnish with slices of lime and cilantro leaves and serve.

Serves 6.

SHRIMP SALAD WITH MINT

16-20 raw large shrimp, peeled and deveined
juice 2 limes
2 teaspoons vegetable oil
2 teaspoons crushed palm sugar
2 tablespoons tamarind water
1 tablespoon fish sauce
2 teaspoons red curry paste
2 stalks lemon grass, very finely chopped
4 tablespoons coconut cream
10 Thai mint leaves, shredded
5 kaffir lime leaves, shredded
1 small crisp lettuce, divided into leaves
1 small cucumber, thinly sliced
Thai mint leaves, to garnish

Put shrimp in a bowl, pour over lime juice and leave for 30 minutes. Remove shrimp, allowing excess liquid to drain into bowl; reserve liquid. Heat oil in a wok, add shrimp and stir-fry for 2-3 minutes until just cooked – marinating in lime juice partially cooks them.

Meanwhile, stir sugar, tamarind water, fish sauce, curry paste, lemon grass, coconut cream, mint and lime leaves into reserved lime liquid. Stir in cooked shrimp. Set aside until cold. Make a bed of lettuce on a serving plate, place on a layer of cucumber slices. Spoon shrimp and dressing on top. Garnish with mint leaves.

Serves 3-4.

MIXED SEAFOOD SALAD

5 fl oz/⅔ cup dry white wine
juice ½ lemon
1 shallot, chopped
8 sprigs fresh Italian parsley, separated into stalks
   and leaves
1 clove garlic, chopped
1½ lb prepared raw seafood such as squid, clams and
   mussels and large shrimp in their shells, shelled
   scallops
7 fl oz/scant cup prepared mayonnaise
½ teaspoon finely grated lemon peel
salt and fresh ground black pepper
1 head lettuce, separated into leaves
lemon slices to garnish

Put wine, 4 fl oz/⅔ cup water, lemon juice, shallot, parsley stalks and 1 clove garlic in a large saucepan. Bring to the boil and boil for 1 minute. Add seafood in succession according to length of cooking time of each type, starting with those that need longest cooking – allow 15 minutes for squid, 5-6 minutes for shrimp, 4-5 for scallops, 2-3 for mussels and clams. Using a slotted spoon, transfer cooked pieces to a large bowl.

Strain cooking liquor into bowl and allow to cool. Cover and put in refrigerator for at least 1 hour.

Chop parsley leaves with remaining clove garlic.

Put parsley and garlic in a bowl and stir in mayonnaise and lemon peel. Season with salt and freshly ground black pepper. Transfer to a serving bowl.

Arrange lettuce leaves as a bed on a serving plate. Drain seafood and pile into center of plate. Season and garnish with lemon slices. Serve mayonnaise separately.

Serves 4-6.

GREEN MUSSEL SALAD

SZECHUAN SHRIMP SALAD

3 lb mussels in their shells
8 tablespoons virgin olive oil
2 tablespoons white wine vinegar
2 teaspoons capers
2 tablespoons finely chopped Spanish onion
½ clove garlic, finely chopped
2 tablespoons chopped fresh parsley
1 teaspoon paprika
small pinch cayenne pepper
salt

1 teaspoon chili oil
1 teaspoon Szechuan peppercorns, toasted and
  ground
pinch of salt
1 tablespoon white rice vinegar
1 teaspoon superfine sugar
12 oz cooked, peeled shrimp, thawed and dried, if
  frozen
4 oz cucumber
1 tablespoon sesame seeds
½ head Chinese leaves, shredded
fresh red chili strips and lemon wedges, to garnish

In a large bowl, mix together the oil, peppercorns, salt, vinegar and sugar.

Clean mussels. Put in a large saucepan with
5 tablespoons water, cover pan and boil for
4-5 minutes, shaking pan occasionally, until
shells open. Drain mussels and discard any
that remain closed. Remove mussels from
shells and discard shells.

Add the shrimp and mix well. Cover and
chill for 30 minutes. Thinly slice the cucumber and slice each piece into thin strips. Pat
dry with kitchen paper and mix into shrimp
with sesame seeds.

In a bowl, mix together remaining ingredients and mussels, cover and place in
refrigerator overnight. Return to room
temperature before serving.

Serves 4.

Arrange the Chinese leaves on 4 serving
plates and top with the shrimp mixture.
Garnish with chili strips and lemon wedges
and serve immediately.

Serves 4.

SEARED SCALLOP SALAD

2 oz sun-dried tomatoes
1 small bunch fresh basil
4 fl oz/½ cup extra virgin olive oil
2 tablespoons balsamic vinegar
salt and freshly ground black pepper
mixed salad leaves
1½ lb shelled scallops
basil sprigs, to garnish

Roughly chop the sun-dried tomatoes. Remove the basil leaves from the stalks and roughly chop the leaves.

Whisk together all but 1 tablespoon of the olive oil, the balsamic vinegar and salt and pepper. Stir in the tomatoes and basil. Set aside. Put the salad leaves in a serving bowl. Heat a large heavy skillet until hot. Add the remaining olive oil and wipe the pan with kitchen paper to remove any excess.

Add the scallops, in 2 batches if necessary, and cook for 20 seconds. Turn and cook for a further 20-30 seconds until well browned. Return all the scallops to the pan. Remove from the heat and add the tomato mixture. Stir gently then pour immediately over the salad leaves. Garnish with basil and serve.

Serves 4.

Note: If the scallops are very large, cut them in half before cooking.

MINTED SEAFOOD SALAD

5 fl oz/⅔ cup dry white wine
1 shallot, chopped
5 whole black peppercorns
1 lb shelled scallops, fresh or frozen and thawed
1 lb cooked large shrimp
4 sticks celery
2 carrots
about 16 whole fresh mint leaves
½ teaspoon finely grated lemon peel
DRESSING:
juice 2 lemons
4 fl oz/½ cup extra virgin olive oil
1 tablespoon white wine vinegar
2 tablespoons chopped fresh Italian parsley
salt and freshly ground black pepper

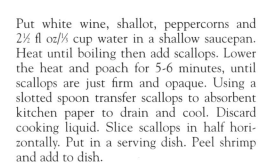

Put white wine, shallot, peppercorns and 2½ fl oz/⅓ cup water in a shallow saucepan. Heat until boiling then add scallops. Lower the heat and poach for 5-6 minutes, until scallops are just firm and opaque. Using a slotted spoon transfer scallops to absorbent kitchen paper to drain and cool. Discard cooking liquid. Slice scallops in half horizontally. Put in a serving dish. Peel shrimp and add to dish.

Cut celery and carrots into thin matchsticks and add to seafood with mint leaves and lemon peel. Toss lightly to mix. To make dressing, mix ingredients together in a small bowl until evenly blended or put in a screw-top jar and shake until blended. Pour over salad and toss. Cover and refrigerate for 30 minutes before serving.

Serves 4-6.

SWEET & SOUR FISH SALAD

HOT SHRIMP SALAD

8 oz trout fillets
8 oz cod fillets
10 fl oz/1¼ cups Chinese Chicken Stock (see page 57)
2 tablespoons dry sherry
2 shallots, sliced
2 pineapple slices, chopped
1 small red bell pepper, diced
1 bunch of watercress
2 teaspoons sunflower oil
1 tablespoon red rice vinegar
pinch of chili powder
1 teaspoon clear honey
salt and freshly ground black pepper
pineapple pieces and watercress leaves, to garnish

mixed salad leaves for serving
2 mangoes, peeled and sliced
2 tablespoons olive oil
5 oz sugar snap peas
4-6 scallions, thinly sliced into 1 in pieces
½ oz/1 tablespoon butter
1 lb cooked jumbo shrimp, peeled and deveined
1 tablespoon anise-flavored liqueur
2 fl oz /¼ cup whipping cream
pinch freshly grated nutmeg
salt and freshly ground black pepper
2 tablespoons chopped fresh dill
fresh dill sprigs, to garnish

Wash and pat dry the fish fillets and place in a non-stick or well seasoned wok. Pour over stock and dry sherry. Bring to the boil and simmer gently for 7-8 minutes until just cooked. Leave to cool in cooking liquor. Drain, remove skin and flake flesh into a bowl.

Arrange the salad leaves on one side of 4 large plates and fan out the mango slices on the other side; set aside. Heat the oil in the wok and swirl to coat wok. Add sugar snap peas and scallions and stir fry for 1-2 minutes until beans turn bright green and scallions begin to soften. With a strainer or slotted spoon, remove to a bowl.

Carefully mix flaked fish with shallots, pineapple and pepper. Arrange watercress on 4 serving plates and top with fish mixture. Mix together the oil, vinegar, chili powder, honey and salt and pepper and pour over the salad. Garnish with pineapple pieces and watercress leaves and serve.

Serves 4.

Add butter to oil in the wok and stir in shrimp. Stir-fry for 1-2 minutes until heated through; do not overcook. Remove to the bowl. Pour in anise-flavor liqueur and stir to deglaze the wok. Cook for 1 minute, then stir in cream and bring to the boil. Season with nutmeg, salt and pepper. Stir in dill, shrimp, sugar snap peas and scallions, tossing to coat. Immediately, spoon mixture onto salad leaves and garnish with dill sprigs.

Serves 4.

SCALLOP, SHRIMP & MINT SALAD

4 fl oz/½ cup dry white wine
½ onion, chopped
1 bay leaf
4 black peppercorns, crushed
1 lb small zucchini
1 lb shelled scallops
1 lb raw large shrimp, peeled
2 tomatoes, peeled, seeded and chopped
about 18 small mint leaves
DRESSING:
3-4 tablespoons lime juice
½ teaspoon finely grated lime rind
½ clove garlic, finely chopped
4 fl oz/½ cup extra virgin olive oil
2 tablespoons chopped fresh parsley
salt and freshly ground black pepper

Heat wine, onion, bay leaf and peppercorns with 18 fl oz/2¼ cups water in a saucepan, simmer for 15 minutes, then add zucchini and cook for about 8 minutes until tender but crisp. Remove zucchini and drain on absorbent kitchen paper. Add scallops and shrimp to pan and poach until scallops just turn opaque, about 2 minutes, and shrimp become pink, 3-4 minutes.

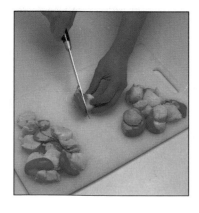

Drain seafood and cool under cold running water. Halve scallops horizontally. Cut zucchini into thin strips. Put into a serving dish with seafood, tomatoes and mint. To make dressing, whisk ingredients together, pour over salad and toss gently. Cover and chill for 30 minutes.

Serves 6.

CHINESE SALAD WITH SALMON

12 oz Chinese noodles
1 tablespoon salted black beans, coarsely chopped
3 oz beansprouts
1 tablespoon groundnut oil
1 lb salmon fillets, cut into 1 in cubes
2 teaspoons grated fresh ginger
2 tablespoons rice wine or medium sherry
2 teaspoons sesame oil
3 oz watercress leaves and fine stalks
½ red bell pepper, seeded and chopped

Cook noodles according to packet directions, drain and rinse well with cold water. Drain again, then put into a serving bowl, cover and refrigerate while preparing remaining ingredients. Soak black beans in 1-2 tablespoons hot water. Bring a pan of water to the boil, add beansprouts and boil for 1 minute. Drain, rinse under cold running water, then set aside. Heat groundnut oil in a skillet, add salmon, in batches if necessary, and fry until just cooked and pale gold. Drain on absorbent kitchen paper.

Stir ginger, rice wine or sherry, sesame oil and half the watercress into pan. Boil for a few seconds, then add black beans and remove from heat. Add beansprouts, pepper and salmon to noodles, pour over warm dressing and garnish with remaining watercress.

Serves 4.

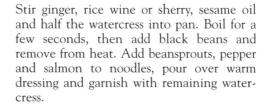

THAI SQUID SALAD

1¾ lb fresh squid
juice of 1 lime
2 tablespoons Thai fish sauce
1 fresh red chili, cored, seeded and finely chopped
1 clove garlic, crushed
1 in piece fresh root ginger, peeled and grated
2 stalks lemon grass, thinly sliced
6 scallions, thinly sliced
2 tablespoons chopped fresh cilantro
10 mint leaves, coarsely chopped
7 oz salad leaves
chili rings, to garnish

To clean squid, pull head and tentacles away from body sac and discard.

Remove innards and discard. Remove transparent 'quill' from body. Remove any purple skin from body. Rinse body sac thoroughly and slit open. Score the inside of body sac in a criss-cross pattern, then cut into ½ × 2 in. strips. Bring a saucepan of water to the boil.

Add squid and simmer for 1 minute, until opaque. Drain and put into a bowl. Add lime juice, fish sauce, chili, garlic, ginger, lemon grass and scallions. Cover and leave to marinate for at least 1 hour. Stir in cilantro and mint. Arrange salad leaves on serving plates, top with squid mixture, garnish with chili rings and serve.

Serves 6.

CHILI-CHICKEN SALAD

8 oz/1¼ cups brown rice
3 tablespoons sesame oil
2 tablespoons peanut oil
5 oz/1 cup cashew nuts or peanuts
5 oz snow peas
1½ lb skinned and boned chicken breasts, cut into thin strips
2 tablespoons sunflower oil
1 in fresh ginger, peeled and thinly sliced
2 cloves garlic, finely chopped
4-6 scallions, sliced
1-2 fresh green chilies, seeded and thinly sliced
3 tablespoons wine vinegar
2 tablespoons chopped fresh mint or cilantro
mixed lettuce leaves
1 orange, peeled, segmented and any juice reserved

Cook rice for 30-35 minutes or according to directions, until tender. Drain and place in a large bowl; toss with sesame oil and set aside. Heat the wok until hot, add peanut oil and swirl to coat wok. Add the nuts and stir-fry for 1-2 minutes until they turn golden. Remove and add to rice. Add snow peas to oil in wok and stir-fry for 1-2 minutes until bright green. Add to the rice. Add chicken to the wok, in 2 batches, and stir-fry for 2-3 minutes until chicken turns white and feels firm to the touch. Add to the rice.

Add sunflower oil to wok and stir in ginger, garlic, scallions and chilies. Stir-fry for 1 minute until onion begins to soften. Pour contents of wok over rice mixture. Return wok to heat and pour in vinegar, swirling to deglaze wok. Pour vinegar over rice mixture, add half the herbs and toss to mix well. Line a shallow serving bowl with lettuce. Spoon rice mixture on to leaves, decorate with orange segments and pour over any juice. Garnish with remaining herbs.

Serves 4.

CHICKEN & WATERCRESS SALAD

YELLOW SALAD

2 cloves garlic, finely chopped
1¼ in. piece galangal, finely chopped
1 tablespoon fish sauce
3 tablespoons lime juice
1 teaspoon crushed palm sugar
2 tablespoons peanut oil
8 oz chicken breast meat, finely chopped
about 25 dried shrimp
1 bunch watercress, about 4 oz, coarse stalks
  removed
3 tablespoons chopped dry-roasted peanuts
2 fresh red chilies, seeded and cut into fine strips

1 clove garlic, crushed
2 teaspoons wholegrain mustard
1 teaspoon clear honey
3 tablespoons white wine vinegar
8 tablespoons olive oil
2 tablespoons chopped fresh chives, plus extra to serve
5 fl oz/⅔ cup natural yogurt
a large pinch of saffron strands
30 fl oz/3¼ cups chicken stock
2 skinned and boned chicken breasts
6 oz/1¼ cups pasta shapes
3 yellow bell peppers, halved and deseeded
2 oz sun-dried tomatoes
6 scallions
1 celery heart, with leaves
salt and freshly ground black pepper

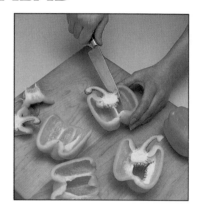

Using a pestle and mortar, pound together garlic and galangal. Mix in fish sauce, lime juice and sugar; set aside. In wok, heat oil, add chicken and stir-fry for about 3 minutes until cooked through. Using a slotted spoon, transfer to absorbent kitchen paper to drain. Put into a serving bowl and set aside.

In a bowl, whisk together the garlic, mustard, honey, vinegar, oil, chives and yogurt and reserve. Soak the saffron strands in the chicken stock in a pan, bring to the boil, then reduce to a simmer. Add the chicken breasts and poach gently for 15 minutes. Drain and set aside to cool slightly. Add the pasta to the poaching liquor and cook for 8-10 minutes until the pasta is *al dente* (cooked but firm to the bite). Drain well and pour over the reserved dressing. Preheat broiler.

Chop half dried shrimp and add to bowl. Mix in watercress, peanuts and half of chilies. Pour over garlic mixture and toss to mix. Sprinkle with remaining chilies and shrimp.

Serves 3-4.

Place the peppers cut-side down under the hot broiler until the skins blacken and blister. Remove and allow to cool, then peel off the blackened skins, cut into thick strips and stir into the pasta. Cut the chicken into strips, slice the tomatoes, scallions and celery heart and stir into the pasta. Season to taste with salt and plenty of ground black pepper, sprinkle with remaining chives and serve warm or cold with chunks of garlic bread.

Serves 4.

MARINATED CHICKEN SALAD

5 fl oz/⅔ cup olive oil
4 tablespoons balsamic vinegar
2 tablespoons chopped fresh basil
2 tablespoons chopped fresh rosemary
2 cloves garlic, crushed
4 skinned and boned chicken breasts
1 red bell pepper, deseeded and quartered
1 yellow bell pepper, deseeded and quartered
2 zucchini, cut into ½ in. thick slices
2 large open cup mushrooms
2 oz/¼ cup toasted pine nuts
8 sun-dried tomatoes
½ teaspoon sugar
salt and pepper

Mix together 4 tablespoons olive oil, 2 table-spoons vinegar, 1 tablespoon basil, 1 table-spoon rosemary and the garlic. Put the chicken into a shallow, flameproof dish and pour over the mixture. Leave for 30 minutes. Preheat broiler. Cook dish of chicken under the hot broiler for 10-14 minutes, turning halfway through until the chicken is brown and crispy; cool. Lay the peppers, zucchini and mushrooms in broiler pan, brush with 2 tablespoons oil and broil for about 10 minutes, turning once: cool.

Peel the skins from the peppers, using a sharp knife, and cut the mushrooms into quarters. Slice the chicken breasts into 1 in. thick slices and arrange with the broiled vegetables in a dish. Sprinkle over the pine nuts and sun-dried tomatoes. In a small jug, mix the remaining herbs with the oil and vinegar. Add the sugar and season with a little salt and pepper. Pour over the chicken and mari-nate for 1 hour, stirring occasionally.

Serves 4.

CHICKEN & GRAPE SALAD

1 lb cold cooked chicken
4 oz/1¼ cups walnut halves
4 oz green seedless grapes, halved
16 stuffed green olives, sliced
3 scallions, sliced
salt and freshly ground black pepper
DRESSING:
5 fl oz/⅔ cup prepared mayonnaise
1 clove garlic, crushed
1 teaspoon paprika
2 tablespoons chopped fresh Italian parsley
few drops hot pepper sauce
2 tablespoons milk
1 head lettuce, separated into leaves

Cut chicken into thin strips and place in a bowl with walnuts, grapes, olives and scal-lions. Season with salt and freshly ground black pepper.

To make dressing, mix ingredients together in a small bowl until evenly blended. Pour over salad and toss gently to mix. Arrange lettuce on a serving plate. Pile chicken salad in center and serve at once.

Serves 4-6.

CHICKEN SATAY SALAD

2 tablespoons dry sherry
4 tablespoons crunchy peanut butter
1 in piece fresh root ginger, finely chopped
2 tablespoons hoisin sauce
3 teaspoons lemon juice
2 tablespoons dark soy sauce
5 fl oz/⅔ cup chicken stock or water
4 tablespoons sunflower seeds
2 teaspoons sesame oil
2 tablespoons vegetable oil
salt and freshly ground black pepper
1 cos lettuce, washed and broken into leaves
4 oz beansprouts
4 oz cooked green beans
4 skinned and boned chicken breasts

Mix together the sherry, peanut butter, ginger, hoisin sauce, 2 teaspoons of the lemon juice and 1 tablespoon of the soy sauce. Mix well, then beat in the stock or water. Put the sunflower seeds in a pan over a high heat. Stir constantly and after about 1 minute the seeds should start to turn golden. Still stirring, add the remaining soy sauce; it will instantly evaporate and coat the seeds. Tip the seeds onto a saucer and leave to cool. Mix together the sesame oil, 1 tablespoon vegetable oil, the remaining lemon juice and salt and pepper.

Put the lettuce leaves and beansprouts into a bowl, pour over the salad dressing and toss gently. Arrange the leaves and beans on 4 serving plates. Slice chicken into thin strips. In a skillet, heat the remaining 1 tablespoon vegetable oil and add the chicken. Stir-fry over a high heat until the chicken starts to brown. Lower the heat and pour over the peanut butter mixture; stir until the sauce is simmering and thick. Spoon over the salad leaves and sprinkle with the sunflower seeds.

Serves 4.

CHICKEN & PEAR SALAD

3 oz rocket
3 oz watercress
3 ripe pears
2 oz/¼ cups butter
2 tablespoons sunflower oil
12 oz cooked smoked chicken breast, cubed
4 oz/1 cup walnut pieces
2 oz Parmesan cheese
WALNUT DRESSING:
2 teaspoons white wine vinegar
2 tablespoons walnut oil
2 tablespoons sunflower oil
salt and freshly ground black pepper

In a large bowl, whisk together wine vinegar, walnut oil, sunflower oil and salt and pepper.

Put rocket and watercress into bowl with dressing and toss to coat thoroughly. Arrange on serving plates. Peel and quarter pears and remove cores. Cut each pear quarter lengthwise in half. Heat half the butter and half the sunflower oil in a skillet. Add pears and cook, turning occasionally, until just beginning to brown around the edges.

Meanwhile, heat remaining butter and oil in another skillet. Add chicken and cook, stirring, until heated through. Add walnuts and heat through. Arrange pears, chicken and walnuts on top of rocket and watercress. Using a vegetable peeler, shave curls of Parmesan cheese over salads and serve.

Serves 6.

BRESAOLA & PEAR SALAD

ITALIAN BEEF SALAD

2 ripe pears
8 slices bresaola
½ head lettuce
fresh Italian parsley sprigs to garnish
DRESSING:
2 oz dolcelatte cheese
½ teaspoon Dijon mustard
2 tablespoons groundnut oil
1 tablespoon lemon juice
½-1 teaspoon granulated sugar
3 tablespoons light cream
salt and freshly ground black pepper

1 small head of escarole, Cos lettuce or other bitter
  leaves, washed and dried thoroughly
2-3 tablespoons olive oil
1 lb fillet steak, frozen for 20 minutes then cut into
  very thin strips
8 anchovy fillets, sliced if large
2 oz Parmesan cheese
2-4 tablespoons lemon juice
1 tablespoon capers, rinsed and drained
salt and freshly ground black pepper
chopped fresh herbs, to garnish

Arrange the escarole, Cos or other leaves on
4 large plates. Set aside.

To make dressing, put dolcelatte in a small
bowl. Using a fork mash cheese then gradually beat in oil and lemon juice until smooth.
Beat in remaining ingredients.

Heat wok until very hot. Add 1 tablespoon
olive oil and a few beef strips. Fry 5-8
seconds until beef just colors, turning each
slice once halfway through cooking. The
beef should be very rare. Remove to one of
the salad plates. Continue cooking beef in
batches, adding oil as necessary, and arranging over leaves.

Peel and core pears and cut lengthwise into
thin slices. Arrange on a serving plate or 4
individual plates with bresaola and lettuce.
Garnish with Italian parsley sprigs. Serve
immediately with dressing.

Serves 4.

Place a few anchovy slices over the beef
slices. Using a swivel-bladed vegetable
peeler, shave paper-thin slices of Parmesan
cheese over the meat. Drizzle each salad with
lemon juice and sprinkle with capers. Season
with salt and pepper. Garnish with fresh
herbs.

Serves 4.

THAI BEEF SALAD

12 oz lean beef, very finely chopped
1 tablespoon fish sauce
2 tablespoons lime juice
2 teaspoons crushed palm sugar
1½ tablespoons long-grain white rice, browned and
    coarsely ground
2 fresh green chilies, seeded and finely chopped
2 cloves garlic, finely chopped
8 Thai mint leaves
4 kaffir lime leaves, torn
8 Thai holy basil leaves
lettuce leaves, to serve
chopped scallions and a chili flower, to garnish

Heat a wok, add beef and dry-fry for about 2 minutes until tender. Transfer to a bowl. In a small bowl, mix together fish sauce, lime juice and sugar. Pour over warm beef, add rice and toss together. Cover and leave until cold.

Add chilies, garlic, mint, lime and basil leaves to bowl and toss ingredients together. Line a plate with lettuce leaves and spoon beef mixture into center. Scatter over scallions and garnish with a chili flower.

Serves 3-4.

PORK & BAMBOO SHOOT SALAD

3 tablespoons vegetable oil
3 cloves garlic, chopped
1 small onion, thinly sliced
8 oz lean pork, very finely chopped
1 egg, beaten
8 oz can bamboo shoots, drained and cut into strips
1 tablespoon fish sauce
1 teaspoon crushed palm sugar
3 tablespoons lime juice
freshly ground black pepper
lettuce leaves, to serve

In a wok, heat 2 tablespoons oil, add garlic and onion and cook, stirring occasionally, until lightly browned. Using a slotted spoon, transfer to absorbent kitchen paper to drain; set aside. Add pork to wok and stir-fry for about 3 minutes until cooked through. Using a slotted spoon, transfer to absorbent kitchen paper; set aside. Using absorbent kitchen paper, wipe out wok.

Heat remaining oil, pour in egg to make a thin layer and cook for 1-2 minutes until just set. Turn egg over and cook for 1 minute more. Remove egg from wok and roll up. Cut across into strips. In a bowl, toss together pork, bamboo shoots and egg. In a small bowl, stir together fish sauce, sugar, lime juice and pepper. Pour over pork mixture and toss. Serve on lettuce leaves and sprinkle with garlic and onion.

Serves 3-4.

BEEF & ORANGE SALAD

1 tablespoon groundnut (peanut) oil
4 × 4 oz lean beef fillet steaks, trimmed and
  tenderized
3 tablespoons dark soy sauce
3 tablespoons dry sherry
1 teaspoon ground cinnamon
1 tablespoon brown sugar
freshly ground black pepper
4 oz canned water chestnuts, rinsed and sliced
6 oz fresh young spinach leaves
4 oz scallions, shredded
2 oranges, peeled and segmented
strips of orange rind, to garnish

Heat oil in a non-stick or well seasoned wok and fry beef steaks for 2 minutes on each side. Drain on kitchen paper and wipe out wok. Mix together soy sauce, dry sherry, cinnamon, brown sugar and pepper. Return steaks to the wok, add water chestnuts and pour over soy sauce mixture. Bring to the boil, reduce heat and simmer for 5-6 minutes, turning steaks halfway through.

Arrange spinach leaves on serving plates and top each with a steak, water chestnuts and sauce. Sprinkle with scallions and top with orange segments. Garnish with strips of orange rind and serve immediately.

Serves 4.

HOISIN BEEF SALAD

12 oz lean roast beef, thinly sliced
½ head Chinese leaves
8 oz carrots
8 oz mooli
4 tablespoons chopped fresh chives
2 tablespoons hoisin sauce
1 teaspoon brown sugar
1 tablespoon red rice vinegar
1 teaspoon sesame oil
carrot and mooli flowers, to garnish

Trim fat from beef slices and cut into ½ in. strips.

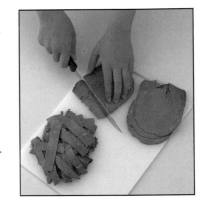

Discard damaged outer layer of Chinese leaves and cut out central core. Shred leaves finely and arrange on 4 serving plates. Peel and grate the carrot and mooli and arrange on top of the Chinese leaves.

Arrange beef strips in the center and sprinkle each plate with chives. In a small bowl, mix together the hoisin sauce, sugar, vinegar and oil and drizzle over the beef. Garnish with carrot and mooli flowers and serve.

Serves 4.

SOUPS

WHITE SOUP WITH GRAPES

7 oz/1¾ cups shelled almonds
4 slices day-old, firm white bread, crusts removed,
   soaked in cold water and squeezed dry
3 cloves garlic, crushed
4 fl oz/½ cup olive oil
2-3 tablespoons sherry vinegar
salt
8 oz muscat or other well-flavored grapes, peeled and
   seeded, if necessary
chopped fresh parsley, to garnish

Place almonds in a bowl and pour over boiling water. Leave for 30 seconds, then remove nuts and squeeze them so the nuts pop out of their skins. Place nuts, bread and garlic in a food processor or blender and mix until smooth. With motor running, slowly pour in the oil. Add sufficient cold water, about 20 fl oz/2½ cups, to give a creamy consistency.

Add vinegar and salt to taste. Add grapes and chill well. Pour into a cold soup tureen or individual soup bowls. Serve garnished with chopped parsley.

Serves 4-6.

GAZPACHO

1½ lb beefsteak tomatoes
½ Spanish onion, chopped
1 green bell pepper, chopped
1 red bell pepper, chopped
2 cloves garlic, chopped
2 slices firm white bread, crusts removed, broken
   into pieces
10 fl oz/1¼ cups tomato juice
3 tablespoons virgin olive oil
2 tablespoons sherry vinegar
salt and freshly ground black pepper
about 8 ice cubes, to serve
ACCOMPANIMENTS:
1 diced small red bell pepper, 1 diced small green bell
   pepper , 1 diced small onion, 1 chopped hard-cooked
   egg and croûtons

Peel, seed and chop tomatoes. Put in a food processor or blender with remaining soup ingredients, except ice cubes. Mix until smooth. Pour soup through a nylon sieve, pressing down well on contents of sieve. If necessary, thin soup with cold water, then chill well.

Place accompaniments in separate bowls. Adjust seasoning of soup, if necessary, then pour into cold soup bowls. Add ice cubes and serve with accompaniments.

Serves 4.

Variation: Do not sieve the soup if more texture is preferred.

CLEAR BEETROOT SOUP

1 onion, coarsely grated
1 large carrot, coarsely grated
1 lb raw beets, peeled and coarsely grated
parsley sprig
1 bay leaf
1⅛ pints/4¼ cups chicken stock
1 egg white
juice of ½ lemon
salt and freshly ground black pepper
thin strips lemon peel, to garnish

Put vegetables into a saucepan with herbs and stock. Bring to the boil, then cover and simmer for 30 minutes.

Strain soup and return it to rinsed-out pan. To clear soup, bring to the boil. Whisk egg white, then pour into pan and simmer gently for 15 minutes.

Strain soup through a cheesecloth-lined sieve into a bowl. Add lemon juice, then cool and chill. Season the soup before serving and garnish with thin strips of lemon peel.

Serves 4-6.

SUMMER AVOCADO SOUP

2 ripe avocados
1 tablespoon lemon juice
1 clove garlic, crushed
5 fl oz/⅔ cup light cream
20 fl oz/2½ cups cold chicken stock
dash Tabasco sauce
salt and freshly ground black pepper
½ avocado, diced, and snipped fresh chives, to garnish

Halve avocados, discard pits and scoop flesh into a blender or food processor. Add lemon juice, garlic and cream and work to a purée.

Blend in stock and season with Tabasco and salt and pepper.

Turn into a bowl, cover with plastic wrap to prevent discoloration and chill for 1 hour. Serve garnished with diced avocado and snipped chives.

Serves 4-6.

CUCUMBER & YOGURT SOUP

1 large cucumber
1 tablespoon olive oil
1 small onion, chopped
20 fl oz/2½ cups hot chicken stock
grated peel and juice of ½ lemon
1 tablespoon chopped fresh dill
3 fl oz/⅓ cup strained Greek yogurt
salt and freshly ground black pepper
dill sprigs, to garnish

Cut 2 in. piece from cucumber, then chop remainder. Put oil in a pan, add onion and cook gently until soft.

Add chopped cucumber, stock, lemon peel and juice and dill. Bring to the boil, then cover and simmer for 15-20 minutes, until cucumber is tender. Purée in a blender or food processor, then turn into a bowl and cool. Stir in half the yogurt and chill.

Check seasoning, then thinly slice reserved piece of cucumber. Serve the soup garnished with thin slices of cucumber floating on the surface and the remaining yogurt spooned on tops with sprigs of dill.

Serves 4-6.

SOUP NORMANDE

1 oz/2 tablespoons butter
1 Spanish onion, chopped
1 teaspoon mild curry powder
1 lb dessert apples
24 fl oz/3 cups chicken stock
2 egg yolks
5 fl oz/⅔ cup thick cream
juice of ½ lemon
salt and freshly ground black pepper
mint leaves, to garnish

Melt butter in a large saucepan, add onion and cook gently until soft. Stir in curry powder.

Reserve 1 apple, then peel, core and chop remainder. Add to pan and cook for 1 minute. Pour in stock and bring to the boil, then cover and simmer for 20 minutes. Purée in a blender or food processor, then return to rinsed-out saucepan.

Beat egg yolks with cream and add to the soup, heating gently until thick. Do not boil. Cool, then chill for at least 2 hours. Peel, core and dice remaining apple and toss in lemon juice. Just before serving, add apple to soup, season and garnish each portion with mint leaves.

Serves 4-6.

MIXED MUSHROOM SOUP

4 dried Chinese mushrooms, soaked in hot water for
    20 minutes
1 oz oyster mushrooms
2 oz button mushrooms
35 fl oz/4½ cups Chinese Chicken Stock (see page
    57)
½ in. piece fresh root ginger, peeled and finely
    chopped
1 clove garlic, finely chopped
2 tablespoons dry sherry
2 tablespoons dark soy sauce
4 oz fresh bean curd, drained and diced
2 teaspoons cornstarch mixed with 4 teaspoons
    water
2 tablespoons shredded basil leaves

Drain soaked mushrooms and squeeze out excess water. Discard stems and slice caps. Slice oyster mushrooms and cut button mushrooms in half.

Pour stock into a saucepan and add ginger, garlic, sherry and soy sauce. Bring to the boil, reduce heat and carefully stir in mushrooms and bean curd. Simmer gently for 5 minutes then add cornstarch mixture and cook, stirring, for a further 2 minutes until thickened. Stir in basil and serve.

Serves 4.

FENNEL & LEMON SOUP

2 tablespoons olive oil
1 onion, roughly chopped
2 fennel bulbs, thinly sliced
20 fl oz/2½ cups chicken stock
grated rind of 1 lemon
5-10 fl oz/⅔-1¼ cups milk
salt and freshly ground black pepper
fennel leaves, to garnish
FRIED LEMON RIND:
1 lemon
vegetable oil for frying

To make the fried lemon rind, use a lemon zester to take as many strips of rind as possible from the lemon.

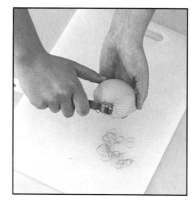

Squeeze the lemon into a small bowl and add the rind to the juice. Leave for 1 hour then drain. Dry the lemon rind on kitchen paper. Heat ½ in. oil in a small saucepan. Add the rind and fry for a few seconds until beginning to color. Remove with a slotted spoon and set aside.

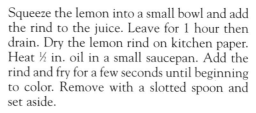

Heat the olive oil in a large saucepan. Add the onion and cook gently for 5 minutes until soft. Stir in the fennel slices. Add the stock and grated lemon rind and bring to the boil. Cover and simmer for 20 minutes until the fennel is tender. Transfer to a food processor or blender and process until smooth. Add sufficient milk to give the desired consistency and season with salt and pepper. Garnish with the fried lemon rind and fennel leaves and serve hot or chilled.

Serves 4.

PEAR VICHYSSOISE

6 pears
juice of ½ lemon
24 fl oz/3 cups chicken stock
1 leek, white part only, trimmed, chopped and
    washed
1 potato, chopped
½ teaspoon ground ginger
3 oz/⅓ cup low-fat fromage frais
pinch grated nutmeg
salt and freshly ground black pepper
1 pear and watercress sprigs, to garnish

Peel and core the 6 pears, putting fruit into a bowl of water with lemon juice.

Put pear skins and cores into a saucepan with half the stock and simmer for a few minutes to extract all the flavor. Strain into a larger pan. Drain pears, chop coarsely and put into pan with leek, potato, remaining stock and ginger. Bring to the boil, then cover and simmer for 20 minutes, until vegetables are tender.

Pureé in a blender or food processor, then pour into a large bowl and set aside to cool, then chill. To serve, whisk fromage frais into the soup, add nutmeg and salt and pepper and garnish with diced or sliced pear and sprigs of watercress.

Serves 4-6.

WATERCRESS SOUP

1 oz/2 tablespoons butter
1 onion, chopped
8 oz potatoes, diced
20 fl oz/2½ cups chicken, veal or vegetable stock
2 bunches watercress, chopped
about 10 fl oz/1¼ cups milk
pinch of freshly grated nutmeg
salt and freshly ground black pepper
fresh chives, to garnish

Heat the butter in a saucepan, add the onion and cook gently, stirring occasionally, for 5 minutes, until soft. Add potatoes.

Stir in stock, bring to the boil and simmer for 15 minutes, until potatoes are tender. Add watercress and simmer for 30 seconds. Transfer to a blender or food processor and process very briefly (otherwise it will become 'gluey'). Press through a sieve and return soup to rinsed-out pan.

Stir in enough milk to give desired consistency. Add nutmeg and salt and pepper and reheat gently without boiling. Garnish with chives and serve.

Serves 4.

Note: For best results, use full-fat milk.

SNOW PEA SOUP

1 oz/2 tablespoons butter
5 scallions, chopped
12 oz snow peas
20 fl oz/2½ cups chicken stock
½ small lettuce, shredded
1 teaspoon sugar
1 tablespoon chopped fresh mint
5 fl oz/⅔ cup crème fraîche
salt and pepper
CROÛTONS:
2 slices bread
vegetable oil for frying

Melt butter in a saucepan, add scallions and cook gently for 3-4 minutes.

Reserve 6 snow peas, then chop remainder and add to pan with stock, lettuce and sugar and simmer for 5 minutes. Purée in a blender or food processor, then sieve and return to pan. Add mint, stir in crème fraîche and salt and pepper and reheat gently: do not boil. Do not reheat too long or the soup will loose its fresh color.

Shred the reserved snow peas and blanch for 30 seconds, then drain. Cut bread into fancy shapes and fry in oil until crisp and golden. Drain on absorbent kitchen paper. Garnish the soup with the shreds of snow peas and croûtons.

Serves 4.

ROASTED BELL PEPPER SOUP

6 large tomatoes
2½ fl oz/⅓ cup olive oil, plus extra for greasing
1 clove garlic, chopped
salt and freshly ground black pepper
4 red bell peppers, quartered
1 onion, finely chopped
6 oz potatoes, cut into ¾ in. cubes
shredded basil leaves, to garnish
BASIL PURÉE:
1 small bunch of basil
2 tablespoons olive oil
1 teaspoon lemon juice

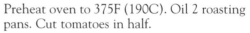

Preheat oven to 375F (190C). Oil 2 roasting pans. Cut tomatoes in half.

Place tomatoes, cut side up, in one of the roasting pans. Drizzle with 2 tablespoons olive oil and scatter with garlic. Season with salt and pepper. Place peppers in the other pan. Drizzle with 2 tablespoons olive oil. Put tomatoes and peppers in oven and cook tomatoes for 45-60 minutes until beginning to blacken around edges. Cook red peppers, turning occasionally, until their skins are charred and blistered. Put in a plastic bag, seal and leave until cool enough to handle. Peel peppers and coarsely chop.

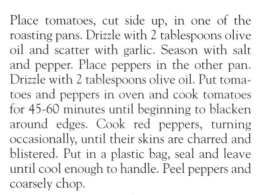

Heat remaining oil in a pan. Add onion and cook, stirring occasionally, for 5 minutes. Add potatoes, peppers and 30 fl oz/3¾ cups water. Cover and simmer for 20 minutes. Transfer to a blender or food processor, add tomatoes and purée until smooth. Press through a sieve, return to rinsed-out pan and heat through. Season. Pound basil leaves with a large pinch of salt. Stir in oil and lemon juice. Add a spoonful of basil purée to each bowl, garnish and serve.

Serves 6.

CONSOMMÉ MADRILÈNE

2 pints/5 cups chicken stock
1 lb tomatoes, chopped
4 sticks celery, finely chopped
2 oz canned pimientos, chopped
1 strip lemon peel
2 egg whites
2 tablespoons dry sherry
2 oz pimientos, diced
1 tomato, skinned and diced
freshly ground black pepper
SOUP NUTS:
2 teaspoons vegetable oil
salt
1 egg
3 oz/¾ cup all-purpose flour
vegetable oil for frying

To make consommé, put stock, tomatoes, celery, chopped pimientos and lemon peel into a large saucepan. Whisk in egg whites and bring to the boil, stirring. Reduce heat, cover and simmer very slowly for 1 hour. To make soup nuts, put oil, ½ teaspoon salt and egg into a food processor. Add flour and mix to a smooth dough. Roll out into thin rolls about ¼ in. thick and leave to dry for a further 10 minutes. Snip with scissors into ¼ in. pieces and leave for a further 30 minutes.

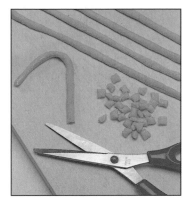

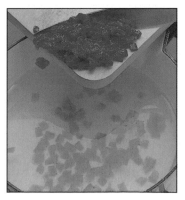

Heat oil in a deep-fat frying pan and fry soup nuts until crisp and golden. Drain on absorbent kitchen paper and use as an accompaniment to the soup. Strain consommé through a large cheesecloth-lined sieve or colander into a bowl. Return to a clean pan and add sherry, diced pimientos and tomato. Add salt and pepper if necessary and reheat.

Serves 4-6.

ZUCCHINI SOUP

2 tablespoons olive or sunflower oil
2 sweet onions, finely chopped
2½ pints/6¼ cups chicken stock
2 lb zucchini, grated
fresh lemon juice, to taste
salt and freshly ground pepper
2 tablespoons chopped fresh chervil or tarragon
5 fl oz/⅔ cup low-fat Greek yogurt, to serve

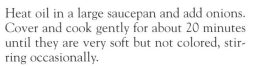

Heat oil in a large saucepan and add onions. Cover and cook gently for about 20 minutes until they are very soft but not colored, stirring occasionally.

Pour in stock and bring to the boil. Stir in zucchini and bring to the boil again then turn down the heat and simmer for 15 minutes. Season to taste with lemon juice, salt and pepper.

Stir in chopped chervil or tarragon, add a swirl of yogurt and serve at once.

Serves 6.

SQUASH SOUP & MINT PURÉE

1 butternut squash, about 1 lb
1 oz/2 tablespoons butter
1 onion, finely chopped
1 clove garlic, crushed
½ teaspoon each ground tumeric and ground cumin
30 fl oz/3¾ cups chicken or vegetable stock
salt and freshly ground black pepper
toasted cumin seeds, to garnish
MINT PURÉE:
1 small bunch fresh mint
2 tablespoons olive oil
1 teaspoon lemon juice

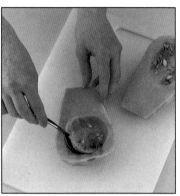

Peel the squash, remove the seeds and roughly chop the flesh.

In a large saucepan, heat the butter. Add the chopped onion and cook gently for 10 minutes until soft. Stir in the garlic, turmeric and cumin and cook, stirring, for 2 more minutes. Add the pieces of squash and stock and season with salt and pepper. Bring to the boil then cover and simmer for 20 minutes until the squash is soft.

Meanwhile, make the mint purée. In a mortar and pestle, pound the mint with a large pinch of salt. Add the olive oil and lemon juice and mix to a purée. In a blender or food processor, process the squash soup until smooth. Check the seasoning and pour into heated bowls. Add a spoonful of purée to each and garnish with toasted cumin seeds.

Serves 4-6.

Note: If butternut squash is not available, other squashes such as pumpkin may be used.

BLUE CHEESE & BROCCOLI SOUP

6 oz potatoes
1 oz/2 tablespoons butter
1 onion, finely chopped
35 fl oz/4½ cups chicken stock
12 oz broccoli
salt and freshly ground black pepper
4 oz blue cheese such as Roquefort, Danish Blue or
  Gorgonzola
CROÛTONS:
2 thick slices white bread, crusts removed
2 tablespoons sunflower oil
½ oz/1 tablespoon butter
1 clove garlic, finely chopped

Peel potatoes and cut into 1 in. dice.

Heat butter in a saucepan. Add onion and cook, stirring occasionally, for 5 minutes, until soft. Add stock and potatoes, bring to the boil, cover and simmer for 10 minutes. Cut broccoli into flowerets and add to pan. Return to the boil, cover and simmer gently for 10 minutes, until vegetables are tender.

Meanwhile, make croûtons. Cut bread into shapes with a pastry cutter. Heat oil, butter and garlic in a skillet and fry bread shapes on both sides until golden and crisp. Remove with a slotted spoon and drain on kitchen paper. Purée soup in a blender or food processor. Return to rinsed-out pan, add salt and pepper, then crumble in cheese. Reheat gently without boiling, until cheese has melted. Garnish with croûtons and serve.

Serves 6.

HERBED PEA SOUP

2 oz/¼ cup unsalted butter
1 leek, finely chopped
1 small round lettuce, separated into leaves
about 30 fl oz/3¾ cups vegetable or chicken stock, or
    water
several sprigs of chervil
few sprigs of parsley
1 lb fresh or frozen peas
salt and freshly ground black pepper
light cream, to garnish

Heat butter in a saucepan, add leek and cook, stirring occasionally, for 5 minutes, until soft. Add lettuce and cook for 1-2 minutes, until leaves have wilted.

Add stock or water, chervil, parsley and fresh peas if using, bring to the boil and simmer for 10 minutes if using fresh peas. If using frozen peas, simmer for 5 minutes, until peas are tender.

Purée soup in a blender or food processor and return to rinsed-out pan. Add salt and pepper and reheat gently without boiling. If soup is too thick, add some boiling stock or water. Swirl in cream and serve.

Serves 4.

EGGPLANT & GARLIC SOUP

2 eggplants, peeled
4 tablespoons olive oil
4 cloves garlic, peeled
2 fl oz/¼ cup water
1 onion, chopped
1 zucchini, chopped
2 ripe tomatoes, skinned, seeded and diced
1 teaspoon chopped fresh thyme
2 teaspoons lemon juice
30 fl oz/3¾ cups vegetable stock
salt and freshly ground black pepper
diced skinned tomatoes, grated lemon zest and thyme
    leaves, to garnish

Preheat broiler. Cut the eggplants lengthwise into ¼ in. slices, brush with a little oil and place under the hot broiler. Cook until lightly charred, then turn over and cook other sides also until lightly charred. Fry the garlic in 1 tablespoon oil for 5 minutes until golden, add the water, then cover and simmer for 5 minutes until soft. Mash with a fork.

Heat the remaining oil in a large saucepan and fry the onion for 3 minutes until soft. Add the zucchini, tomatoes and thyme and fry for a further 3 minutes. Add the eggplant, mashed garlic, lemon juice and stock. Bring to the boil, cover and simmer gently for 15 minutes. Purée the soup in a blender or food processor until smooth. Return to the pan, season to taste and heat through for 5 minutes. Garnish and serve hot.

Serves 6.

SAFFRON SOUP & QUENNELLES

OYSTER & LEEK SOUP

1 onion, chopped
8 oz potatoes, chopped
8 oz white fish fillet, skinned and chopped
1½ pints/3¾ cups fish stock
¼ teaspoon powdered saffron
5 fl oz/⅔ cup light cream
salt and freshly ground black pepper
dill sprigs, to garnish
TROUT QUENNELLES:
8 oz pink trout fillets, skinned
1 teaspoon anchovy essence
2 oz/1 cup day-old white breadcrumbs
2 eggs, separated

18 oysters, unopened
1 oz/2 tablespoons butter
3 leeks, trimmed and thinly sliced
1 shallot, finely chopped
4 fl oz/½ cup dry white wine
16 fl oz/2 cups light fish stock
8 fl oz/1 cup light cream
salt and freshly ground black pepper
four 2 in. rounds fried bread, to garnish

Insert point of an oyster knife or sharp, short-bladed vegetable knife at hinge of each oyster shell and twist open, holding over a bowl to catch juices. Remove each oyster and put into bowl.

Put onion, potatoes and fish in a saucepan with fish stock, cover and gently simmer for 25 minutes, until potatoes are cooked. Meanwhile, prepare quennelle mixture. Put the trout into a blender or food processor with the anchovy essence, breadcrumbs and egg yolks and work until smooth. Turn into a bowl and chill until the soup is ready. Blend soup to a purée, then sieve and return to pan. Add saffron and cream and reheat very gently. Add salt and pepper if necessary.

Melt butter in a saucepan, add leeks and cook gently for 5 minutes, until beginning to soften. Lift out with a slotted spoon and set aside. Add shallot to pan and cook until soft. Pour in the wine and simmer for 5 minutes, uncovered. Add stock and simmer for a further 5 minutes. Meanwhile, put half the oysters in a blender or food processor with their juice and work until coarsely chopped. Cut remaining oysters in half.

Whisk egg whites until stiff and fold into the trout mixture. Bring a pan of salted water or fish stock to the boil, then reduce to a simmer. Drop heaped teaspoons of trout mixture into the water and cook for 2-3 minutes, until they float to surface. Lift out with a slotted spoon and place on top of the reheated soup. Garnish with fresh dill.

Add chopped and halved oysters to soup with three-quarters of the leeks and cream and season with salt and pepper. Reheat very slowly: do not boil but maintain a heat below simmering for 3-4 minutes, until oysters are just cooked. Reheat remaining leeks in a small pan, then divide between croûtons. Float one on each portion of soup.

Serves 6.

Serves 4.

CURRIED COCONUT SOUP

2 tablespoons olive oil
1 onion, chopped
1 clove garlic, crushed
1 teaspoon grated fresh root ginger
2 teaspoons curry powder
3 oz/½ cup long-grain rice
40 fl oz/5 cups vegetable stock
6 oz spinach
2 oz creamed coconut
1 tablespoon chopped fresh cilantro
salt and freshly ground black pepper

Heat the oil in a large saucepan and fry the onion, garlic, ginger and curry powder for 5 minutes.

Add the rice and stir-fry for 2 minutes until transparent. Add the stock, bring to the boil, cover and simmer gently for 10 minutes. Wash the spinach, discard tough stalks and dry well, then cut into thin shreds. Add to the pan and cook for a further 5 minutes.

Place the creamed coconut in a small bowl and stir in 5 fl oz/⅔ cup boiling water, stirring until melted. Stir into the pan with the cilantro and heat through for 2-3 minutes, without boiling. Taste and adjust seasoning. Serve hot.

Serves 6-8.

FRAGRANT THAI BROTH

30 fl oz/3¾ cups vegetable stock
2 slices fresh root ginger
2 sprigs cilantro
1 stalk lemon grass, lightly crushed
1 red chili
1 clove garlic, crushed
4 oz/1 cup diced plain tofu
2 tablespoons light soy sauce
2 oz dried wholewheat noodles
2 carrots, cut into matchsticks
4 oz shiitake mushrooms, wiped and sliced
2 teaspoons tamarind paste or lemon juice
cilantro leaves, to garnish

Pour the stock into a pan and add the ginger, cilantro sprigs, lemon grass, chili and garlic. Bring slowly to the boil, cover and simmer gently for 25 minutes. Meanwhile, marinate the tofu in the soy sauce for 25 minutes.

Cook noodles according to packet instructions, then drain well and transfer to warmed soup bowls. Strain stock into a clean pan, add soy sauce and the tofu, carrots and mushrooms. Simmer for 2-3 minutes until tender. Arrange the tofu and vegetables over the noodles. Whisk the tamarind paste or lemon juice into the broth, return to the boil and pour over the noodles. Garnish with cilantro leaves and serve at once.

Serves 4.

PROVENÇAL FISH SOUP

2 tablespoons olive oil
1 leek, sliced
2 sticks celery, chopped
1 onion, chopped
2 cloves garlic, chopped
4 ripe tomatoes, chopped
1 tablespoon tomato paste
5 fl oz/⅔ cup dry white wine
bouquet garni
1 teaspoon saffron strands
2¼ lb mixed fish fillets and shellfish, fish trimmings, bones and heads
salt and freshly ground black pepper
croûtons and grated Gruyère cheese, to serve
ROUILLE:
1 slice white bread, crusts removed
1 red bell pepper
1-2 fresh red chilies, cored, seeded and chopped
2 cloves garlic, crushed
olive oil

To make the rouille, soak the bread in cold water for 10 minutes then squeeze dry. Preheat the broiler. Quarter the pepper and remove the core and seeds. Broil, skin side up, until the skin is charred and blistered. Put into a plastic bag and leave until cool enough to handle. Peel off the skin.

Roughly chop the pepper and put in a food processor or blender with the bread, chilies and garlic. Process, adding a little olive oil, if necessary, to form a coarse paste. Transfer to a small bowl and set aside.

Heat the olive oil in a large saucepan. Add the leek, celery, onion and garlic. Cook gently for 10 minutes until soft. Add the tomatoes, tomato paste, wine, bouquet garni, saffron, any shellfish and the fish trimmings. Bring to the boil, cover and simmer for 30 minutes.

Strain through a colander into a clean saucepan, pressing out as much liquid as possible. Discard the shellfish, trimmings and vegetables. Cut the fish fillets into large chunks and add to the strained soup. Cover and simmer gently for 10 minutes until the fish is cooked through. Strain through a colander into a clean saucepan. Put the cooked fish in a food processor or blender with 10 fl oz/1¼ cups of the soup. Process until well blended but still retaining some texture.

Stir the fish back into the remaining soup. Season and reheat gently. Serve the soup with the rouille, croûtons and grated cheese handed separately.

Serves 4-6.

Note: The fish and shellfish mixture should contain white fish fillets, a small piece of smoked cod and a few mussels and shrimp.

MUSSEL SOUP

2 tablespoons olive oil
3 cloves garlic, 2 chopped and 1 whole
8 oz ripe tomatoes, chopped
pinch of chili powder
6 slices country bread
16 fl oz/3 cups fish or vegetable stock
3 lb mussels, scrubbed and de-bearded
3 tablespoons chopped fresh parsley

Heat the oil in a large flameproof casserole, add chopped garlic and cook until golden. Stir in the tomatoes and chili powder. Cover and simmer for 25 minutes until the oil separates.

Cut whole garlic clove in half. Toast bread on both sides and rub each side with a cut side of the garlic clove.

Add stock to the casserole and bring to boil. Add mussels, cover and cook for 3-5 minutes until all the mussels are open, occasionally shaking the pan. Scatter parsley over the top and serve with the garlic bread.

Serves 6.

Variation: Substitute clams for the mussels.

LEMON GRASS SOUP

6-8 oz raw large shrimp
2 teaspoons vegetable oil
20 fl oz/2½ cups light fish stock
2 thick stalks lemon grass, finely chopped
3 tablespoons lime juice
1 tablespoon fish sauce
3 kaffir lime leaves, chopped
½ fresh red chili, seeded and thinly sliced
½ fresh green chili, seeded and thinly sliced
½ teaspoon crushed palm sugar
cilantro leaves, to garnish

Peel shrimp and remove dark veins running down their backs; reserve shrimp.

In a wok, heat oil, add shrimp shells and fry, stirring occasionally, until they change color. Stir in stock, bring to boil and simmer for 20 minutes. Strain stock and return to wok; discard shells. Add lemon grass, lime juice, fish sauce, lime leaves, chilies and sugar. Simmer for 2 minutes.

Add shrimp and cook just below simmering point for 2-3 minutes until shrimp are cooked. Serve in warmed bowls garnished with cilantro.

Serves 4.

CREAM OF SHRIMP SOUP

1 lb raw shrimp
2 oz/¼ cup butter
1 small onion, chopped
1½ oz/⅓ cup all-purpose flour
3 tablespoons white wine
5 fl oz/⅔ cup light cream
SHELLFISH STOCK:
8 oz fish scraps and bones
1 strip lemon peel
1 stick celery, chopped
1 small onion, quartered
5 fennel seeds
salt and freshly ground black pepper

VIETNAMESE FISH SOUP

1 tablespoon vegetable oil
2 cloves garlic, finely chopped
2 shallots or 1 small onion, chopped
1 tablespoon each chili sauce and tomato paste
2 tomatoes, cubed
3 tablespoons fish sauce
2 tablespoons sugar
24 fl oz/3 cups chicken stock
2 tablespoons tamarind water or lime juice
8 oz firm fish fillet, cut into small slices
4 oz fresh scallops, sliced
4 oz raw peeled shrimp
12 clams or mussels, scrubbed clean
2-3 tablespoons dry white wine or sherry
salt and freshly ground black pepper
cilantro sprigs, to garnish

Peel shrimp and set aside. To make stock, put shrimp shells into a large saucepan with 2 pints/5 cups water and remaining stock ingredients and slowly bring to the boil, removing any scum which rises to surface. Lower heat and simmer for 25 minutes, then strain through a cheesecloth-lined sieve. Return to rinsed-out pan and simmer to reduce to 24 fl oz/3 cups.

Heat oil in a wok or pan and lightly brown garlic and shallots or onion. Add the chili sauce, tomato paste, cubed tomato, fish sauce and sugar. Blend well, then simmer mixture for 2-3 minutes. Add the stock with tamarind water or lime juice and bring to the boil.

Melt butter in a saucepan, add onion and cook until soft. Stir in flour, cook for 1 minute, then gradually blend in stock. Add wine and three-quarters of the shrimp, bring to the boil, then simmer for 10 minutes. Cool soup slightly, then purée in a blender or food processor. Return to pan and add cream and salt and pepper if necessary. Reheat gently for 3-4 minutes, then serve, garnished with reserved shrimp.

Serves 4.

When ready to serve, add the seafood and wine or sherry to the stock, bring back to boil, cover and simmer for 3-4 minutes until clam or mussel shells have opened; discard any that remain closed after cooking. Taste soup and adjust the seasoning. Serve hot, garnished with cilantro sprigs.

Serves 4-6.

Note: Take care not to overcook seafood. If using ready-shelled clams or mussels, reduce the cooking time by half.

SMOKED SALMON & DILL SOUP

1 oz/2 tablespoons butter
2 shallots, finely chopped
½ oz/2 tablespoons all-purpose flour
20 fl oz/2½ cups milk
½ fish stock cube
1 cucumber, peeled and chopped
6 oz smoked salmon bits
1 tablespoon chopped fresh dill
5 fl oz/⅔ cup light cream
salt and freshly ground black pepper

Melt butter in a pan, add shallots and cook until soft. Stir in flour and cook for 1 minute, then gradually stir in milk. Bring to boil and crumble in stock cube, then add cucumber.

Simmer stock for 10 minutes. Reserve a few of better bits of salmon for garnish, then chop remainder and add to soup and cook for 2-3 minutes.

Purée in a blender or food processor until smooth. Return to pan, add dill and cream and salt and pepper if necessary and gently reheat. Serve garnished with small pieces of reserved smoke salmon.

Serves 4.

HOT & SOUR TURKEY SOUP

4 oz lean turkey, minced
1 oz dried Chinese mushrooms, soaked in hot water
for 20 minutes
4 oz Szechuan preserved vegetables, shredded
35 fl oz/4½ cups Chinese Chicken Stock (see page
57)
2 teaspoons brown sugar
2 tablespoons red rice vinegar
large pinch of ground white pepper
1 tablespoon dark soy sauce
2 teaspoons cornstarch blended with 4 teaspoons
water
2 scallions, finely chopped
2 tablespoons chopped fresh cilantro

Blanch the turkey in a saucepan of boiling water for 3 minutes. Drain and set aside. Drain mushrooms and squeeze out excess water. Discard stems and slice the caps.

Place all the ingredients except the cornstarch mixture, scallions and cilantro, in a saucepan. Bring to the boil and simmer for 3 minutes. Add the cornstarch mixture and cook, stirring, until thickened. Add chopped scallions and cilantro and serve.

Serves 4.

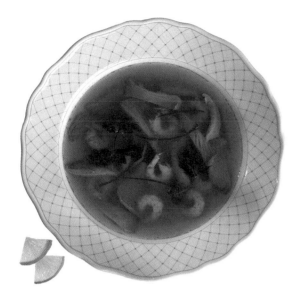

HOT & SOUR SHRIMP SOUP

8 oz cooked shrimp in shells
2 stalks lemon grass
50 fl oz/6¼ cups vegetable stock
4 kaffir lime leaves
2 slices fresh root ginger, peeled
2 fl oz/¼ cup Thai fish sauce
2 fl oz/¼ cup lime juice
2 cloves garlic, very finely chopped
2 shallots, very finely chopped
1 fresh red chili, cored, seeded and cut into thin
    strips
4 oz oyster mushrooms, sliced
12 cilantro sprigs

Peel shrimp. Reserve shrimp and put shells in a large saucepan.

Lightly crush lemon grass and add to pan with stock, lime leaves and ginger. Bring to the boil and simmer for 20 minutes. Strain into a clean saucepan, discarding shrimp shells and herbs.

Add fish sauce, lime juice, garlic, shallots, chili and mushrooms to pan. Bring to the boil and simmer gently for 5 minutes. Add peeled shrimp and cook for 1 minute, to heat through. Add cilantro sprigs and serve.

Serves 6.

CHICKEN SOUP WITH KREPLACH

8 oz/2 cups all-purpose flour
salt and freshly ground black pepper
3 eggs, beaten
2 tablespoons chopped fresh parsley
2 tablespoons chopped fresh oregano
1 tablespoon oil
1 small onion, finely chopped
6 oz skinned and boned chicken, ground
finely grated rind of 1 lemon
2 tablespoons Greek yogurt
20 fl oz/2½ cups consommé

Sift the flour and a pinch of salt into a bowl and make a well in the center. Add the eggs and half of the parsley and oregano.

Using a fork, gradually blend in the flour to form a soft dough. If the dough is too sticky, add a little more flour. Knead the dough on a lightly floured surface for 3-4 minutes. Wrap in plastic wrap and refrigerate for 30 minutes. In small pan, heat the oil. Add the onion and cook until soft. Add the chicken and cook for a further 2-3 minutes. Add the lemon rind, remaining herbs and yogurt. Season and put on one side to cool. On a floured board, roll out the dough to about ⅛ in. thickness. Cut the dough into 2-2½ in. squares.

Place a spoonful of the filling on each square, brush the edges with a little water and fold the dough in half over the filling to make a triangle. Pinch the edges together to seal, then pull 2 corners together and pinch them to make them stick. Repeat with the remaining dough and filling. Bring a pan of salted water to the boil and cook the kreplach for 5-7 minutes or until the dough is cooked. Heat the consommé, add the kreplach, heat through and serve.

Serves 4.

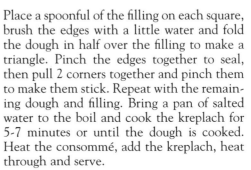

CHICKEN & ASPARAGUS SOUP

AVGOLEMONO

8 oz fresh asparagus
35 fl oz/4½ cups Chinese chicken Stock (see page 57)
2 tablespoons light soy sauce
2 tablespoons dry sherry
2 teaspoons brown sugar
2 oz vermicelli rice noodles
½ in. piece fresh root ginger, peeled and chopped
12 oz lean cooked chicken, finely shredded
salt and ground white pepper
2 scallions, finely chopped, to garnish

2 pints/5 cups chicken stock
salt and freshly ground black pepper
2 oz/⅓ cup long-grain rice
2 eggs
finely grated peel of ½ lemon
juice of 1 lemon
3 tablespoons chopped fresh parsley
parsley sprigs and thin lemon slices, to garnish

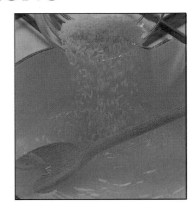

Put stock into a saucepan and bring to the boil. Add salt and pepper and rice and simmer for 15 minutes or until rice is tender.

Trim ends from asparagus stalks and slice stalks into 1½ in. pieces. Pour stock into a large saucepan along with soy sauce and sherry. Stir in brown sugar. Bring to the boil and add asparagus and noodles. Simmer, covered, for 5-6 minutes.

Break the eggs into a bowl, add lemon peel and juice and beat together. Whisk in a ladleful of hot stock, then pour mixture back into pan, stirring constantly.

Stir in the chopped ginger and shredded chicken and season well. Simmer gently for 3-4 minutes to heat through. Garnish with chopped scallions and serve.

Serves 4.

Reheat over a low heat until the soup thickens and looks creamy: do not boil. Stir in chopped parsley and serve at once, garnished with a parsley sprig and a lemon slice on each portion.

Serves 4-6.

Note: This soup can also be served cold.

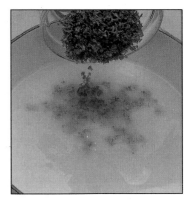

CHICKEN & BOK CHOY SOUP

6 oz lean chicken
6 oz bok choy
35 fl oz/4½ cups Chinese Chicken Stock (see page 57)
1 in piece fresh root ginger, peeled and finely chopped
2 tablespoons rice wine
1 tablespoon light soy sauce
salt and freshly ground black pepper
strips of fresh root ginger, to garnish

Cut the chicken into thin strips. Blanch in a saucepan of boiling water for 2 minutes until just firm and opaque. Drain.

Trim and shred bok choy. Blanch in a saucepan of boiling water for 20 seconds until wilted. Rinse in cold water and drain.

Pour stock into a saucepan and stir in chopped ginger, wine and soy sauce. Bring to the boil, reduce to a simmer and add prepared bok choy and chicken. Simmer for 5 minutes, season well and serve garnished with ginger strips.

Serves 4.

CHICKEN & MUSHROOM SOUP

2 cloves garlic, crushed
4 cilantro sprigs
1½ teaspoons black peppercorns, crushed
1 tablespoon vegetable oil
35 fl oz/4¼ cups chicken stock
5 pieces dried Chinese black mushrooms, soaked in cold water for 20 minutes, drained and coarsely chopped
1 tablespoon fish sauce
4 oz chicken, cut into strips
2 oz scallions, thinly sliced
cilantro sprigs, to garnish

Using a pestle and mortar or small blender, pound or mix garlic, cilantro stalks and leaves and peppercorns to a paste. In a wok, heat oil, add paste and cook, stirring, for 1 minute. Stir in stock, mushrooms and fish sauce. Simmer for 5 minutes.

Add chicken, lower heat so liquid barely moves and cook gently for 5 minutes. Scatter scallions over surface and garnish with cilantro sprigs.

Serves 4.

CHINESE CHICKEN STOCK

2¼ -2¾ lb chicken, giblets removed
2 slices fresh root ginger
1 clove garlic
2 scallions
large pinch of salt
large pinch of ground white pepper

Skin the chicken and trim away any visible fat. Wash and place in a large saucepan with remaining ingredients and 70 fl oz/9 cups of cold water.

Bring to the boil, skimming away surface scum using a large flat ladle. Reduce heat, cover and simmer gently for 2 hours. Allow to cool.

Line a sieve with clean muslin and place over a large bowl. Ladle stock through sieve and discard chicken and vegetables. Cover and chill. Skim away any fat that forms on the surface before using. Store in refrigerator for up to 3 days or freeze for up to 3 months.

Makes 62 fl oz/7¾ cups.

BEAN CURD SOUP

35 fl oz/4½ cups well-flavored vegetable stock
8 oz bean curd, cut into ½ in. cubes
1 fresh red chili, cored, seeded and finely chopped
6 shallots, finely chopped
1 small carrot, finely chopped
2 scallions, sliced into rings
4 tablespoons light soy sauce
2 teaspoons light brown sugar
salt

Pour stock into a saucepan. Add bean curd, chili, shallots, carrot, scallions, soy sauce and sugar.

Bring to the boil, uncovered. Stir briefly then simmer for 2-3 minutes.

Add salt to taste. Ladle the soup into warmed soup bowls. Serve as part of a main meal to counterbalance hot dishes.

Serves 4.

STARTERS

BABA GANOUSH

2 small eggplants
1 clove garlic, crushed
4 tablespoons tahini
1 oz/¼ cup ground almonds
juice of ½ lemon
½ teaspoon ground cumin
salt and freshly ground black pepper
1 tablespoon chopped fresh mint leaves
2 tablespoons olive oil
fresh mint leaves, to garnish
selection of vegetables such as baby artichokes,
  radishes, sliced bell peppers to serve

Place eggplants under a hot broiler, turning often, until black.

Remove the skins, chop the flesh roughly and leave to drain in a colander for 10 minutes. Squeeze out as much liquid from the eggplants as possible and place the flesh in a food processor or blender. Add cumin, salt and pepper and process to a smooth paste.

Stir the chopped mint leaves into the dip. Spoon into a bowl and drizzle with olive oil. Scatter mint leaves on top. Place the bowl on a serving platter and serve with the vegetable selection.

Serves 6.

BAKED STUFFED ARTICHOKES

4 large young artichokes
3 tablespoons fresh white breadcrumbs
1 oz/¼ cup pecorino cheese, grated
juice 1 lemon
5 tablespoons olive oil
½ oz/1 tablespoon butter
2 tablespoons olive oil
3 slices lean bacon, chopped
1 small onion, finely chopped
2 sticks celery, finely chopped
2 zucchini, finely chopped
1 clove garlic, crushed
1 tablespoon chopped fresh sage
1 tablespoon chopped fresh Italian parsley
salt and freshly ground black pepper
fresh Italian parsley sprigs to garnish

Preheat oven to 400F (200C). Cook artichokes in a saucepan of boiling salted water for 30 minutes. Remove and place upside down to drain. Pull away and discard outer leaves and, using a teaspoon, remove central hairy choke. Heat butter and 2 tablespoons olive oil in a saucepan. Add bacon, onion, celery, zucchini and garlic and cook gently for 5 minutes, stirring frequently, until vegetables are just soft. Stir in herbs. Purée half the mixture in a food processor or blender. Return to pan. Season with salt and freshly ground black pepper.

Place artichokes close together in an ovenproof dish. Fill centres of artichokes with vegetable mixture. In a small bowl, mix together breadcrumbs and cheese. Pile on top of filling. Sprinkle with lemon juice and remaining 3 tablespoons olive oil. Cover with foil and bake in the preheated oven for 15 minutes. Remove foil. Bake for a further 10 minutes until lightly browned. Serve garnished with Italian parsley sprigs.

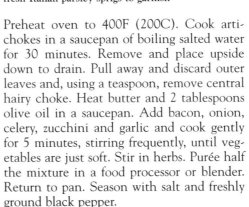

Serves 4.

ARTICHOKES WITH AÏOLI

PICKLED VEGETABLES

6 globe artichokes
1 teaspoon lemon juice
1 slice lemon
1 teaspoon sunflower oil
AÏOLI:
5 fl oz/⅔ cup mayonnaise
2 cloves garlic, crushed
1 teaspoon Dijon mustard

Cut off artichoke stalks and any tough leaves. Trim base so that artichokes will stand upright. Trim about ½ in. off leafy top with a sharp knife.

8 oz baby carrots
8 oz radishes, trimmed
1 fennel bulb, sliced
2 teaspoons salt
4 tablespoons white wine vinegar
4 tablespoons sugar
1 tablespoon green peppercorns in brine, drained
1 tablespoon capers
freshly ground black pepper
cilantro leaves, to garnish

Peel and trim the carrots, leaving some green leaves attached at the top. Place in a bowl.

Add lemon juice to a large bowl of cold water and soak artichokes for 20-30 minutes. Put artichokes into a pan of boiling salted water. Add lemon slice and oil and cook for 30-40 minutes, until a base leaf can be pulled off easily. Drain artichokes, turn upside down on a rack and leave to cool.

Add the radishes and fennel slices to the carrots in the bowl. Sprinkle the salt over and leave for 2 hours. Drain the vegetables and rinse with cold water. Pat dry and return to the bowl.

To make aïoli, mix together mayonnaise, garlic and mustard. Pull out central leaves of artichokes, scrape out fibrous hairs with a teaspoon and discard. Place artichokes on serving plates and serve with aïoli.

Serves 6.

Variation: Artichokes may also be served with a vinaigrette dressing or a herb mayonnaise. Alternatively, serve hot, with melted butter or hollandaise sauce.

In a saucepan, heat the vinegar and sugar, without boiling, until the sugar is dissolved. Pour the vinegar mixture over the vegetables and add the peppercorns, capers and pepper. Leave until cold then cover and refrigerate overnight. Serve the vegetables garnished with cilantro leaves.

Serves 6.

EGGPLANT STACKS

2½ fl oz olive oil
1 onion, finely chopped
1 clove garlic, crushed
1 red bell pepper, seeded and chopped
14 oz can chopped tomatoes
1 oz sun-dried tomatoes in oil, drained and chopped
1 tablespoon raisins
½ teaspoon sugar
2 teaspoons balsamic vinegar
salt and freshly ground black pepper
1 teaspoon dried mint
4 long-shaped eggplants
fresh mint sprigs, to garnish

ROAST VEGETABLE CUPS

2 eggplants, cut into ¼ in. cubes
4 zucchini, cut into ¼ in. cubes
1 red onion, chopped
2 cloves garlic, crushed
4 tablespoons olive oil
juice of ½ lemon
2 teaspoons dried oregano
salt and freshly ground black pepper
1½ oz/3 tablespoons butter, melted
6 sheets filo pastry, 16 × 12 in.
strips of sun-dried tomatoes and toasted pine nuts, to
    garnish

In a saucepan, heat 2 tablespoons of the olive oil. Add the onion and garlic and cook for 10 minutes or until soft. Add the bell pepper, canned tomatoes, sun-dried tomatoes, raisins, sugar, vinegar, salt, pepper and mint. Simmer gently, uncovered, for 20 minutes or until the mixture has thickened. Meanwhile, cut the eggplants into ¼ in. thick slices. Brush each slice on both sides with the remaining olive oil.

Preheat the oven to 400F (200C). Place the eggplants, zucchini and onion in a large roasting pan. Add the garlic, olive oil, lemon juice, oregano, salt and pepper and mix well. Roast for 30 minutes, stirring occasionally, until tender and slightly browned. Meanwhile, prepare the filo cups. Invert 12 individual ramekins on a baking sheet. Brush lightly with melted butter. Brush 1 sheet of pastry with melted butter and cut into 6 squares. Press 1 square, butter side up, over an upturned ramekin.

Heat a ridge cast iron grill pan and cook the eggplant slices for 3-4 minutes on each side until soft and browned. Keep hot while cooking the remaining slices. Spoon a little of the tomato mixture on an eggplant slice. Top with a second slice. Keep warm. Repeat with the remaining eggplant slices and tomato mixture. Serve garnished with mint sprigs.

Serves 6.

Repeat with a second square at an angle so that the points form petals. Repeat with a third square. Cover remaining ramekins in the same way. Remove vegetables from oven and keep warm. Reduce oven temperature to 375F (190C). Bake the cups for 10 minutes until crisp and golden. Ease off the ramekins and place on a serving dish. Divide roast vegetables between the cups. Garnish with sun-dried tomatoes and pine nuts and serve with salad.

Makes 12.

BROILED VEGETABLES

1 red bell pepper
2 baby zucchini
2 baby eggplants
1 fennel bulb
8 baby sweetcorn
salt and freshly ground black pepper
zucchini flowers and basil sprigs, to garnish
MARINADE:
5 fl oz/⅔ cup olive oil
2 cloves garlic, crushed
1 teaspoon chopped fresh parsley
1 teaspoon chopped fresh mint
1 teaspoon chopped fresh oregano

To make marinade, in a bowl mix together olive oil, garlic, parsley, mint and oregano. Cut red pepper into quarters, lengthwise. Remove seeds and core. Cut zucchini in half lengthwise. Cut eggplants in half lengthwise. Cut fennel bulb into quarters. Put pepper, zucchini, eggplants, fennel and sweetcorn into the bowl with the marinade. Leave for at least 1 hour.

Preheat broiler or barbecue. Broil vegetables for about 10 minutes, or until tender. Turn them every few minutes and brush with marinade. Season with salt and pepper. Garnish with zucchini flowers and basil sprigs.

Serves 4.

Variation: A wide variety of vegetables can be broiled. Try mushrooms, tomatoes, chicory, onions and squashes.

FENNEL WITH FETA & PEARS

2 fennel bulbs
4 tablespoons olive oil
6 oz feta cheese
1 ripe pear
4 sun-dried tomatoes in oil, drained and sliced
1 oz/¼ cup pitted black olives
a few basil leaves
1 teaspoon lemon juice
½ teaspoon clear honey
salt and freshly ground black pepper

Preheat broiler. Trim the fennel, discarding any damaged outer leaves. Cut each bulb, lengthwise, into 6 thin slices.

Brush with a little of the olive oil and place under the hot broiler for 2-3 minutes until browned. Turn fennel, brush with oil and broil for a further 2-3 minutes until charred and just tender. Leave to cool slightly.

Slice the feta into thin slabs and quarter, core and thinly slice the pear. Arrange the fennel, cheese and pear on serving plates and top with the tomatoes, olives and basil. Blend the remaining oil, lemon juice, honey and seasonings together, drizzle over the salad and serve.

Serves 4.

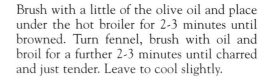

ANCHOVY-STUFFED MUSHROOMS

1 oz fresh bread without crusts, crumbled
4 tablespoons milk
1 lb medium cap mushrooms
4 oz/4 slices green (unsmoked) bacon, finely chopped
4 canned anchovy fillets, finely chopped
1 clove garlic, finely chopped
1 egg, beaten
3 tablespoons finely chopped fresh parsley
pinch chopped fresh oregano
salt and freshly ground black pepper
4 tablespoons dry breadcrumbs
4 tablespoons olive oil
oregano sprigs, to garnish

Preheat the oven to 400F (200C). Oil a large baking tray. Put fresh bread in a small bowl, add milk and leave to soak. Remove stalks from mushrooms and chop finely. Put into a bowl with bacon, anchovy fillets, garlic, egg, parsley, oregano and salt and pepper. Squeeze soaked bread dry, add to bacon mixture and mix together well.

Divide bread mixture between open side of mushroom caps, piling mixture into small mounds. Place on baking tray and sprinkle with dry breadcrumbs. Trickle oil over mushrooms, bake on top shelf of oven for 20-30 minutes until top of stuffing is crisp. Leave to stand for a few minutes before serving, garnished with oregano.

Serves 4-6.

AVOCADO & REDCURRANTS

3 ripe avocados
redcurrants, to garnish
DRESSING:
6 oz redcurrants
2 tablespoons balsamic vinegar
4 fl oz/½ cup light olive oil or sunflower oil
salt and freshly ground black pepper
½-1 teaspoon sugar

To make dressing, purée redcurrants in a blender or food processor. Press through a nylon sieve to remove seeds.

Return redcurrant purée to blender with vinegar. With motor running, gradually pour in oil. Season with salt and pepper and add sugar to taste.

Halve avocados lengthwise. Removes pits and peel. Thinly slice flesh lengthwise. Fan out slices on serving plates. Stir dressing and pour around avocados. Garnish with redcurrants and serve immediately.

Serves 6.

Note: Be sure to use a nylon sieve as a metal one may taint the flavor of the redcurrants.

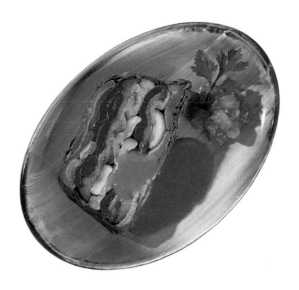

RATATOUILLE TERRINE

10-12 large spinach leaves
salt and freshly ground black pepper
3 yellow bell peppers, quartered
3 red bell peppers, quartered
1 clove garlic, crushed
4 fl oz/½ cup olive oil
2 eggplants
4 zucchini
red and yellow bell pepper strips and flat-leaf parsley
  sprigs, to garnish
2 tomatoes, peeled, seeded and diced, to serve
TOMATO VINAIGRETTE:
1 large ripe tomato
4 teaspoons balsamic vinegar
4 fl oz/½ cup olive oil

Put a layer of yellow peppers in base of lined terrine, then add a layer of red peppers, followed by layers of eggplant, zucchini, red pepper, eggplant, zucchini, finishing with a layer of yellow pepper. Lightly season each layer with salt and pepper.

Remove stalks from spinach and rinse leaves thoroughly. Blanch spinach in boiling water for 1 minute. Drain, rinse in cold water and drain again. Spread spinach leaves on a clean tea towel, place another tea towel on top and pat dry. Line a 35 fl oz/4½ cup terrine or loaf pan with cling film. Line terrine with blanched spinach leaves, leaving ends overhanging sides of terrine. Season lightly with salt and pepper.

Fold overhanging spinach over top of terrine. Cover with cling film. Press down with a weight and chill for 8 hours.

Preheat broiler. Broil and peel peppers. Mix together garlic and olive oil. Cut zucchini and eggplant lengthwise into ½ in. slices. Brush with garlic oil and broil on both sides until soft and beginning to brown.

To make tomato vinaigrette, put tomato, vinegar, olive oil and salt and pepper in a blender or food processor and process until smooth. Press through a sieve. Turn terrine on to a serving dish and remove cling film. Garnish with pepper strips. Slice terrine with a very sharp knife, garnish with flat-leaf parsley and serve with tomato vinaigrette and diced tomato.

Serves 6-8.

CARROT & GINGER SOUFFLÉS

1½ oz/½ cup ground almonds, toasted
12 oz carrots, trimmed and chopped
1 tablespoon olive oil
1 small onion, finely chopped
2 teaspoons grated fresh root ginger
1½ oz/3 tablespoons butter
1½ oz/3 tablespoons all-purpose flour
8 fl oz/1 cup milk
2 oz Cheshire cheese, grated
3 eggs, separated

Preheat oven to 375F (190C) and lightly oil eight 8 fl oz/1 cup ramekin dishes.

Sprinkle the inside of each ramekin with the ground almonds to coat the sides. Shake out the excess and reserve. Cook the carrots in a pan of boiling water for 15 minutes until soft. Heat the oil in a small pan and gently fry the onion and ginger together for 10 minutes until softened. Drain the carrots and purée with the onion mixture in a blender or food processor until smooth.

Melt the butter in a small pan, stir in the flour and cook for 1 minute. Gradually add the milk, stirring, until thickened. Remove from the heat, stir in the cheese, cool and beat in the egg yolks, carrot purée and the remaining almonds. Stiffly whisk the egg whites and fold in. Spoon into the prepared ramekins, place in a roasting pan and add enough boiling water to come two-thirds of the way up the sides of the dishes. Bake for 30 minutes, then serve at once.

Serves 8.

ZUCCHINI TIMBALES

sunflower oil for greasing
1½ lb zucchini
3 eggs, beaten
1 tablespoon chopped fresh basil
4 oz/½ cup ricotta cheese
salt and freshly ground black pepper
TOMATO SALSA:
12 oz tomatoes, peeled and diced
1 red onion, finely chopped
1 tablespoon chopped fresh basil
1 tablespoon olive oil
1 teaspoon lime juice

To make tomato salsa, mix together tomatoes, onion, basil, olive oil, lime juice and salt and pepper. Chill until required. Oil six 4 fl oz/½ cup ramekins. Trim ends from zucchini. Using a vegetable peeler, cut very thin ribbons from two of the zucchini. Cut remaining zucchini into slices. Steam ribbons over a saucepan of boiling water for 2 minutes, until soft. Spread on kitchen paper and pat dry. Steam sliced zucchini for 3-5 minutes, until soft. Preheat oven to 400F (200C).

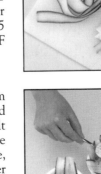

Press out as much moisture as possible from zucchini slices and place in a blender or food processor with the eggs, basil, ricotta and salt and pepper. Process to a coarse purée. Line ramekins with zucchini strips. Fill with purée, fold over ends of zucchini strips and cover with foil. Place ramekins in a roasting pan and pour in ½ in. boiling water. Bake for 10-15 minutes, until set. Leave for 5 minutes, turn out and serve with tomato salsa.

Serves 6.

CAPONATA

2 eggplants
salt and freshly ground black pepper
4 fl oz/½ cup olive oil
1 onion, finely chopped
1 clove garlic, chopped
4 sticks celery, sliced, leaves reserved for garnish
14 oz can chopped tomatoes
2 teaspoons sugar
2 tablespoons balsamic vinegar
1 tablespoon pine nuts, lightly toasted
1 tablespoon capers
12 pitted black olives, halved

Cut eggplants into ¼ in. thick slices.

Place eggplants in a colander, sprinkle generously with salt and leave for 1 hour. Preheat oven to 300F (150C). Heat 2 tablespoons olive oil in a saucepan, add onion and garlic and cook, stirring occasionally, for 5 minutes, until soft. Add celery and cook, stirring occasionally, for a further five minutes. Stir in tomatoes, sugar and vinegar and bring to the boil. Simmer, uncovered, for 15-20 minutes, until thickened. Season with salt and pepper and stir in pine nuts, capers and olives.

Rinse eggplant thoroughly and pat dry with kitchen paper. Arrange in a shallow ovenproof dish. Spoon a little tomato mixture on to each eggplant slice. Drizzle remaining oil over and around eggplant. Cover with foil and cook in oven for 45-60 minutes, until eggplants are tender. Leave to cool. Garnish with celery leaves and serve at room temperature.

Serves 6.

STUFFED ZUCCHINI RINGS

3 oz bulgar wheat
6 zucchini about 6 in long
1 tablespoon olive oil
1 small onion, finely chopped
2 teaspoons tomato paste
1 teaspoon chopped fresh mint
salt and freshly ground black pepper
2 tablespoons lemon juice
fresh vine leaves, to serve
fresh herbs, to garnish

Put bulgar wheat in a bowl. Pour in enough boiling water to come well above the wheat. Leave to soak for 1 hour. Drain thoroughly.

Preheat oven to 350F (180C). Cut rounded ends off zucchini. With a small apple corer, carefully remove centers from zucchini. In a skillet, heat oil. Cook onion until soft. Remove from heat. Stir in bulgar wheat, tomato paste, mint, salt and pepper. Press stuffing firmly into the hollowed-out zucchini.

Place zucchini in an ovenproof dish. Pour over lemon juice and 4 tablespoons water. Cover dish and bake in the oven for 45 minutes or until zucchini are cooked but still firm enough to slice neatly. With a sharp knife, cut zucchini into ⅛ in. slices. Serve on a plate lined with vine leaves, garnished with fresh herbs.

Serves 6.

GREEN & GOLD ROULADE

1 lb carrots, sliced
4 oz/½ cup cream cheese
salt and freshly ground black pepper
sunflower oil for greasing
1 lb frozen chopped spinach
4 eggs, separated
large pinch of grated nutmeg
flat-leaf parsley springs and carrot ribbons, to garnish
HERB SAUCE:
6 fl oz/¾ cup crème fraîche
1 tablespoon chopped fresh parsley
3 tablespoons chopped fresh chives
chopped fresh chives, to garnish

Cook carrots in a saucepan of boiling salted water for 15 minutes, until tender. Drain.

Purée carrots in a blender or food processor. Add cream cheese and salt and pepper and process until well blended. Set aside.

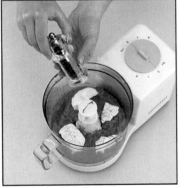

Preheat oven to 400F (200C). Lightly oil a 13 × 9 in. jelly roll pan and line with baking parchment. Lightly oil baking parchment. Cook spinach according to directions on packet. Drain well, pressing out as much water as possible. Place in a bowl and leave to cool slightly. Stir in egg yolks, nutmeg and salt and pepper.

In a large bowl, whisk eggs whites until soft peaks form, then fold into spinach mixture. Gently spread into prepared pan and bake for 15-20 minutes, until firm.

Meanwhile, make herb sauce. Mix together crème fraîche, parsley and chives, cover and chill until required. Gently reheat carrot mixture without boiling. Turn spinach roll on to a sheet of baking parchment, peel off lining paper and spread spinach roll with carrot mixture.

Roll up by gently lifting baking parchment. Garnish herb sauce with chopped chives. Garnish roulade with flat-leaf parsley and carrot ribbons, slice and serve on warmed plates with herb sauce.

Serves 6.

ASPARAGUS NIÇOISE

1 tablespoon lemon juice
1 lb asparagus spears
8 oz cherry tomatoes, halved
12 black olives, pitted and halved
basil sprigs, to garnish
DRESSING:
1 teaspoon Dijon mustard
1 tablespoon white wine vinegar
salt and freshly ground black pepper
2½ fl oz/⅓ cup extra virgin olive oil
1 hard-cooked egg, finely chopped

Add the lemon juice to a saucepan of boiling salted water. Snap the tough ends from the asparagus. Tie the spears in a bundle.

Stand the bundle upright in the pan so that the tips stand out of the water. Cover with a dome of foil and simmer for 10 minutes or until tender. Drain well and leave to cool. Take 16 stalks and cut in half lengthwise, cutting as far as the base of the tip so that the tip remains intact. Cut the remaining stalks into 1 in. lengths and put in a bowl with the tomatoes and olives.

Arrange 4 asparagus spears on each of 4 serving plates to make a square, with a tip at each corner and the halved stalks splayed out at right angles. To make the dressing, whisk together the mustard, vinegar and salt and pepper then whisk in the oil. Stir in the chopped hard-cooked egg. Pour the dressing over the tomato and asparagus mixture and toss together. Arrange the mixture in the center of the asparagus squares. Garnish with basil sprigs and serve.

Serves 4.

EGGPLANT ROLLS

2 × 8 oz eggplants
3 tablespoons olive oil
4 oz mozzarella cheese, diced
2 tomatoes, peeled, seeded and diced
1 tablespoon chopped fresh basil
salt and freshly ground black pepper
basil sprigs, to garnish
RED BELL PEPPER SAUCE:
1 tablespoon olive oil
1 small onion, chopped
2 red bell peppers, diced
6 fl oz/¾ cup vegetable stock

To make red pepper sauce, heat oil in a saucepan. Add onion and cook gently for 5 minutes until soft. Add peppers and cook gently for 5 minutes. Pour in the stock, bring to the boil and simmer for 10 minutes. Transfer to a food processor or blender and process until smooth. Press through a sieve into a bowl. Season and set aside. Cut each eggplant lengthwise into eight ¼ in. slices. Preheat the oven to 375F (190C). Preheat the broiler.

Brush the eggplant slices on both sides with the oil then broil, turning once, until soft and beginning to brown. Mix together the mozzarella, tomatoes, basil and salt and pepper. Put a little on one end of each eggplant slice and roll up. Put the rolls, seam side down, in an ovenproof dish. Bake for 10-15 minutes. Reheat the sauce. Arrange 4 rolls on each plate, garnish with basil sprigs and serve with the red pepper sauce.

Serves 4.

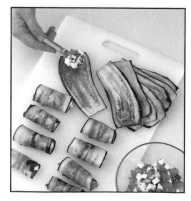

QUAILS' EGGS IN FILO NESTS

12 quails' eggs
1 oz/2 tablespoons butter, melted
3 sheets filo pastry, 16 × 12 in.
tarragon leaves, to garnish
MUSHROOM DUXELLE:
12 oz button mushrooms
1 oz/2 tablespoons butter
2 shallots, finely chopped
pinch of freshly grated nutmeg
salt and freshly ground black pepper
CREAM SAUCE:
2 egg yolks
4 teaspoons lemon juice
4 oz/½ cup butter
2½ fl oz/⅓ cup thick cream
1 tablespoon chopped fresh tarragon

Preheat oven to 375F (190C). To make mushroom duxelle, finely chop mushrooms in a food processor or by hand. Heat butter in a saucepan. Add shallots and cook, stirring occasionally, for 5 minutes, until soft. Add chopped mushrooms and cook gently, stirring occasionally, for 5 minutes, until soft. Increase the heat and cook until any liquid has evaporated. Season with nutmeg and salt and pepper and set aside.

Bring a saucepan of water to the boil. Lower quails' eggs into water and boil for 1 minute. Put eggs in a colander and rinse with cold water. Carefully peel eggs. Heat some water in a saucepan, but do not boil. Put peeled eggs in the water to keep warm.

To make filo nests, turn six 3 in. ramekins upside down and lightly brush all over with melted butter. Cut the pastry into eighteen 5 in squares. Brush a square with butter and press, butter side up, over an upturned ramekin. Butter a second square of filo and press over the first piece, arranging it at an angle so that the points form petals. Repeat with a third piece. Cover remaining ramekins in the same way. Bake for 10-15 minutes, until crisp and golden. Carefully lift off pastry nests and place, right side up, on a baking sheet. Keep warm.

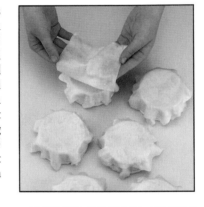

To make cream sauce, put egg yolks in a bowl set over a pan of simmering water. Whisk in lemon juice and heat gently until warm. Put butter in a small saucepan and heat very gently until melted. Gradually whisk in egg yolk mixture until mixture thickens. Stir in cream, tarragon and salt and pepper. Reheat mushroom duxelle.

Put a filo nest on each of 6 warmed serving plates. Divide mushroom duxelle between nests. Arrange 2 quails' eggs in each nest. Spoon over cream sauce, garnish with tarragon leaves and serve at once.

Serves 6.

Note: Filo pastry is available in different sizes, so you may have to adjust the number of sheets needed, depending on their size.

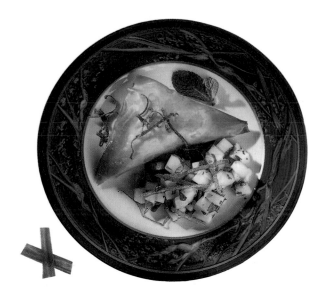

FRUITY ROQUEFORT PARCELS

1 ripe mango
4 oz Roquefort cheese
1 teaspoon lime juice
freshly ground black pepper
8 sheets filo pastry, 8 × 12 in.
2 oz/¼ cup butter, melted
strips of lime rind and mint leaves, to garnish
CUCUMBER SALSA:
½ cucumber, peeled, seeded and diced
grated rind of 1 lime
1 teaspoon lime juice
1 teaspoon chopped fresh mint

Peel mango, cut flesh away from pit and cut flesh into small dice.

Cut Roquefort cheese into small dice. Mix together mango, cheese, lime juice and pepper. Lightly brush a sheet of filo pastry with melted butter. Layer 3 more sheets on top, brushing each one with butter. Layer remaining 4 sheets in the same way. Cut each piece of pastry into three 4 in. wide strips. Brush a baking sheet with butter. Preheat oven to 425F (220C).

Place a spoonful of mango filling in one corner of a strip and diagonally fold over the corner. Continue folding over the filled corner of pastry to form a triangular parcel. Place on baking sheet and brush lightly with butter. Repeat with remaining pastry and filling. Bake for 7-10 minutes, until golden brown. To make cucumber salsa, mix together cucumber, lime rind and juice and mint. Garnish triangles with lime rind and mint leaves and serve with cucumber salsa.

Serves 6.

PEARS WITH STILTON SAUCE

3 large pears
1 tablespoon lemon juice
chervil leaves, to garnish
STILTON SAUCE:
4 fl oz/½ cup crème fraîche
2 tablespoons milk
3 oz Stilton cheese
1-2 teaspoons lemon juice
2 teaspoons poppy seeds
salt and freshly ground black pepper

To make Stilton sauce, put crème fraîche and milk in a saucepan and heat gently. Crumble in Stilton and stir until melted.

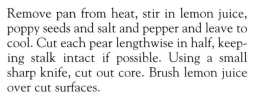

Remove pan from heat, stir in lemon juice, poppy seeds and salt and pepper and leave to cool. Cut each pear lengthwise in half, keeping stalk intact if possible. Using a small sharp knife, cut out core. Brush lemon juice over cut surfaces.

Divide Stilton sauce among 6 serving plates. Slice each pear-half lengthwise and arrange on top of sauce, in a fan shape. Garnish with chervil leaves and serve.

Serves 6.

GOATS' CHEESE SOUFFLÉS

8 fl oz/1 cup milk
1 shallot, finely chopped
1 bay leaf
6 black peppercorns
3 tablespoons butter
1½ oz/⅓ cup all-purpose flour
4 oz goats' cheese
3 eggs, separated
1 tablespoon chopped fresh chives
salt and freshly ground black pepper
5 fl oz/⅔ cup thick cream
1 oz/¼ cup coarsely grated Parmesan cheese
lamb's lettuce and hazelnuts, to garnish

Preheat oven to 350F (180C). Butter six 5 fl oz/⅔ cup) ramekins. Put milk, shallot, bay leaf and peppercorns in a saucepan and bring slowly to the boil. Strain into a jug. Melt butter in a saucepan, add flour and cook, stirring, for 1-2 minutes. Remove from heat and gradually stir in milk. Simmer gently for 2-3 minutes. Crumble in goats' cheese and stir until melted. Stir in egg yolks, chives and salt and pepper. Remove from heat. Whisk egg whites until holding soft peaks and fold into cheese mixture.

Spoon into prepared ramekins. Stand dishes in a roasting pan and pour boiling water into tin to come one-third up the sides of ramekins. Bake for 15-20 minutes, until firm. Leave to cool. When ready to serve, preheat oven to 400F (200C). Run a knife round sides of ramekins and turn soufflés into a shallow ovenproof dish. Pour over cream, sprinkle with Parmesan and bake for 10-15 minutes, until golden. Garnish with lamb's lettuce and hazelnuts and serve.

Serves 6.

GOATS' CHEESE & FIG DRESSING

2 oz/⅓ cup couscous
1½ oz pine nuts, finely chopped
salt and freshly ground black pepper
1 tablespoon all-purpose flour
1 egg, beaten
2 × 3½ oz soft goats' cheeses, cut in half horizontally
vegetable oil for frying
salad leaves, to serve
FIG DRESSING:
6 tablespoons olive oil
3 tablespoons lemon juice
3 tablespoons orange juice
1 teaspoon cumin seeds, roughly crushed
2 teaspoons pink peppercorns, roughly crushed
2 ripe figs

Place the couscous in a bowl and just cover with boiling water. Leave to soak for a few minutes. Fluff up the grains with a fork, then spread out on a baking sheet to dry for about 20 minutes. The grains should not dry completely. Place in a bowl, stir in the pine nuts and season with salt and pepper. Sift the flour on to a plate and pour the beaten egg into a shallow dish. Roll each cheese slice in the flour, then dip into the egg. Roll in the couscous to coat completely. Wrap each coated slice in cling film and chill for 1 hour.

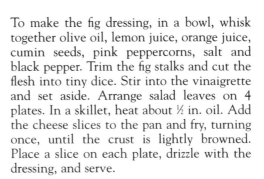

To make the fig dressing, in a bowl, whisk together olive oil, lemon juice, orange juice, cumin seeds, pink peppercorns, salt and black pepper. Trim the fig stalks and cut the flesh into tiny dice. Stir into the vinaigrette and set aside. Arrange salad leaves on 4 plates. In a skillet, heat about ½ in. oil. Add the cheese slices to the pan and fry, turning once, until the crust is lightly browned. Place a slice on each plate, drizzle with the dressing, and serve.

Serves 4.

RICOTTA MOLDS

MONKFISH TEMPURA

12 oz/1½ cups ricotta cheese
1 tablespoon finely chopped fresh Italian parsley
1 tablespoon chopped fresh fennel
1 tablespoon snipped fresh chives
1 tablespoon gelatine
5 fl oz/⅔ cup prepared mayonnaise
salt and freshly ground black pepper
fresh chives, fennel and Italian parsley sprigs to garnish
PEPPER SAUCE:
2 large red bell peppers, broiled, deseeded and chopped
3 tablespoons extra virgin olive oil
few drops balsamic vinegar
salt and freshly ground black pepper

1 lb monkfish fillets
sunflower oil for deep-frying
BATTER:
4 oz/1 cup all-purpose flour
1 egg, beaten
1 egg yolk
RED PEPPER SALSA:
½ red onion, finely diced
1 fresh green chili, cored, seeded and chopped
1 red bell pepper, finely diced
2 tablespoons lemon juice
1 tablespoon chopped fresh parsley
salt

Mix together all ingredients for red pepper salsa. Cover and chill until required.

In a bowl, mix together ricotta and herbs. Oil six 4-5 fl oz/½ cup molds. In a small bowl, soak gelatine in 3 tablespoons cold water for 2 minutes. Place bowl over a saucepan of simmering water, stirring until dissolved. Cool slightly then stir into cheese mixture with mayonnaise and salt and freshly ground black pepper. Divide between molds and chill until set.

Cut monkfish into strips. To make batter, sift flour into a bowl and whisk in egg, egg yolk and 6 fl oz/¾ cup iced water. Heat 2 in. sunflower oil in a large, deep skillet or wok.

To make sauce, put peppers and oil in a food processor or blender and process until smooth. Add a few drops of balsamic vinegar and season with salt and freshly ground black pepper. Chill until required. To serve, turn out molds on to individual plates; spoon the pepper sauce around the molds and garnish with fresh herbs.

Serves 6.

Dip monkfish strips into batter and fry, in batches, until crisp and pale golden. Drain on kitchen paper and keep warm while cooking remainder. Divide among serving plates and serve with red pepper salsa.

Serves 6.

SEAFOOD DIAMONDS

12 oz puff pastry, thawed if frozen
1 egg, beaten
8 oz smoked haddock fillet
8 oz monkfish fillet
8 oz leeks
1 oz/2 tablespoons butter
2 teaspoons all-purpose flour
5 fl oz/⅔ cup dry white wine
large pinch of saffron strands
2 teaspoons lemon juice
salt and freshly ground black pepper
2 fl oz/¼ thick cream
4 oz cooked, peeled shrimp
salad leaves, to garnish

Preheat oven to 425F (220C). Roll out pastry on a lightly floured surface until ⅛ in. thick. Cut out twelve diamonds and arrange on a baking sheet. Brush pastry with beaten egg. Bake in the oven for 10 minutes, until well risen and golden brown. Split each diamond in half horizontally and keep warm.

Put smoked haddock in a saucepan, cover with cold water, bring to the boil and simmer for 5 minutes, until just cooked. Remove haddock, reserving cooking liquid. Flake fish into a bowl, discarding skin. Cut monkfish into ¾ in. cubes. Add monkfish to cooking liquid and cook for 5 minutes. Remove with a slotted spoon, reserving cooking liquid, and add monkfish to bowl.

Cut leeks lengthwise in half and thinly slice. Heat butter in a saucepan, add leeks and cook, stirring occasionally, for 5-10 minutes, until soft. Stir in flour and cook, stirring, for 1 minute. Stir in 5 fl oz/⅔ cup reserved fish cooking liquid, bring to the boil and simmer for 2 minutes.

Put wine and saffron in a small saucepan, bring to the boil and boil rapidly until reduced to 2 tablespoons. Strain into leek sauce. Stir in lemon juice and salt and pepper. Add cream, haddock, monkfish and shrimp and heat gently to warm through.

Arrange bottom halves of 2 pastry diamonds on each warmed serving plate. Spoon over fish mixture and top with glazed pastry lids. Garnish and serve.

Serves 6.

CEVICHE

1 lb monkfish or halibut fillets, thinly sliced
1 fresh red chili, seeded and thinly sliced
2 teaspoons coriander seeds, toasted and finely
    crushed
salt
juice 4 limes
2½ tablespoons virgin olive oil
½ red onion, thinly sliced
1 beefsteak tomato, peeled, seeded and cut into thin
    strips
1 red bell pepper, seeded and chopped
1 tablespoon chopped fresh cilantro
lime wedges, to garnish
lamb's lettuce and red chicory salad, to serve

Lay fish in a shallow, non-metallic dish. Scatter over chili and coriander seeds and sprinkle with salt. Pour over lime juice. Cover and leave at room temperature for 1 hour, or 2-4 hours in refrigerator.

Drain off juices from fish and mix 2½ table-spoons with the oil; discard remaining juices. Scatter onion, tomato, pepper and chopped cilantro over fish. Trickle oil mixture over the vegetables and fish. Serve garnished with lime wedges and accompanied by lamb's let-tuce and red chicory salad.

Serves 4.

SALMON MOUSSE

12 oz skinless salmon fillet
4 oz/½ cup curd cheese
4 fl oz/½ cup plain yogurt
2 eggs, beaten
salt and freshly ground black pepper
2 teaspoons lemon juice
1 tablespoon chopped fresh dill
dill sprigs, to garnish
SORREL SAUCE:
1 tablespoon butter
4 oz sorrel, washed, dried and very finely chopped
5 fl oz/⅔ cup whipping cream

Preheat oven to 325F (160C). Lightly oil six 4 fl oz/½ cup molds. Cut salmon into cubes and put in a blender or food processor with curd cheese, yogurt, eggs and salt and pepper. Process until smooth. Add lemon juice and dill and process briefly. Spoon mixture into prepared molds then place in a roasting pan. Pour in boiling water to come one-third of the way up sides of molds. Cover each one with foil and bake for about 20 minutes, until a skewer inserted in center comes out clean.

Meanwhile, make sorrel sauce. Heat butter in a saucepan, add sorrel and cook, stirring, for 2-3 minutes, until softened. Stir in cream and salt and pepper, bring to the boil and simmer for 2-3 minutes, to thicken slightly. Turn each mousse on to a warmed serving plate, pour a little sorrel sauce around the mousse, garnish with dill sprigs and serve.

Serves 6.

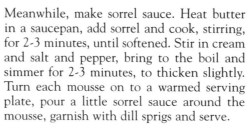

THAI CRAB CAKES

1 oz/2 tablespoons butter
1 oz/¼ cup all-purpose flour
5 fl oz/⅔ cup milk
12 oz dressed crab
2 teaspoons chopped fresh cilantro
5 oz/2½ cups fresh breadcrumbs
grated rind of ½ lime
2 teaspoons lime juice
4 scallions, finely chopped
1 teaspoon Thai green curry paste
2 teaspoons Thai fish sauce
1 egg, beaten
2½ fl oz/⅓ cup sunflower oil
lime slices and cilantro leaves, to garnish

SMOKED TROUT MOUSSE

1¼ lb thinly sliced smoked trout
5 oz/2⅓ cups cream cheese
5 fl oz/⅔ cup Greek yogurt
juice of ½ lemon
salt and freshly ground black pepper
pinch of cayenne pepper
tarragon sprigs, to garnish
CUCUMBER VINAIGRETTE:
2½ fl oz/⅓ cup light olive oil
juice of ½ lemon
1 tablespoon chopped fresh tarragon
⅛ cucumber, seeded and finely diced

Line six 4 fl oz/½ cup ramekins with cling film. Line with half the smoked trout.

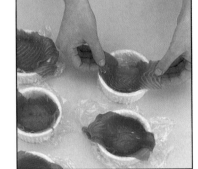

Heat butter in a saucepan. Add flour and cook, stirring, for 1 minute. Remove from heat and gradually stir in milk. Simmer stirring, for 2-3 minutes, until thickened. Remove from heat. Stir in crab, cilantro, 1 oz/½ cup breadcrumbs, lime rind and juice, scallions, curry paste and fish sauce. Leave to cool, spread mixture into a round and cut into 12 wedges. With floured hands, shape each wedge into a round cake.

Put remaining smoked trout in a blender or food processor with cream cheese, yogurt, lemon juice, salt and cayenne pepper. Process until smooth. Spoon into lined ramekins, fold overhanging trout and cling film over the top and chill for at least 4 hours.

Put remaining breadcrumbs on a plate and put beaten egg in a shallow dish. Dip each crab cake in beaten egg and then in breadcrumbs, to coat thoroughly. Chill for 15 minutes. Heat oil in a skillet and fry crab cakes for 3-4 minutes on each side, until crisp and golden. Garnish with lime slices and cilantro leaves and serve.

Serves 6.

To make the cucumber vinaigrette, whisk together oil and lemon juice. Stir in tarragon, cucumber and salt and pepper. Turn each mousse out on to a serving plate and remove cling film. Garnish with tarragon sprigs and serves with cucumber vinaigrette.

Serves 6.

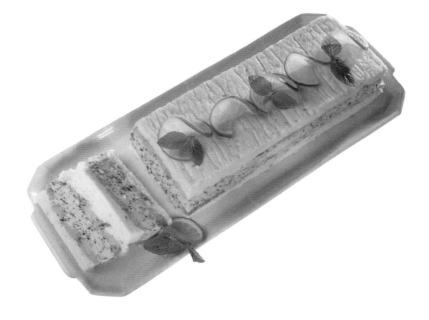

LAYERED FISH TERRINE

1 lb salmon, skinned and boned
salt and freshly ground white pepper
5 fl oz/⅔ cup medium-bodied dry white wine
2 small bunches watercress, trimmed
½ oz/1 tablespoon butter
1 shallot, finely chopped
1 lb firm white fish, such as hake, monkfish or cod, skinned, boned and cubed
2 egg whites
7½ fl oz/scant 1 cup heavy cream, chilled
lime slices and mint sprigs, to garnish

In a small saucepan, heat butter. Add shallot and cook gently until softened but not browned. Purée shallot with cubed white fish in a food processor. Add egg whites and season with salt and pepper. Mix for 1 minute, then slowly pour in cream. Remove and reserve two thirds of fish mixture. Add watercress to food processor and purée briefly. Chill both mixtures for 30 minutes.

Cut salmon into long strips, put in a dish, season lightly and pour the wine over it. Cover and leave for about 1 hour.

Preheat oven to 350F (180C), lightly oil a 10 × 3½ in. terrine. Spread half the plain fish mixture in the terrine, then half the salmon strips followed by all the green mixture. Cover this with remaining salmon strips, then remaining white mixture.

Meanwhile, boil a saucepan of lightly salted water, add watercress and blanch for 1 minute. Drain watercress, rinse under cold running water, drain again, then dry on absorbent kitchen paper; set aside.

Cover terrine with foil, place in a roasting pan and pour in enough boiling water to come halfway up sides of terrine. Bake in oven for about 40 minutes until a cake tester inserted in center comes out clean. Transfer terrine to a wire rack to cool, then refrigerate. Serve cut into slices, garnished with lime slices and sprigs of mint.

Serves 4-6.

MUSSEL & FENNEL TARTLETS

1 lb shortcrust pastry
3 lb mussels, trimmed
4 fl oz/½ cup dry white wine
1 oz/2 tablespoons butter
1 bunch of scallions, finely chopped
1 clove garlic, crushed
1 large fennel bulb, halved and thinly sliced
2 teaspoons lemon juice
2 fl oz/¼ cup thick cream
salt and freshly ground black pepper
fennel leaves, to garnish

Preheat oven to 400F (200C). Roll out pastry on a lightly floured surface and use to line six 4 in. loose-bottomed tartlet pans. Line with foil or baking parchment.

Fill with baking beans and bake in the oven for 10 minutes. Remove foil and beans and bake for 2-3 minutes, until pastry is cooked and golden. Keep warm. Put mussels in a large saucepan with 2 tablespoons white wine. Bring to the boil, cover tightly and cook over a high heat, shaking pan occasionally, for 4-5 minutes, until mussels open. Drain, reserving cooking liquid and discarding any mussels that have not opened. Remove mussels from shells, discarding shells, and keep warm.

Heat butter in a saucepan. Add scallions, garlic and fennel and cook, stirring occasionally, for 5 minutes, until soft. Add remaining white wine, lemon juice and 2½ fl oz/⅓ cup reserved mussel cooking liquid. Simmer until reduced by half. Add cream and boil for a few minutes until thickened. Season with salt and pepper. Add mussels to fennel mixture and heat gently to warm through. Spoon into pastry cases. Garnish with fennel and serve.

Serves 6.

SALMON MILLE FEUILLES

6 fl oz/¾ cup plain yogurt, preferably Greek style, chilled
¾ teaspoon chopped fresh dill
salt and freshly ground black pepper
8 sheets filo pastry
melted butter
4 oz smoked salmon trimmings, minced
2 tablespoons heavy cream, chilled
1 bunch chives, roughly chopped
12 large slices smoked salmon
dill sprigs, to garnish
lemon wedges, to serve

Mix together half of yogurt with dill and salt and pepper. Cover and chill. Preheat oven to 425F (220C). Cut twenty-four 3 in. circles from filo pastry. Lay half the circles on a baking sheet, brush with melted butter, then cover each circle with another. Brush with melted butter and bake for 5 minutes until golden. Transfer to a wire rack to cool. Put salmon trimmings in a blender then, with motor running, slowly pour in cream and remaining yogurt until just evenly mixed. Add chives and pepper to taste.

Cut salmon into twelve 3 in. circles. Place pastry circle on a plate, spread with a twelfth of the smoked salmon cream, then cover with a smoked salmon circle. Repeat twice more to make one mille feuille. Make 3 more mille feuilles in the same way. Chill. Serve garnished with dill sprigs and accompanied by sauce and lemon wedges.

Serves 4.

FISH & WATERCRESS TERRINE

¼ cucumber, very thinly sliced
1 lb sole fillets
2½ fl oz/⅓ cup dry white wine
1 tablespoon lemon juice
2 bay leaves
4 black peppercorns
1 tablespoon powdered gelatine
8 oz/1 cup cream cheese
4 oz watercress, stalks removed
4 fl oz/½ cup thick cream
salt and freshly ground black pepper
4 oz thinly sliced smoked salmon
lemon slices, lemon rind and sprigs of watercress, to
   garnish
WATERCRESS SAUCE:
1 oz watercress, stalks removed
8 fl oz/1 cup crème fraîche
1 tablespoon lemon juice

Spread cucumber slices on kitchen paper, sprinkle with salt and leave to drain. Line a 35 fl oz/4½ cup terrine or loaf pan with cling film. Place sole in a saucepan. Add wine, 2½ fl oz/⅓ cup water, lemon juice, bay leaves and peppercorns. Bring slowly to the boil, cover and simmer gently for 10 minutes, until fish flakes easily. Remove fish, reserving cooking liquid and flake fish, discarding skin.

Put 2½ fl oz/⅓ cup warm water in a large bowl, sprinkle over gelatine and leave for 5 minutes, until absorbed. Bring fish cooking liquid to the boil and boil rapidly until reduced by half. Strain into bowl of gelatine and stir until gelatine has dissolved.

Put sole in a blender of food processor with cream cheese and process until blended. With motor running, pour gelatine mixture on to fish mixture and blend. Remove three-quarters of mixture, transfer to a bowl and set aside. Add watercress to blender and process briefly. Transfer to a bowl. Lightly whip cream. Fold just under half of cream into watercress mixture and remainder into white fish mixture.

Season both mixtures with salt and pepper. Dry cucumber with kitchen paper and arrange half in base of terrine. Spread half white fish mixture over base of pan and cover with half smoked salmon. Cover with watercress mixture and then the remaining smoked salmon. Top with remaining white fish mixture. Cover with remaining cucumber. Cover pan and chill for 4 hours.

To make watercress sauce, put watercress, crème fraîche, lemon juice and salt and pepper in a blender or food processor and process until smooth. Turn out terrine and slice. Garnish and serve with watercress sauce.

Serves 6-8.

CRAB ROLLS

8 oz cooked chicken, very finely chopped
4 oz cooked crabmeat, flaked
4 scallions, finely chopped
1 oz beansprouts, finely chopped
1 small carrot, grated
2 teaspoons fish sauce
freshly ground black pepper
about 9 rice paper wrappers, each about 7 in in
  diameter
vegetable oil for deep frying
Thai holy basil leaves, Thai mint leaves and lettuce
  leaves, to serve
dipping sauce to serve

In a bowl, mix together chicken, crabmeat, scallions, beansprouts, carrot, fish sauce and black pepper. Brush both sides of each wrapper liberally with water and set aside to soften. Cut each into 4 wedges. Place a small amount of filling near wide end of one wedge, fold end over filling, tuck in sides and roll up. Repeat with remaining wedges and filling.

In a wok, heat oil to 375F (190C). Fry rolls in batches for 2-3 minutes until crisp and golden. Drain on absorbent kitchen paper. Serve hot. To eat, sprinkle each roll with herbs, then wrap in a lettuce leaf and dip into dipping sauce.

Makes about 36.

SAFFRON MUSSELS

6 lb mussels
3 tablespoons dry cider
SAFFRON SAUCE:
2 tablespoons olive oil
3 shallots, finely chopped
1 clove garlic, crushed
6 fl oz/¾ cup dry (alcoholic) cider
large pinch of saffron strands
freshly ground black pepper
1 oz/2 tablespoons butter
2 tablespoons chopped fresh parsley

Discard broken mussels and any which do not close when tapped sharply. Scrape off any barnacles, remove 'beards' and scrub.

To make saffron sauce, heat olive oil in a saucepan. Add shallots and garlic and cook, stirring occasionally, for 5 minutes, until soft. Set aside. Put mussels and cider in a large saucepan. Bring to the boil, cover tightly and cook over a high heat, shaking pan occasionally, for 4-5 minutes, until mussels have opened.

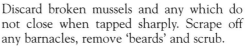

Remove mussels with a slotted spoon, discarding any that have not opened. Transfer to warmed serving plates and keep warm. Line a sieve with cheesecloth, place over a measuring jug and strain cooking liquid. Add 5 fl oz/⅔ cup cooking liquid to shallots and garlic. Add cider, saffron and pepper. Bring to the boil and boil until reduced by one-third. Whisk in butter. Stir in parsley, pour over mussels and serve.

Serves 6.

MEDITERRANEAN SCALLOPS

GARLIC & LEMON SHRIMP

1½ lb shelled scallops
3 tablespoons olive oil
1 clove garlic, crushed
4 teaspoons fresh thyme leaves
salt and freshly ground black pepper
MEDITERRANEAN VEGETABLES:
2 tablespoons olive oil
1 shallot, finely chopped
1 clove garlic, crushed
1 eggplant, diced
2 zucchini, diced
1 red and 1 yellow bell pepper, diced
juice of ½ lemon
1 tablespoon chopped fresh oregano

8 oz small to medium raw shrimp
salt and freshly ground pepper
4 tablespoons olive oil
2 tablespoons sunflower oil
3 large cloves garlic, coarsely chopped
1 dried red chili pepper, stem and seeds removed,
 chopped
fresh lemon juice
2 tablespoons chopped fresh parsley
crusty bread, to serve

Shell shrimp and pat dry on absorbent kitchen paper. Lay shrimp in a dish and sprinkle lightly with salt.

Rinse scallops, dry with kitchen paper and cut in half. Place in a bowl with oil, garlic, thyme and salt and pepper. Mix well, cover and chill. To prepare Mediterranean vegetables, heat oil in a skillet, add shallot and garlic and cook, stirring occasionally, for 5 minutes, until soft. Add eggplant, zucchini, and peppers and stir-fry over a high heat until softened but still retaining some texture. Keep warm.

Heat the oil in a non-stick skillet, add garlic and chili and fry for 1-2 minutes until garlic is golden. Immediately add shrimp and cook over high heat for 2 minutes until the shrimp are just tender. Add lemon juice to taste and check the seasoning.

Heat a large heavy skillet. Add scallops in one layer and cook for 1 minute. Turn and cook other side for 1 minute. Add lemon juice, oregano and salt and pepper to vegetables. Arrange vegetables in scallop shells or on serving plates, place scallops on top and serve.

Serves 6.

Note: If the scallops have their coral with them you can use that too.

Stir in chopped fresh parsley, then serve the shrimp in ramekins, hot or cold with plenty of crusty bread.

Serves 4.

SHRIMP & FETA PURSES

1½ oz/3 tablespoons butter, melted
4 oz/1 cup cooked, peeled shrimp, thawed if frozen
6 oz feta cheese, crumbled
1 oz sun-dried tomatoes, roughly chopped
1 teaspoon chopped fresh chives
1 teaspoon chopped fresh fennel
salt and freshly ground black pepper
6 sheets filo pastry, about 16 × 12 in.
fennel leaves and lemon twists, to garnish

Preheat the oven to 400F (200C). Brush a baking sheet with melted butter. Dry the shrimp on kitchen paper and roughly chop.

Mix together the shrimp, feta cheese, sun-dried tomatoes, chives, fennel and salt and pepper. Cut each sheet of filo pastry into 12 squares. Brush each square with melted butter and layer 3 more squares on top, arranging them at different angles to form petals.

Place a spoonful of the shrimp mixture in the middle of the pastry. Pull up the edges of the pastry and pinch together at the top to form a purse. Put on a baking sheet and brush with melted butter. Bake for 10-15 minutes until golden brown. Garnish with fennel leaves and lemon twists and serve.

Serves 6.

SHRIMP-STUFFED EGGS

4 hard-cooked eggs, peeled
4 tablespoons mayonnaise
2 oz peeled shrimp, chopped
salt, cayenne pepper and lemon juice, to taste
lettuce leaves, to serve
whole shrimp, paprika and parsley sprigs, to garnish

Slice the eggs in half lengthwise. Using a teaspoon, scoop the yolks into a small bowl; reserve the white shells.

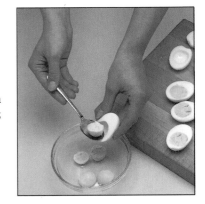

Add the mayonnaise to the bowl and, using a fork, mash with the yolks and shrimp. Add salt, cayenne pepper and lemon juice to taste.

Divide the shrimp mixture between the egg whites. Arrange on lettuce leaves and garnish with whole shrimp, paprika and parsley sprigs.

Serves 4.

SHRIMP WITH MELON

12 cooked Mediterranean jumbo shrimp
1 small Charentais melon
1 small Galia or Ogen melon
juice 1 small lemon
salt and freshly ground black pepper
fresh mint leaves, to garnish

Peel shrimp leaving tail tips on, if desired.

Cut melons into thin wedges and remove skins.

Arrange shrimp and the two varietes of melon on a serving plate or individual plates and sprinkle with lemon juice. Season with salt and freshly ground black pepper. Serve garnished with fresh mint leaves.

Serves 4-6.

BROILED BUTTERFLY SHRIMP

1 lb jumbo shrimp
juice of 1 lemon
5 tablespoons extra virgin olive oil
½ clove garlic, crushed
2 tablespoons sun-dried tomato paste
pinch cayenne pepper
1 tablespoon chopped fresh basil
salt and freshly ground black pepper
fresh basil leaves to garnish

Remove heads and fine legs from shrimp. Using sharp scissors cut shrimp lengthwise almost in half, leaving tail end intact.

Place in a shallow dish and pour over half of the lemon juice and 2 tablespoons of the olive oil. Stir in garlic. Leave for at least 30 minutes. Preheat broiler. Arrange shrimp in one layer on a rack and cook under the hot broiler for about 3 minutes until shrimp have curled or 'butterflied' and are bright pink.

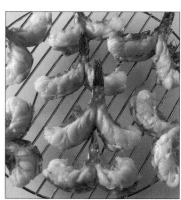

In a small bowl, mix together remaining lemon juice and 3 tablespoons olive oil, the sun-dried tomato paste, cayenne, basil, salt and freshly ground black pepper. Either spoon over shrimp or serve separately for dipping. Garnish shrimp with basil sprigs.

Serves 4.

SPICY JUMBO SHRIMP

2 cloves garlic, crushed
1 small bunch of cilantro, finely chopped
juice of 2 limes
1 fresh red chili, cored, seeded and finely chopped
2½ fl oz/⅓ cup sunflower oil
24 large raw shrimp
GUACAMOLE:
1 clove garlic, crushed
4 tomatoes, peeled and finely chopped
1 fresh green chili, cored, seeded and finely chopped
juice of 1 lime
2 tablespoons chopped fresh cilantro
salt and freshly ground black pepper
1 large ripe avocado

In a shallow non-metallic dish, mix together garlic, cilantro, lime juice, chili and sunflower oil. Add shrimp and mix well. Cover and chill for 1-2 hours, turning occasionally. To make guacamole, put garlic, tomatoes, chili, lime juice, cilantro and salt and pepper in a bowl and mix well. Halve avocado lengthwise and remove pit. Using a teaspoon, scoop out flesh, taking care to scrape away dark green flesh closest to skin. Mash into tomato mixture. Preheat broiler.

Remove shrimp from marinade and arrange on broiler rack. Broil for 2-3 minutes on each side, basting with marinade. Serve with guacamole and tortilla chips.

Serves 6.

Note: Don't prepare the guacamole more than 30 minutes in advance or the avocado will discolor.

SHRIMP & LETTUCE PARCELS

2 crisp lettuces
1 tablespoon olive oil
1 bunch of scallions, chopped
1 clove garlic, crushed
1 red bell pepper, diced
8 oz large cooked, peeled shrimp
4 teaspoons chopped fresh chives
salt and freshly ground black pepper
10 fl oz/1¼ cups dry white wine
10 fl oz/1¼ cups fish stock
4 oz/½ cup butter, diced
1 teaspoon pink peppercorns
chives and red bell pepper strips, to garnish

Separate 12 large leaves from lettuces and wash thoroughly. Bring a large pan of water to the boil, add lettuce leaves and blanch for 30 seconds. Drain and plunge into a bowl of cold water. Spread on a tea towel and leave to drain. Heat oil in a saucepan, add scallions, garlic and red pepper and cook, stirring occasionally, for 3 minutes. Add shrimp, half chives and salt and pepper.

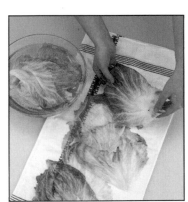

Divide filling among lettuce leaves and wrap up to form parcels. Put wine and stock in a saucepan. Bring to the boil and boil rapidly until reduced by half. Add parcels and heat gently to warm through. Remove with a slotted spoon, transfer to warmed serving plates and keep warm. Whisk butter into sauce, a little at a time, until thickened. Stir in remaining chives and pink peppercorns. Pour around parcels, garnish with chives and red pepper strips and serve.

Serves 6.

OYSTERS ROCKEFELLER

few handfuls rock salt
24 oysters, opened, on the half shell
4 oz/½ cup butter
2 shallots, finely chopped
1 stick celery, finely chopped
8 oz spinach, finely chopped
1 tablespoon chopped fresh parsley
1½ teaspoons chopped fresh tarragon
2 tablespoons fresh breadcrumbs
1 tablespoon Pernod or pastis
dash Tabasco sauce and Worcestershire sauce
salt and freshly ground black pepper

Spread a generous layer of rock salt over bottom of broiler. Nestle oysters in salt.

In a saucepan or skillet, heat a quarter of the butter, add shallots and celery and cook gently until softened but not colored. Stir in spinach, parsley and tarragon and cook over a moderate heat until surplus moisture from spinach has evaporated.

Preheat broiler. Purée spinach mixture in a blender, then mix in breadcrumbs, remaining butter, Pernod or pastis, Tabasco and Worcestershire sauces and season with salt and pepper. Place a tablespoon of spinach mixture on each oyster and broil for about 3 minutes until beginning to turn golden. Serve at once.

Serves 4.

Note: Garnish with lemon slices and sprig of parsley, if wished.

OYSTERS IN COFFINS

2 miniature brioche
2 oz/¼ cup sweet butter, melted
6 large oysters
4 tablespoons sour cream
cayenne pepper and white pepper
finely grated lemon rind and slices, to garnish
tomato, onion and tarragon salad, to serve

Preheat oven to 425F (220C). Remove top knobs from brioche. Scoop out insides to leave a thin shell, taking care not to pierce walls. Brush brioches inside and out with half the melted butter. Place on a baking sheet and bake for 5-10 minutes until crisp.

Meanwhile, scrub oysters then, holding one at a time, curved side down in a cloth, prise open shells at hinge using a strong, short-bladed knife. Loosen each oyster and pour the liquid into pan with remaining melted butter. Boil for a few minutes until liquid is reduced then, over a low heat, add sour cream. Heat gently without boiling. Season with cayenne and white pepper.

Place 3 oysters in each brioche and pour the sauce over them. Garnish with lemon rind and slices and serve with tomato, onion and tarragon salad.

Serves 2.

SMOKED SALMON RAVIOLI

4 oz smoked salmon, chopped
4 oz/½ cup cream cheese
2 teaspoons lemon juice
salt and freshly ground black pepper
flat-leaf parsley and lemon slices, to garnish
PASTA:
8 oz/2 cups strong white flour
½ teaspoon salt
2 eggs, beaten
GREEN PEPPERCORN SAUCE:
1 oz/2 tablespoons butter
2 shallots, finely chopped
4 fl oz/½ cup white wine
5 fl oz/⅔ cup light cream
2 teaspoons green peppercorns, lightly crushed

To make pasta, sift flour and salt into a food processor. Add eggs and process to a crumbly consistency. Gather dough together to form a ball, wrap in cling film and set aside for 30 minutes.

On a floured surface, roll out dough into 2 thin sheets, 9 × 12 in. Cut each sheet into twelve 73 in. squares.

Put smoked salmon in a bowl with cream cheese and lemon juice. Season with salt and pepper and mix well. Place a small spoonful of salmon mixture on each square of dough.

Fold over dough and press edges together to form triangles. Spread ravioli on a tea towel and leave for a few minutes to dry, turning frequently. To make green peppercorn sauce, heat butter in a saucepan. Add shallots and cook very gently for 10 minutes, until soft.

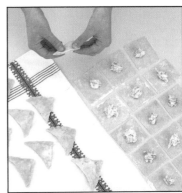

Add wine and boil until reduced by half. Add cream, peppercorns and salt and boil until slightly thickened. Keep warm, stirring from time to time. Bring a large pan of salted water to the boil, add ravioli, a few at a time, and cook for 5-10 minutes, until just tender. Drain. Arrange ravioli on warmed serving plates. Pour over sauce, garnish with flat-leafed parsley and lemon slices and serve.

Serves 6.

ORIENTAL CHICKEN PARCELS

CHICKEN & CRAB ROLLS

2 tablespoons dry sherry
2 tablespoons soy sauce
2 tablespoons sesame oil
12 oz skinned and boned chicken breasts
1 in. piece fresh root ginger, finely chopped
8 scallions, finely chopped
1 stick celery, finely sliced
oil for brushing

Cut the chicken into 16 equal-sized pieces and put into a shallow dish. Mix together the sherry, soy sauce and sesame oil, pour over the chicken and leave to marinate for 45 minutes.

Cut 16 squares of kitchen foil, each large enough to wrap around a piece of chicken and brush each square of foil with a little oil. Put a piece of chicken on each piece of foil and top with a little of the ginger, scallion and celery. Spoon over any remaining marinade and fold the foil over to make parcels, making sure the edges are well sealed.

Place the parcels in a bamboo or metal steamer and cook for 10 minutes or until the chicken is cooked through. Serve in the foil.

Serves 4.

12 spring roll wrappers
8 oz cooked chicken, finely chopped
4 oz dressed crab
4 scallions finely chopped
1 small carrot, grated
2 teaspoons Thai fish sauce
2 teaspoons soy sauce
1 clove garlic, crushed
2 small sticks celery, finely diced
12 small, crisp lettuce leaves
sunflower oil for deep-frying
scallion tassels, to garnish
chili dipping sauce, to serve

Place spring roll wrappers between 2 damp tea towels, to soften.

In a bowl, mix together chicken, crab, scallions, carrot, fish sauce, soy sauce, garlic and celery. Place a lettuce leaf in middle of each spring roll wrapper. Place a spoonful of chicken mixture on each lettuce leaf. Fold over 3 sides of wrapper to enclose filling. Roll up firmly.

Heat oil in a wok or deep-fat fryer to 375F (190C), or until a cube of bread will brown in 40 seconds. Add rolls and fry, in batches, for 3 minutes, or until crisp and golden. Drain on kitchen paper. Garnish with scallion tassels and serve with chili dipping sauce.

Serves 6.

CHICKEN MOUSSELINES

12 oz skinned and boned chicken breasts
1 oz/2 tablespoons butter, softened
1 large egg, beaten
5 fl oz/⅔ cup thick cream
1 tablespoon chopped fresh chives
1 teaspoon finely grated lemon rind
salt and freshly ground black pepper
FILLING:
2¼ oz full fat soft cheese
2 teaspoons lemon juice
SAUCE:
2 red bell peppers, deseeded and halved
1 oz sun-dried tomatoes in oil, drained
3 tablespoons Greek yogurt
1 teaspoon red wine vinegar

Preheat broiler. For the sauce, place the pepper halves under a very hot broiler and cook until the skins are blackened, allow to cool and peel.

Place the chicken and butter into a blender or food processor and process until smooth. With the blades running, pour in the egg and 3 fl oz/⅓ cup of the cream. Stir in the chives, lemon rind and seasoning and spoon into six 4 fl oz/½ cup capacity molds, tapping them well on the worktop to level the surface. For the filling, cream together the soft cheese, the remaining 2 fl oz/¼ cup cream and the lemon juice and put into a large piping bag fitted with a large plain top.

In a blender or food processor, process the peppers, tomatoes, yogurt and vinegar until smooth, then pour into a pan and heat gently. Pour some sauce into 6 individual side plates, remove the chicken mousselines from the pan and drain off any excess liquid which has collected in the molds.

Plunge the piping top deep into the center of the filled molds and pipe one-quarter of the filling into each; use a wet finger to smooth the chicken back over the filling where the top has been. Cover each with a small round of baking parchment and place in a shallow pan half-filled with boiling water. Cover and simmer for 15 minutes.

Peel off the baking parchment and tip the mousselines on top of the sauce. Serve at once, garnished with herbs. Serve any extra sauce separately.

Serves 6.

WRAPPED TERRINE

4 oz large spinach leaves, stalks removed
4 oz carrots, peeled
4 oz French beans, topped and tailed
1 lb skinned and boned chicken meat
2 oz/1 cup fresh white breadcrumbs
3 fl oz/⅓ cup thick cream
4 teaspoons creamed horseradish sauce
2 teaspoons lemon juice
2 tablespoons dry sherry
¼ teaspoon ground nutmeg
salt and freshly ground black pepper
2 eggs, separated

Preheat oven to 350F (180C). Blanch spinach for 30 seconds, refresh and drain well.

Cut the carrots into even-sized sticks, about the same length as the beans. Blanch the carrots and beans for 3-4 minutes in separate pans of boiling, salted water, then plunge into cold water to refresh and drain thoroughly. Put the chicken, breadcrumbs, cream, horseradish, lemon juice, sherry, nutmeg and seasoning into a blender or food processor and blend until smooth, then stir in the egg yolks and mix well.

Stiffly whisk the egg whites and fold them into the chicken mixture. Lightly oil a 40 fl oz/5 cup capacity loaf pan and line with the spinach leaves, slightly overlapping them each time and leaving enough to overhang the top rim of pan to cover the top. Spread one-third of the chicken mixture over the base of the pan and level the surface.

Cover with a neat layer of carrots, top with half the remaining chicken mixture and cover with a layer of beans.

Top with the final layer of chicken mixture and fold the overhanging spinach leaves over the mixture to neaten. Cover with a piece of baking parchment and a layer of foil, then stand in a deep baking pan. Add enough boiling water to three-quarters fill the pan.

Cook in oven for 50 minutes until firm, then leave to cool. Pour off any excess juices from the pan, turn out terrine on to a serving platter and garnish with lemon twists. Serve cold with a garlic and lemon mayonnaise.

Serves 6.

CARIBBEAN TURKEY MOUSSE

LAYERED COUNTRY TERRINE

12 oz ground turkey
1 small mango, peeled and roughly chopped
2 egg whites and 1 egg, beaten
grated rind and juice of 1 lime
¼ in. piece fresh root ginger, peeled and grated
salt and freshly ground black pepper
4 fl oz/½ cup thick cream
sunflower oil for greasing
strips of lime rind and mint leaves, to garnish
MANGO SALSA:
1 large mango, chopped
juice of 1 lime
1 fresh red chili, cored, seeded and finely chopped
1 small red onion, finely chopped
2 tablespoons chopped fresh mint

8 slices rindless, smoked streaky bacon
4 oz chicken livers
4 oz ground pork
4 oz herby sausagemeat
1 clove garlic
1 onion, finely chopped
3 tablespoons chopped fresh parsley
1 oz/½ cup fresh white breadcrumbs
2 fl oz/¼ cup brandy
1 small egg, beaten
¼ teaspoon freshly grated nutmeg
1 teaspoon finely grated lemon rind
salt and freshly ground black pepper
2 skinned and boned chicken breasts
1 bay leaf

Put ground turkey in a blender or food processor. Add mango, egg whites and egg, lime rind and juice and ginger. Process until just smooth, then season with salt and pepper. With motor running, gradually add cream until just blended. Do not overprocess. Transfer mixture to a bowl, cover and chill for 30 minutes. Preheat the oven to 325F (170C). Lightly grease six 3 in. ramekins.

Preheat oven to 350F (180C). Place the bacon on a board and stretch with the back of a knife. Use 4 rashers to line a 40 fl oz/5 cup loaf pan, reserving 4 rashers for the top. Roughly chop the chicken livers, mix them together with the pork, sausagemeat, garlic, onion and parsley. Soak the breadcrumbs in the brandy, then add to the meat mixture with the egg, nutmeg, lemon rind and seasonings.

Divide turkey mixture between ramekins. Smooth top and cover each one with foil. Place in a roasting pan and pour in boiling water to come halfway up the sides of ramekins. Bake for 20-25 minutes, until a skewer inserted in center comes out clean. To make mango salsa, mix together mango, lime juice, chili, onion, mint and salt and pepper. Chill until required. Turn mousses on to serving plates, garnish and serve hot or cold with mango salsa.

Spread one third of the meat mixture over the bacon in the pan. Cut the chicken into very thin slices and layer half over the meat mixture. Cover with half the remaining mixture, then cover with the remaining chicken and the rest of the meat mixture. Lay the reserved bacon on top and add the bay leaf. Cover with foil. Stand the terrine in a baking pan three-quarters full of boiling water. Bake for 1½ hours. Allow to cool. Serve with crusty bread, salad and spiced chutney.

Serves 6.

Serves 4-6.

MALAYSIAN SPRING ROLLS

5 oz boneless, chicken breast
4 oz raw shrimp in shell
2 tablespoons groundnut oil
½ in. piece of fresh root ginger, grated
1 clove garlic, finely crushed
3 shallots, very finely chopped
1 small carrot, grated
1 stick celery, very finely chopped
1 fresh red chili, cored, seeded and finely chopped
2 scallions, chopped
1 teaspoon sesame oil
2 teaspoons soy sauce
12 spring roll wrappers
1 egg, beaten
4 fl oz/½ cup vegetable oil

Fold bottom corner up and over filling. Moisten side corners with beaten egg. Fold sides over to cover bottom corner and filling. Press firmly to seal. Moisten top corner with beaten egg.

Skin and finely chop chicken. Peel and finely chop shrimp. In a wok or sauté pan, heat groundnut oil. Add chicken and stir-fry until beginning to turn opaque. Stir in shrimp and continue to stir-fry until shrimp begin to turn pink. Add remaining ingredients except wrappers, egg and vegetable oil, and fry for 1 minute. Transfer to a bowl and leave until cold.

Roll wrapper over tightly to make a neat cylinder. Press top corner of roll to seal. Place seam side down and cover with a damp towel. Repeat with remaining wrappers and filling.

Spread 1 spring roll wrapper on the wok surface; keep remaining wrappers between 2 damp tea towels. Put 1-2 tablespoons filling on lower half of wrapper.

In a wok, or sauté pan, heat vegetable oil. Fry rolls in batches for 3-5 minutes, turning occasionally, until golden and crisp. Remove with a slotted spoon and drain on paper towels. Keep warm while frying remaining rolls. Serve with Dipping Sauce.

Serves 6.

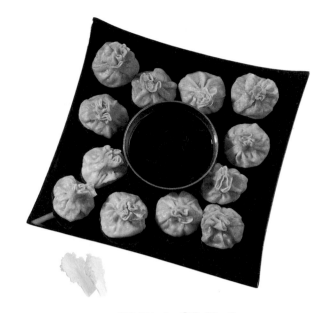

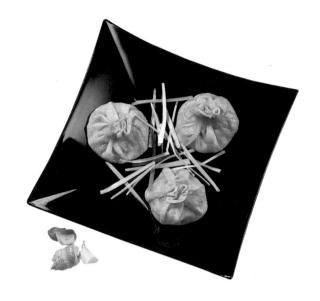

DIM SUM

9 oz/2¼ cups all-purpose flour
8 oz/1 cup ground pork
3 scallions, 1 reserved for garnish, 2 chopped,
   including some green
2 large Chinese cabbage leaves, shredded, plus extra
   leaves for lining steamer basket
1 in. piece of fresh root ginger, grated
1 tablespoon cornstarch
1 tablespoon each light soy sauce and rice wine
2 teaspoons dark sesame oil
½ teaspoon superfine sugar

Sift flour into a bowl. Make a well in center and slowly pour in 8 fl oz/1 cup boiling water. Mix in flour with a fork or chopsticks.

Continue to mix to form a rough dough, adding more flour, if necessary. Cover bowl and leave for 1 minute, to cool. Using your hands, form dough into a soft, loose ball. Knead on a lightly floured surface for about 5 minutes until smooth and elastic. Cover and leave to rest for 30 minutes. In a bowl, combine remaining ingredients using chopsticks or a fork. Set aside.

Divide dough in half. Roll each half to a 9 in. cylinder. Using a floured sharp knife, cut each cylinder into 12 thick slices. Cover with a damp cloth.

Roll each slice into a ball then roll out to a 4 in. circle, making edges slightly thinner than center. Place 1 tablespoon filling in center. Brush edges of circle with a little water.

Lift wrapper around filling, gathering and pinching wrapper to form a purse or dolly bag shape. Put on a tray and cover with a damp cloth. Repeat with remaining dough and filling.

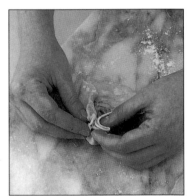

Place some dim sum in a steamer basket lined with cabbage leaves, without crowding dim sum. Cover with a lid. Steam over simmering water for 12-15 minutes until tender but chewy. Garnish with reserved scallion and serve warm with soy sauce mixed with shredded fresh red chili for dipping.

Serves 6-8.

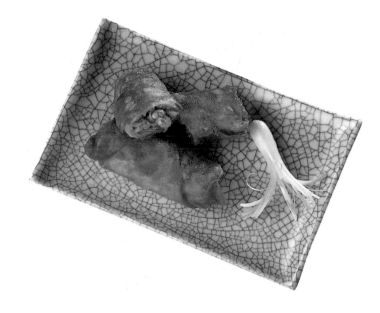

BROILED PROSCIUTTO & FIGS

SPRING ROLLS

8 fresh ripe figs
3 tablespoons olive oil
12 thin slices of prosciutto or Parma ham
3 tablespoons freshly grated Parmesan cheese
crushed black pepper, to serve

Take each fig and stand it upright. Using a sharp kitchen knife, make 2 cuts across and downwards in each fig not quite quartering it, but keeping it intact. Ease the figs open and brush with olive oil.

2 tablespoons vegetable oil
1 clove garlic, finely chopped
1 in. piece fresh root ginger, finely chopped
4 oz chicken breast, shredded
2 oz snow peas, finely sliced
6 oz shiitake mushrooms, sliced
8 scallions, finely chopped
2 oz cooked peeled shrimp, chopped
1 tablespoon soy sauce
1 teaspoon sesame oil
10 oz filo pastry
1 egg white, for brushing
oil for deep frying
bottled chili and hoisin sauces to serve

Place the figs cut side down on a barbecue or ridged griddle and cook for 5-10 minutes until hot and golden brown, turning once. Alternatively, place under a searing hot broiler and broil until browning and hot through. While the figs are cooking, place half the prosciutto slices on the barbecue or griddle and broil for 2-3 minutes until starting to crisp. Remove and keep warm while cooking the remaining slices.

In wok or large skillet, heat the oil, add the garlic and ginger and stir-fry for 15 seconds, then add the chicken breast and continue cooking for 2-3 minutes. Add the snow peas, mushrooms, scallions and shrimp, followed by the soy sauce and sesame oil. Mix well and transfer to a bowl to cool. Cut the filo pastry into sixteen 7 in. squares. On a board, place one square of pastry diagonally towards you and cover with another square of pastry to give 2 layers.

Arrange 3 pieces of the ham and 2 figs per person on warm plates. Sprinkle with grated Parmesan and season with plenty of crushed black pepper. Serve at once.

Serves 4.

Place a large tablespoon of mixture just below the center of the pastry. Fold the bottom corner over and then the 2 side flaps to give an elongated open envelope. Brush with egg white and roll up, pressing gently. Repeat with the remaining filo pastry and filling. Half-fill a deep fat pan or fryer with oil and heat to 375F (190C). Fry the rolls, in 2 batches, for about 4 minutes or until golden. Leave to drain on absorbent kitchen paper. Serve with chili and hoisin sauces.

Serves 4.

PARMA HAM BASKETS

2 sheets filo pastry, 16 × 12 in.
1 oz/2 tablespoons butter, melted
1 tablespoon olive oil
1 red onion, finely chopped
1 teaspoon sugar
5 oz Parma ham, coarsely chopped
10 sun-dried tomatoes, coarsely chopped
7 oz salad leaves
basil leaves, to garnish
DRESSING:
2 fl oz/¼ cup olive oil
2 teaspoons wine vinegar
salt and freshly ground black pepper

Preheat oven to 375F (190C). Cut filo pastry into twenty-four 4 in. squares.

Lightly brush a 12-cup bun pan with butter. Brush 12 sheets of pastry with butter. Line each cup in bun pan with a square of pastry. Brush remaining sheets of pastry with melted butter and place on top, arranging them so that the points are like petals. Bake in the oven for 10 minutes, until golden. Keep warm. Heat oil in a saucepan, add onion and cook, stirring occasionally, for 5 minutes, until soft. Add sugar and cook for 3 minutes. Stir in Parma ham and sun-dried tomatoes. Heat gently to warm through.

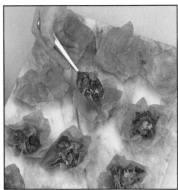

To make dressing, put olive oil, wine vinegar and salt and pepper in a large bowl and whisk together. Add salad leaves and toss well. Arrange salad on 6 serving plates. Fill tartlet cases with ham mixture. Arrange on serving plates, garnish with basil leaves and serve.

Serves 6.

CHICKEN & MANGO YAKITORI

3 large skinned and boned chicken breasts, weighing about 6 oz each
1 large ripe mango
2½ fl oz/⅓ cup chicken stock
2½ fl oz/⅓ cup sake or sweet white wine
3 fl oz/⅓ cup dark soy sauce
1½ tablespoons brown sugar
1 fl oz/2 tablespoons sweet sherry
1 clove garlic, crushed

Cut the chicken into long, thin strips about ¼ in. wide. Peel and pit the mango and cut the flesh into ¼ in. pieces. Thread a strip of chicken on to a skewer, followed by a piece of mango.

Wrap the chicken over the mango, then thread another piece of mango on to the skewer and continue threading the ingredients in this way so that the chicken weaves over and under the mango. Place all the remaining ingredients in a small pan and heat gently until the sugar has dissolved, then bring to the boil for 1 minute. Set aside to cool. Preheat broiler.

Put a small amount of the sauce aside to use as a dip. Brush a little of the remaining sauce over the kabobs. Place under the hot broiler for 30 seconds, then brush with a little more sauce and return to the broiler and cook for a further 30 seconds. Repeat this process for 2-3 minutes or until the kabobs are cooked. Serve hot.

Makes 16-20.

VEAL & SPINACH TERRINE

1 lb fresh spinach
1 lb ground veal
4 oz lean unsmoked bacon, finely chopped
3 oz/¾ cup provolone cheese, grated
1 oz/½ cup fresh white breadcrumbs
1 tablespoon chopped fresh Italian parsley
2 eggs, beaten
salt and freshly ground black pepper
fresh Italian parsley sprigs to garnish

Preheat oven to 320F (170C). Grease and line base of a 2 lb terrine or loaf pan. Rinse spinach thoroughly; do not dry. Cook in a large saucepan without additional water for about 2 minutes until wilted. Tip into a sieve and press out excess water using a wooden spoon. Chop finely.

In a large mixing bowl mix spinach with remaining ingredients. Spoon into the terrine or loaf pan. Cover with foil and cook in the preheated oven for 1-1¼ hours until firm. Remove from oven but cool in pan. Turn out and serve sliced, garnished with Italian parsley sprigs.

Serves 6.

PORK & NOODLE PARCELS

3 cloves garlic, chopped
4 cilantro roots, chopped
6 oz lean pork, ground
1 small egg, beaten
2 teaspoons fish sauce
freshly ground black pepper
about 2 oz egg thread noodles (1 'nest')
vegetable oil for deep frying
dipping sauce to serve
cilantro sprig, to garnish

Using a pestle and mortar or blender, mix together garlic and cilantro roots. In a bowl, mix together pork, egg, fish sauce and pepper, then stir in garlic mixture.

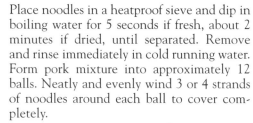

Place noodles in a heatproof sieve and dip in boiling water for 5 seconds if fresh, about 2 minutes if dried, until separated. Remove and rinse immediately in cold running water. Form pork mixture into approximately 12 balls. Neatly and evenly wind 3 or 4 strands of noodles around each ball to cover completely.

In a wok, heat oil to 350F (180C). Using a slotted spoon, lower 4-6 balls into oil and cook for about 3 minutes until golden and pork is cooked through. Using a slotted or draining spoon, transfer to absorbent kitchen paper to drain. Keep warm while cooking remaining balls. Serve hot with dipping sauce. Garnish with cilantro sprig.

Makes about 12 parcels.

CARPACCIO

MOROCCAN LAMB ROLLS

10 oz piece beef fillet
3 oz piece Parmesan, thinly sliced
8 oz button mushrooms, thinly sliced
Leaves from 8 sprigs fresh Italian parsley
DRESSING:
4 fl oz/½ cup extra virgin olive oil
juice 2 lemons
1 clove garlic, chopped
salt and freshly ground black pepper

Put beef in freezer for 30 minutes. Using a very sharp knife, cut beef into wafer thin slices.

Lay beef slices in center of a large serving plate and arrange Parmesan slices, mushrooms and parsley around edge.

To make dressing, whisk together all dressing ingredients in a small bowl or put in a screw-top jar and shake until thoroughly blended. Pour over beef, Parmesan, mushrooms and parsley.

Serves 6.

1 tablespoon pine nuts
2 fl oz/¼ cup olive oil
1 onion, finely chopped
12 oz lean ground lamb
½ teaspoon ground cinnamon
1 tablespoon chopped fresh mint
salt and freshly ground black pepper
6 sheets filo pastry, 16 × 12 in.
fresh mint, to garnish
TAHINI & LEMON DIP:
2 tablespoons tahini
juice of 1 lemon
2 cloves garlic, crushed

In a skillet, heat pine nuts until golden. Remove from the pan and set aside.

In a skillet, heat 2 tablespoons of the oil. Add the onion and cook for 10 minutes until soft. Stir in the lamb and cook, stirring, for a few minutes until browned. Add the cinnamon, mint, pine nuts, salt and pepper. Cook for a further 10 minutes then leave to cool. Preheat the oven to 350F (180C). Cut each sheet of filo pastry across into 3 strips. Brush the strips with the remaining oil.

Spread a spoonful of the lamb filling in a line on one end of each filo strip, leaving a small margin on either side. Roll over twice and fold the long sides over the edge, then continue rolling to make a tube. Place the rolls on a baking sheet. Bake in the oven for 20-30 minutes until crisp and golden. Meanwhile, make the tahini and lemon dip. In a bowl, mix together the tahini, lemon juice and garlic. Garnish the lamb rolls with mint and serve with the dip.

Makes 18.

MAIN COURSES

STEAK WITH BÉARNAISE SAUCE

olive oil for brushing
4 sirloin steaks, about 1 in thick
salt and freshly ground black pepper
BÉARNAISE SAUCE:
4 oz/½ cup unsalted butter, diced
3 stalks each tarragon and chervil
2 teaspoons chopped shallot
4 black peppercorns, crushed
2 tablespoons dry white wine
2 tablespoons white wine vinegar
2 egg yolks
1 teaspoon each chopped fresh tarragon, parsley and
    chervil

Preheat broiler. Oil broiler rack, add steaks
and season with black pepper.

Broil for 1-3 minutes on each side, according
to taste. Meanwhile, make sauce. Melt butter in a small saucepan then set aside and
cool slightly. Put tarragon and chervil stalks,
shallot, peppercorns, wine and vinegar in a
small saucepan, bring to the boil and boil
until reduced to 2 teaspoons. Strain.

Put egg yolks in a blender or food processor
with 2 teaspoons water and process briefly to
combine. With motor running at low speed,
pour in reduced liquid. With motor still running at low speed, pour in melted butter in a
steady stream, to make a thick sauce. Add
herbs and salt and pepper and serve immediately with steaks.

Serves 4.

BEEF FILLET BORDELAISE

7 oz bone marrow (optional)
2 oz/¼ cup butter
2 oz shallots, finely chopped
6 fl oz/¾ cup red Bordeaux wine
bouquet garni
1 tablespoon olive oil
1 lb piece beef fillet
salt and freshly ground black pepper
1 tablespoon chopped fresh parsley

Put marrow, if using, in a saucepan, cover
with water and bring to the boil. Remove
from heat and set aside. Heat half butter in a
saucepan, add shallots and cook, stirring
occasionally, for 3-5 minutes, until soft.

Add wine and bouquet garni, bring to the
boil and boil until reduced by half.
Meanwhile, heat oil in a skillet, add beef and
fry for 2-4 minutes on each side, according to
taste. Transfer to a warmed plate, season and
keep warm. Remove bouquet garni from
sauce and season sauce with salt and pepper.
Reduce heat and whisk in remaining butter.

Cut beef diagonally into 4 thick pieces.
Drain marrow, cut diagonally into 4 slices
and add to sauce. Pour sauce over beef,
sprinkle with parsley and serve immediately.

Serves 2.

DEVILLED STEAKS

STEAKS WITH SHERRY DIP

1 tablespoon olive oil
4 fillet steaks, about 4 oz each
salt and freshly ground black pepper
2 tablespoons sherry vinegar
6 tablespoons dry red wine
4 tablespoons strong beef stock
2 cloves garlic, chopped
1 teaspoon crushed fennel seeds
1 tablespoon sun-dried tomato paste
large pinch chili powder
chopped fresh parsley and parsley sprigs, to garnish

Heat oil in a non-stick skillet until smoking, then add the steaks.

4 × 4 oz lean fillet steaks
freshly ground black pepper
1 tablespoon dry sherry
1 in. piece fresh root ginger, peeled and finely
   chopped
1 teaspoons sesame oil
4 scallions, finely chopped, and scallion strips, to
   garnish
DIP:
2 teaspoons sunflower oil
4 oz scallions, finely chopped
½ in. piece fresh root ginger, peeled and finely
   chopped
4 tablespoons dry sherry
2 tablespoons dark soy sauce

Cook for 2 minutes, turn over and cook for a further 2 minutes for medium/rare steaks. Cook for a little longer if well-done steaks are preferred. Remove from the pan, season and keep warm while making sauce. Pour vinegar, red wine and stock into the pan and boil for 30 seconds. Stir in garlic and fennel seeds. Whisk in the sun-dried tomato paste and chili powder, to taste. Simmer until the sauce is syrupy.

Trim any fat and silver skin from the steaks and lightly tenderize with a meat tenderizer. Season both sides with black pepper. Mix together sherry, ginger and sesame oil. Preheat broiler. Place the steaks on a broiler rack and brush with the sherry mixture. Broil for 3-4 minutes on each side, basting to prevent drying out. Drain on kitchen paper.

Place steaks on warm plates. Pour any juices into the sauce, bring to the boil, taste and season. Pour sauce over the steaks. Garnish with chopped parsley and parsley sprigs and serve with broiled tomatoes and roast diced potatoes.

Serves 4.

Meanwhile, make the dip. Heat the oil in a non-stick or well seasoned wok and stir-fry spring onions and ginger for 2 minutes until soft. Drain well on kitchen paper and place in a bowl. Mix in sherry and soy sauce. Garnish steaks with chopped scallions and scallion strips and serve with the dip and a salad.

Serves 4.

STIR-FRIED CITRUS BEEF

12 oz lean rump or sirloin steak
2 tablespoons dark soy sauce
1 tablespoon dry sherry
2 pieces preserved mandarin peel, shredded
grated rind of l lime
grated rind and juice of 1 orange
1 whole cinnamon stick, broken
2 teaspoons cornstarch
2 teaspoons sunflower oil
4 scallions, shredded
freshly ground black pepper
8 × 1 oz clusters vermicelli egg noodles
lime and orange slices and strips of rind, to garnish

Trim any fat from the beef and cut beef into ¼ in. pieces. Place in a bowl.

Add the soy sauce, sherry, mandarin peel, lime rind, orange rind and juice, cinnamon stick and cornstarch and mix well. Cover and chill for 30 minutes. Heat oil in a non-stick or well-seasoned wok and stir-fry beef mixture for 2-3 minutes. Add the scallions and seasoning and simmer for a further 2-3 minutes until the beef is tender. Discard cinnamon stick.

Meanwhile, bring a large saucepan of water to the boil, add noodle clusters, reduce heat and simmer gently for 2-3 minutes, taking care they retain their shape. Remove from the pan with a slotted spoon, drain well and arrange on serving plates. Top with the beef mixture, garnish and serve with steamed carrots.

Serves 4.

STEAKS WITH CHILI SAUCE

4 × 4 oz lean fillet steaks
1 teaspoon dark soy sauce
1 clove garlic, finely chopped
1 teaspoon sesame oil
2 tablespoons chopped fresh chives, to garnish
SAUCE:
1 teaspoon sunflower oil
1 fresh green chili, seeded and finely chopped
1 shallot, finely chopped
1 teaspoon chili sauce
2 tablespoons red rice vinegar
4 tablespoons dry sherry
1 teaspoon brown sugar

Trim any fat from the steaks. Tenderize lightly with a meat tenderizer or rolling pin.

Preheat broiler. Place steaks on broiler rack. Mix together the soy sauce, garlic and sesame oil and brush over steaks. Broil for 3-4 minutes on each side, brushing with the soy sauce mixture to prevent drying out.

Meanwhile, make the sauce. Heat oil in a non-stick or well-seasoned wok and stir-fry the chili and shallot over a low heat for 1 minute. Add remaining ingredients and simmer gently for 2-3 minutes. Drain cooked steaks on kitchen paper. Sprinkle with chives and serve with the sauce and a salad.

Serves 4.

TERIYAKI STEAKS

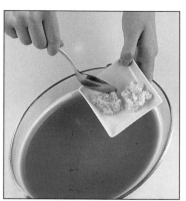

2 fl oz/¼ cup mirin or dry sherry sweetened with
  1 teaspoon sugar
2 fl oz/¼ cup light soy sauce
½ in. piece fresh root ginger, peeled and ground
1 clove garlic, finely chopped
1 teaspoon sugar
½ teaspoon red pepper sauce (or to taste)
4 sirloin or fillet steaks, cut into strips
2 tablespoons sesame oil
4 scallions, thinly sliced
fresh cilantro leaves, to garnish

In a shallow baking dish, combine mirin or
sweetened dry sherry, soy sauce, ginger,
garlic, sugar and red pepper to taste.

Add the steak strips and turn to coat well.
Leave to stand for 1 hour, turning strips once
to twice.

Heat the wok until very hot. Add sesame oil
and swirl to coat. Drain meat, reserving
marinade, and add to wok. Stir-fry for 2-3
minutes until browned on all sides. Pour
over marinade and add scallions. Cook for 3-
5 minutes until steaks are cooked to desired
extent and most of marinade has evaporated,
glazing the meat. Garnish with cilantro
leaves and serve with marinated cucumber or
mooli salad and rice.

Serves 4.

SPICY SESAME BEEF

1 tablespoon cornstarch
3 tablespoons light soy sauce
1 lb rump, sirloin or fillet steak, cut crosswise into
  thin strips
12 oz broccoli
2 tablespoons sesame oil
1 in piece of fresh root ginger, peeled and cut into
  julienne strips
2 cloves garlic, finely chopped
1 fresh chili, seeded and thinly sliced
1 red bell pepper, thinly sliced
14 oz baby corn
4 fl oz/½ cup beef or chicken stock, or water
4-6 scallions cut into 2 in. pieces
toasted sesame seeds, to garnish

In a bowl, combine cornstarch and soy sauce.
Add beef strips and toss to coat well. Leave
to stand for 20 minutes. Cut large flowerets
from the broccoli and divide into small
flowerets. With a swivel-bladed vegetable
peeler, peel the stalk and cut diagonally into
1 in. pieces. Heat the wok until very hot.
Add sesame oil and swirl to coat. Add beef
strips and marinade and stir-fry for 2-3
minutes until browned.

With a slotted spoon, remove beef strips to a
bowl. Add ginger, garlic and chili to the wok
and stir-fry for 1 minute. Add broccoli, red
pepper and baby corn and stir-fry for 2-3
minutes until broccoli is tender but still crisp.
Add the stock and stir for 1 minute until
sauce bubbles and thickens. Add scallions and
reserved beef strips and stir-fry for 1-2 minutes
until beef strips are heated through. Sprinkle
with sesame seeds and serve with rice or
noodles.

Serves 4.

BRISKET WITH JUNIPER

3 lb boned and rolled beef brisket
2 tablespoons all-purpose flour
10 juniper berries, crushed
1 teaspoon chopped fresh rosemary
1 teaspoon chopped fresh thyme
1 teaspoon grated nutmeg
salt and freshly ground black pepper
2 teaspoons cider vinegar
1 tablespoon soft brown sugar
2 lb small onions
1 lb button mushrooms
8 fl oz/1 cup red wine

Make sure the meat is trimmed of excess fat and neatly tied, then place it in the soaked clay pot. Mix together with flour, juniper berries, rosemary, thyme, nutmeg and plenty of seasoning. Add the cider vinegar and brown sugar. Rub this seasoning mixture all over the meat. Pour the red wine into the bottom of the pot and add 8 fl oz/1 cup water. Add the onions. Cover the pot and place in the cold oven. Set the oven at 450F (230C). Cook for 2 hours.

Baste the meat and add the mushrooms, and cook, covered, for a further 1 hour, basting 2 or 3 times, until the meat is succulent and tender. Uncover the pot and cook for a further 15 minutes to brown the meat on top. Serve with boiled or mashed potatoes, rice or pasta.

Serves 6.

BEEF STROGANOFF

2 tablespoons groundnut oil
1¾ lb fillet or boneless sirloin steak, cut crosswise
    into ½ in. strips
1 oz/2 tablespoons butter
1 onion, thinly sliced
8 oz mushrooms, thinly sliced
salt and freshly ground black pepper
1 tablespoon flour
4 fl oz/½ cup beef or veal stock
1 tablespoon Dijon mustard (optional)
8 fl oz/1 cup sour cream
pinch of cayenne pepper
dill sprigs, to garnish

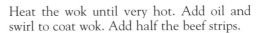

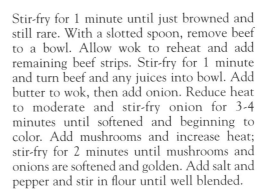

Heat the wok until very hot. Add oil and swirl to coat wok. Add half the beef strips.

Stir-fry for 1 minute until just browned and still rare. With a slotted spoon, remove beef to a bowl. Allow wok to reheat and add remaining beef strips. Stir-fry for 1 minute and turn beef and any juices into bowl. Add butter to wok, then add onion. Reduce heat to moderate and stir-fry onion for 3-4 minutes until softened and beginning to color. Add mushrooms and increase heat; stir-fry for 2 minutes until mushrooms and onions are softened and golden. Add salt and pepper and stir in flour until well blended.

Add beef stock and bring to the boil, then simmer for 1 minute until sauce thickens. Stir in mustard, if using, and gradually add the sour cream. (Do not allow sour cream to boil.) Return beef strips and any juices to sauce and cook gently for 1 minute until beef is heated through. Sprinkle a little cayenne pepper over and garnish with dill sprigs. Serve with rice.

Serves 6.

MIXED GRIDDLE

10 oz sirloin or topside of beet cut into 3 × 1½ in.
  pieces, half-frozen
1 squid, cleaned (optional)
4-8 scallops or raw jumbo shrimp, peeled
4-8 fresh shiitake or button mushrooms, stalks
  removed
1 red or green bell pepper, deseeded
9 oz bean sprouts, trimmed
1 lemon, cut into wedges
2-3 scallions, finely chopped
vegetable oil for frying
DIPPING SAUCE:
6 in large mooli, peeled
1 fresh or dried chili
shoyu

Cut beef into wafer-thin slices. Skin the squid by holding the two flaps together and peeling down; cut in half lengthwise. Put fillets on a cutting board skinned-side up and make fine cross slits on them with a sharp knife. Cut fillets and flaps into 1 in. square pieces. Separate the tentacles, if large. Arrange the meat and the fish on separate platters. If the mushrooms are large, cut them in half. Slice pepper into thin strips. Arrange all the vegetables on a platter.

To make 'autumn maple leaf' relish grate the daikon, finely chop the fresh chili and mix together. Arrange mooli relish, lemon wedges and the scallion in a serving bowl or on small plate. Place the hot-plate in the center of the dining table set with small individual bowls. Serve the meat, fish and vegetable platters and condiments: diners mix their own sauce, adding shoyu to taste, and fry their portion for themselves.

Serves 4-6.

STEAK WITH TOMATO & OLIVES

four 4 oz minute steaks
2 tablespoons olive oil
2 cloves garlic, chopped
1 onion, thinly sliced
1 carrot, finely diced
14 oz can chopped tomatoes
1 teaspoon balsamic vinegar
½ teaspoon dried oregano
1 tablespoon chopped fresh basil
salt and freshly ground black pepper
12 Greek-style black olives, pitted
basil leaves, to garnish

Lightly brush both sides of the steaks with a little of the olive oil. Set aside.

In a non-stick saucepan, heat remaining oil and add garlic. Cook gently until golden. Add onion and carrot and 2 tablespoons water. Cover saucepan and cook gently for 10 minutes until onions are soft, stirring once. Stir in the tomatoes, vinegar, herbs and seasoning, then simmer, uncovered, for 15 minutes until thick and reduced. Stir in the olives and keep warm.

Heat a ridged griddle until smoking and grill steaks for 1 minute per side. Remove to 4 warm plates and season with salt and pepper. Serve with a tomato and olive sauce if liked. Garnish with basil leaves and serve with roast sliced potatoes and broccoli.

Serves 4.

BEEF WITH WATER CHESTNUTS

1 lb lean rump or sirloin steak
1 tablespoon dark soy sauce
1 tablespoon dry sherry
1 teaspoon chili sauce
2 teaspoons brown sugar
2 teaspoons cornstarch
8 oz broccoli
4 oz canned water chestnuts, drained
1 tablespoon sunflower oil
salt and freshly ground black pepper
strips of fresh red chili, to garnish

Trim any fat from the beef and cut into ¾ in. pieces.

Place beef in a bowl, and mix with soy sauce, sherry, chili sauce, sugar and cornstarch. Cover and chill for 30 minutes. Meanwhile, cut the broccoli into small flowerets. Bring a small saucepan of water to the boil and cook the broccoli for 3 minutes. Drain and rinse in cold water. Halve the water chestnuts.

Heat the oil in a non-stick or well-seasoned wok. Add the beef mixture and stir-fry for 2-3 minutes. Add the broccoli and water chestnuts, season and stir-fry for 3 minutes. Garnish with strips of red chili and serve with noodles.

Serves 4.

PROVENÇAL BEEF DAUBE

1 large onion, chopped
10 fl oz/1¼ cups red wine
3 cloves garlic, crushed
2 fresh bay leaves
1 sprig of thyme
salt and freshly ground black pepper
2¼ lb stewing beef, cubed
2 tablespoons olive oil
6 oz streaky bacon, diced
1 tablespoon plain flour
2 tablespoons balsamic vinegar
2 ripe tomatoes, chopped
6 in strip pared orange rind
12 black olives, pitted and halved
10-20 fl oz/1¼-2½ cups beef stock

Put the onion, wine, garlic, bay leaves, thyme and salt and pepper in a large shallow dish and mix well. Add the beef and stir well to coat. Cover and leave in a cool place overnight. Preheat the oven to 325F (160C). Remove the beef from the marinade, reserving the marinade, and pat the beef dry on kitchen paper. Heat the oil in a flameproof casserole, add the bacon and cook until golden. Remove with a slotted spoon and set aside.

Add the beef to the casserole and cook until browned all over. Sprinkle on the flour and cook for 1 minute, stirring. Add the reserved marinade and vinegar. Add the tomatoes, orange rind and olives. Pour in enough stock to cover the beef and season with salt and pepper. Cover tightly and cook in the oven for 3 hours or until the beef is tender. If necessary, add more stock during cooking. Discard the bay leaves, thyme and orange rind and serve.

Serves 4-6.

SPICY BRAISED BEEF

2 cloves garlic, crushed
½ teaspoon ground cinnamon
¼ teaspoon ground cloves
salt and freshly ground black pepper
3 lb beef topside joint
3 tablespoons olive oil
4 onions, thinly sliced
4 fl oz/½ cup red wine
2 tablespoons tomato paste
1 lb spaghetti
1 tablespoon balsamic vinegar

Mix together the garlic, cinnamon, cloves and salt and pepper. Make incisions in the beef and push in the garlic mixture.

Leave in a cool place for 1 hour. Heat the oil in a casserole into which the meat will just fit. Add the meat and cook, turning, until browned all over. Remove from the casserole. Add the onions and cook gently until soft and lightly browned. Replace the meat, add the wine and enough water to barely cover. Mix the tomato paste with a little water. Stir into the casserole. Season, cover and simmer, turning the meat frequently, for about 1½ hours until tender.

Bring a large saucepan of salted water to the boil. Cook the spaghetti according to the packet instructions until just tender. Drain. Remove the meat from the casserole and keep warm. Add the vinegar to the sauce. Boil briskly until reduced to a smooth glossy sauce. Slice the beef and arrange on warmed serving plates. Pour a little sauce over the beef, stir the remainder into the spaghetti and serve with the beef.

Serves 6.

BEEF TAGINE WITH PRUNES

8 oz/1¼ cups pitted prunes
1 teaspoon ground ginger
1 tablespoon ground coriander
pinch saffron threads
salt and freshly ground black pepper
3 tablespoons olive oil
2¾ lb stewing beef, cubed
2 onions, sliced
2 cloves garlic, crushed
chicken stock or water
1 cinnamon stick
1 tablespoon clear honey
1 teaspoon harissa
1 tablespoon sesame seeds
3 tablespoons chopped fresh parsley
1 teaspoon orange flower water, to serve

Place the prunes in a bowl and cover with boiling water. Leave to soak for 2 hours. In a large bowl, mix together the ginger, coriander, saffron, salt, pepper and 2 tablespoons of the oil. Add the beef and mix well, rubbing the spices into the meat with your fingers. Transfer to a tagine or casserole. In a large skillet, heat the remaining oil. Add the onions and garlic and cook for 10 minutes until soft. Add to the spiced beef, then pour in enough stock or water to barely cover the meat. Add the cinnamon stick.

Cover the tagine and simmer gently for 2 hours until the beef is tender. Check from time to time and add more liquid, if necessary. Drain the prunes and add to the casserole; simmer for 20 minutes longer. Stir in the honey and harissa and cook for a further 15 minutes. Dry fry the sesame seeds in a skillet until lightly browned. To serve, stir in the parsley, sprinkle with orange flower water and scatter the sesame seeds on top. Serve with couscous.

Serves 6.

BEEF IN BAROLO WINE

2¼ lb braising beef joint
6 cloves garlic, crushed
1 onion, roughly chopped
1 carrot, chopped
1 stick of celery, chopped
2 bay leaves
2 large thyme sprigs
2-3 peppercorns, lightly crushed
2 cloves
2 allspice berries, crushed
4 fl oz/½ cup Barolo wine, or other full-bodied red wine
2 tablespoons tomato paste
5 fl oz/⅔ cup strong beef stock
salt and freshly ground black pepper

ROAST HOISIN BEEF

1½ lb lean topside or silverside of beef
freshly ground black pepper
2 cloves garlic, finely chopped
½ in. piece of fresh root ginger, peeled and finely chopped
2 teaspoons sesame oil
4 tablespoons hoisin sauce
16 fl oz/2 cups beef stock
4 carrots
1 mooli
1 large green bell pepper
1 large yellow bell pepper
4 scallions, shredded
scallion rings, to garnish

Place meat in a large polythene bag with the garlic, onion, carrot, celery, bay leaves, thyme, peppercorns, cloves, allspice and wine. Shake the bag, seal and refrigerate for several hours or overnight, turning meat occasionally. Next day, preheat oven to 325F (170C). Open bag, remove the meat from marinade and pat dry. Heat oil in a large flameproof casserole and brown the meat all over. Pour in reserved marinade, tomato paste and stock. Cover tightly and bake in oven for 2-3 hours until beef is tender.

Preheat oven to 350F (180C). Trim any fat from the beef and place in a non-stick roasting pan. Season with black pepper. Mix together the garlic, ginger, sesame oil and hoisin sauce and spread over beef. Pour half the stock into the pan and roast for 1 hour, basting occasionally to prevent drying out.

Lift meat out of casserole and keep warm. Skim off any fat, remove bay leaves from the sauce. Purée in a blender or food processor until smooth. Taste and season. The sauce should be quite thick; if it is not, boil to reduce it. Slice the meat thinly and serve with the sauce, accompanied by snow peas and polenta.

Serves 8.

Meanwhile, peel carrots and mooli. Halve carrots and slice lengthwise. Slice daikon widthwise. Quarter and seed the peppers. Arrange around beef, pour in the remaining stock and cook for 45-60 minutes or until tender. Drain beef and vegetables. Slice beef and serve with the vegetables, topped with shredded scallions and garnished with scallion rings.

Serves 4.

BEEF TATAKI

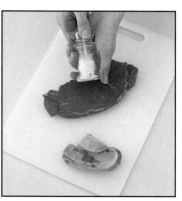

1 lb lean sirloin steak
salt and vegetable oil for brushing
2 scallions, finely chopped
1 in. piece of fresh root ginger, peeled and grated
1 tablespoon wasabi paste
½ cucumber
lime slices and watercress, to garnish
MOOLI DIP:
3 in mooli, peeled and grated
3 tablespoons shoyu
juice of ½ lime

Preheat broiler. Trim fat from meat, sprinkle with salt and brush with oil.

Quickly brown under a high heat broiler for 2-3 minutes on each side. Remove from the heat and immediately plunge into ice cold water to stop further cooking. Traditionally the meat should be golden brown outside but rare inside. Drain, pat dry and set aside while preparing the mooli dip. Mix the mooli, shoyu and lime juice in a serving bowl. Arrange the chopped scallions, grated ginger and wasabi in separate heaps on a small plate. Cut the cucumber in half lengthways, then slice crossways into paper-thin 'half-moons'.

Slice the meat very thinly against the grain. Arrange each piece folded on a half-moon slice of cucumber, slightly overlapping in a circle on a large serving platter. Garnish with lime slices and watercress. Serve with the bowl of mooli dip, accompanied by the plate of condiments. Each diner has a small plate for mixing their own dip sauce.

Serves 4-6.

Note: Serve this dish with 'autumn maple leaf' relish, see page 102, if liked.

BEEF CURRY

2 tablespoons vegetable oil
3 tablespoons red curry paste
12 oz lean beef, cut into cubes
1 stalk lemon grass, finely chopped
4 oz long beans, or green beans, cut into 1½ in. lengths
about 8 pieces dried Chinese black mushrooms, soaked, drained and chopped
3 tablespoons roasted peanuts
1 fresh green chili, seeded and chopped
1 tablespoon fish sauce
2 teaspoons crushed palm sugar
15 Thai mint leaves

In a wok, heat oil, add curry paste and stir for 3 minutes. Add beef and lemon grass and stir-fry for 5 minutes. Add beans and mushrooms, stir-fry for 3 minutes, then stir in peanuts and chili.

Stir for 1 minute, then stir in 4 tablespoons water, the fish sauce and sugar and cook for about 2 minutes until beans are tender but crisp. Transfer to a warmed serving dish and scatter over mint leaves.

Serves 3-4.

CURRIED COCONUT BEEF

53 fl oz/6⅔ cups coconut milk
4 fresh bay leaves
3 lb braising steak, cut into 2 in. cubes
CURRY PASTE:
6 shallots, chopped
6 cloves garlic, smashed
6 fresh red chilies, cored, seeded and chopped
3 in piece galangal, chopped
2 stalks lemon grass, chopped
1 in. piece cinnamon
12 whole cloves
1 teaspoon ground turmeric

Mix all curry paste ingredients in a blender. Add a little coconut milk, if necessary.

In a saucepan, combine curry paste and coconut milk. Add bay leaves and bring to the boil over high heat, stirring occasionally. Lower heat to medium and cook sauce, stirring occasionally, for 15 minutes.

Stir in beef. Simmer, uncovered, stirring occasionally, for 2 hours. Reduce heat to very low and cook beef for a further 1½-2 hours until sauce is quite thick. Stir frequently to prevent sticking. Skim fat and oil from surface. Serve with boiled rice.

Serves 8.

BARBECUED SPARE RIBS

2 tablespoons chopped cilantro stalks
3 cloves garlic, chopped
1 teaspoon black peppercorns, cracked
1 teaspoon grated kaffir lime peel
1 tablespoon green curry paste
2 teaspoons fish sauce
1½ teaspoons crushed palm sugar
6 fl oz/¾ cup coconut milk
2 lb pork spare ribs, trimmed
scallion brushes, to garnish

Using a pestle and mortar or small blender, pound or mix together cilantro, garlic, peppercorns, lime peel, curry paste, fish sauce and sugar. Stir in coconut milk. Place spare ribs in a shallow dish and pour over spiced coconut mixture. Cover and leave in a cool place for 3 hours, basting occasionally.

Preheat a barbecue or moderate broiler. Cook ribs for about 5 minutes a side, until cooked through and brown, basting occasionally with coconut mixture. Garnish with scallion brushes.

Serves 4-6.

Note: The ribs can also be cooked on a rack in a roasting pan in an oven preheated to 400F (200C) for 45-60 minutes, basting occasionally.

BEEF & SEAFOOD FONDUE

8 oz beef fillet, sliced paper thin
4 oz firm white fish fillet, thinly sliced
4 oz cleaned squid
6 raw peeled shrimp, cut in half lengthwise
1 tomato and 1 onion, thinly sliced
freshly ground black pepper
1 tablespoons sesame oil
2 teaspoons vegetable oil
1 clove garlic, chopped
2 shallots, chopped
1 tablespoon each tomato paste and sugar
1 teaspoon salt
2 tablespoons rice vinegar
24 fl oz/3 cups stock or water

Arrange the beef and seafood on a platter in separate sections. Place tomato and onion slices in the center and sprinkle pepper and sesame oil all over them. Set aside while you prepare the broth.

Heat vegetable oil in a saucepan and stir-fry the garlic and shallots for about 30 seconds, then add the tomato paste, sugar, salt and rice vinegar. Blend well, then add the stock or water, bring to the boil and transfer to a Chinese hot pot or fondue.

FONDUE ACCOMPANIMENTS:
2 oz bean thread vermicelli, soaked then cut into
  short lengths
6-8 Chinese dried mushrooms, soaked and each cut
  in half or quartered
2 cakes tofu, cut into small cubes
4 oz bok choy (Chinese cabbage), cut into small
  pieces
dried rice paper or lettuce leaves
fresh mint and cilantro leaves
Sherry Dip (see page 98)

Arrange the vermicelli, mushrooms, tofu cubes and bok choy on a serving platter in separate sections.

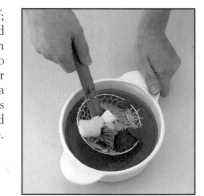

If using large sheets of rice paper, cut in half; if using lettuce leaves, separate them, and place on a serving dish. Place spicy sauce in individual small saucers for dipping. To serve, bring boiling broth in the hot pot or fondue to the table; each person picks up a slice of beef or some seafood with vegetables and dips them into the broth to be cooked very briefly – usually no more than 1 minute.

Meanwhile, dip a piece of rice paper in hot water to soften it. Quickly remove the food from the broth and place in the middle of the rice paper or a lettuce leaf, add a few mint and cilantro leaves, then fold over to make into a neat parcel. Dip the parcel in the dip before eating.

Serves 4-6.

VEAL WITH MUSHROOMS

2 tablespoons olive oil
6 slices streaky bacon, cut into thin strips
4 x 8 oz slices veal shank
12 oz carrots, cut into thick strips
4 plum tomatoes, peeled, quartered and seeded
20 fl oz/2½ cups beef stock
4 fl oz/½ cup red wine
1 lb mixed mushrooms
2 oz/¼ cup butter, diced
2 oz chopped fresh parsley

Heat the oil in a flameproof casserole. Add the bacon and cook for 3-4 minutes. Remove and drain on kitchen paper. Add the veal and cook until browned on both sides.

Remove the veal and drain on kitchen paper. Add the carrots and tomatoes to the casserole and cook for 2-3 minutes. Return the veal to the casserole. Pour over the stock and the red wine. Bring to the boil, cover and simmer for 40 minutes. Add the mushrooms and bacon and cook for 10 minutes, until the veal is cooked through and tender.

Lift out the veal and remove the carrots, mushrooms and bacon with a slotted spoon. Keep warm. Strain the sauce and return to the casserole. Bring to the boil and boil until reduced by one-third. Whisk in the butter, a little at a time. Stir in the parsley. Return the bacon and vegetables to the sauce and cook gently for 2 minutes, to warm through. Arrange the veal on warmed serving plates, pour the sauce over and serve.

Serves 4.

VIETNAMESE BEEF PARCELS

2 cloves garlic, chopped
3 shallots, chopped
2 tablespoons chopped lemon grass
1 tablespoon sugar
1 tablespoon fish sauce
1 tablespoon sesame oil
½ teaspoon freshly ground black pepper
1 lb fillet steak, cut across the grain into thin slices about 2 in. long
8 sheets dried rice paper, halved if large
fresh mint and cilantro leaves
Sherry Dip (see page 98)

Using a pestle and mortar, pound the garlic, shallots, lemon grass and sugar to a paste.

Place paste in a mixing bowl with fish sauce, sesame oil and pepper. Blend well. Add beef and leave to marinate for at least 1 hour, the longer, the better. Meanwhile, prepare the barbecue, or preheat broiler, or preheat oven to 450F (230C). Cook beef on barbecue for 1 minute, under broiler for 2-3 minutes, or in oven for 6-8 minutes, turning once.

To serve, dip each piece of dried rice paper in warm water to soften it, then place a slice of beef on one end of the paper, put a mint leaf and some cilantro on top of the beef and roll into a neat parcel. Dip the parcels in the Sherry Dip before serving.

Serves 4.

Note: This dish can also be served as an appetizer, in which case it will serve 6-8.

SHABUSHABU (BEEF HOT POT)

1 lb sirloin or topside of beef
2 leeks, white part only
8 fresh or dried shiitake or 12 button mushrooms, stalks removed
9 oz (1 cake) firm tofu
4-6 Chinese cabbage (hakusai) leaves
10 oz spinach, trimmed
4 in. piece dried konbu (kelp)
10 oz udon noodles, cooked (optional)
finely chopped scallion, to garnish

CITRUS DIP:
½ mooli, peeled
1 dried or fresh red chili
2 scallions, finely chopped
juice of ½ lemon and ½ lime
4 fl oz/½ cup shoyu

SESAME DIP:
4 tablespoons sesame paste or smooth peanut butter
4 fl oz/½ cup dashi or chicken stock
3 tablespoons shoyu
1 tablespoon mirin or sweet sherry
1 tablespoon sugar
2 tablespoons sake or white wine
2 teaspoons chili oil or chili powder (optional)

Trim off any fat from the beef and cut into 3 × 1½ in. flat pieces (any length). Place in separate freezer bags and freeze for 1-2 hours.

Remove from the freezer and leave until half thawed, then cut the beef into wafer-thin slices and arrange in a circular fan on a large platter. Slice leeks diagonally. If the shiitake mushrooms are large cut in half. If using dried shiitake, soak in warm water with a pinch of sugar for 45 minutes, then remove stalks before use. Cut the tofu into 16 cubes. Cut the Chinese cabbage leaves and spinach into bite-size pieces. Arrange the vegetables and tofu on a large platter.

To prepare the citrus dip, grate the mooli very finely and chop the fresh red chili, them mix together. Put the relish, chopped scallion, a mixture of the lemon and lime juices, and the shoyu in separate small bowls. To make the sesame dip, mix all the ingredients together and stir until the sesame paste (or peanut butter) is of a smooth runny consistency. Divide between 4-6 individual dipping bowls.

Put the konbu in a large pot (ideally a clay pot, an enamelled cast-iron casserole or a copper-based Mongolian hot-pot) and fill two thirds full with water. Bring to the boil and remove the konbu. Put in some of the leek, Chinese leaves, shiitake mushrooms, spinach and tofu and when it begins to come back to boil, transfer the pot to a portable gas ring or electric hotplate on the dining table. Diners make their own citrus dip in individual dipping bowls by mixing 1-2 teaspoons each of the relish, scallion and citrus juice with some shoyu.

Diners serve themselves by cooking the meat in the pot, adding more vegetables, and eating them dipped in either of the sauces. When ingredients are finished, skim and season the soup with shoyu and a little salt and sugar. If using noodles, warm them in the soup, seasoned with a little shoyu to taste, so that diners can end the meal with plain noodles garnished with chopped spring onion.

Serves 4-6.

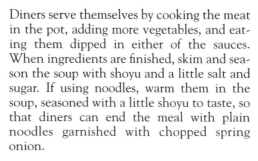

STUFFED VEAL

1½ lb boned breast or loin of veal or oyster cut from
    leg of veal
salt and freshly ground black pepper
1 tablespoon lemon juice
8 oz sausagemeat
1 egg
1 onion, finely chopped
6 tablespoons fresh breadcrumbs
2 tablespoons chopped fresh parsley
1 tablespoon chopped fresh thyme
grated rind of ½ lemon
8 fl oz/1 cup dry white wine
12 fl oz/1½ cups light cream
2 tablespoons chopped fresh dill (optional)
dill sprigs, to garnish (optional)

Trim the veal of excess fat, then season it well all over and sprinkle with lemon juice. Mix together the sausagemeat, egg, onion, breadcrumbs, herbs, lemon rind and plenty of seasoning. When all the ingredients are thoroughly combined, spread the stuffing over the meat and roll it up neatly. Tie securely and place in the soaked clay pot. Pour in the wine.

Cover the pot and place in the cold oven. Set oven at 400F (200C). Cook for 2 hours, or until the veal is tender, basting occasionally. Uncover the pot and cook for a further 15 minutes to brown the meat. Transfer the meat to a serving platter. Strain the cooking juices into a saucepan and add the cream. Heat gently without boiling, then stir in the dill, if used, and taste for seasoning. Carve the veal, garnish with dill, if used, and serve the sauce separately.

Serves 6.

SPICY BEEF STEW

1 tablespoon vegetable oil
2 cloves garlic, chopped
1 onion, chopped
1 stalk lemon grass, chopped
1 lb stewing beef, cut into bite-size cubes
20 fl oz/2½ cups stock or water
5-6 tablespoons soy or fish sauce
1 teaspoon chili sauce
2 teaspoons five-spice powder
1 tablespoon sugar
2-3 scallions, chopped
freshly ground black pepper
cilantro sprig, to garnish

Heat oil in a clay pot or flameproof casserole and stir-fry garlic, onion, and lemon grass for about 1 minute. Add the beef and stir-fry for 2-3 minutes, or until the color of the meat changes. Add the stock or water, bring to boil, then add the soy or fish sauce, chili sauce, five-spice powder and sugar. Blend well, then reduce heat, cover and simmer gently for about 45-50 minutes.

Add scallions, season with pepper and cook for a further 5 minutes. Garnish with cilantro sprigs and serve straight from the pot, accompanied by carrots and baby corn.

Serves 4.

Variation: Substitute curry powder for the five-spice powder to make beef curry.

MOROCCAN COUSCOUS

2¼ lb trimmed lamb shoulder, cut into pieces
2 onions, chopped
2 oz/⅓ cup garbanzos, soaked
1 teaspoon ground ginger
salt and freshly ground black pepper
pinch saffron threads
4 each small turnips and carrots, in large pieces
1 lb/2½ lb regular couscous (not instant)
1 oz smen or butter, melted
a little rosewater
2 oz/⅓ cup raisins
4 medium zucchini, halved lengthwise
1 butternut squash, peeled and cubed
2 tomatoes, quartered
2 tablespoons each chopped fresh cilantro and
  parsley

Place the lamb, with the onions and garbanzos in the bottom of a couscoussière or large stockpot. Stir in the ginger, saffron and 1 teaspoon pepper. Cover with water, bring to the boil and simmer, covered, for 45 minutes. Add the turnips and carrots.

Place the couscous grains in a large bowl. Dissolve 1 teaspoon salt in 5 fl oz/⅔ cup) water and sprinkle over the couscous. Stir with your fingers, rubbing to separate the grains and break up any lumps. When the couscous has soaked up all the water, place in the top of a couscoussière, or in a colander lined with cheesecloth. Set the couscoussière or colander on top of the simmering stew.

If any steam escapes, wrap a strip of cloth around the top of the pan before placing the couscous on top. Steam, covered, for 20 minutes, occasionally drawing a fork through the couscous grains to separate them. Turn the couscous out on to a large wooden or earthenware dish. Sprinkle with a little salted water, as before, and separate the grains with your fingers.

Lightly rub in the melted smen or butter and the rosewater and put the couscous back in the top part of the couscoussière or colander. Add the raisins, zucchini, squash, tomatoes, salt, cilantro and parsley to the simmering stew then replace the couscous over the pan. Steam for a further 30 minutes, occasionally fluffing the couscous grains with a fork.

To serve, pile the couscous on to a large wooden or earthenware serving dish. With a slotted spoon, transfer the lamb and vegetables to the center of the dish. Pour over some of the broth. Stir some harissa into the remaining broth and serve it separately.

Serves 6.

Variation: The selection of vegetables can include beans, peas, eggplant, but traditionally 7 vegetables are used.

RACK OF LAMB WITH ONIONS

ROAST STUFFED LEG OF LAMB

grated rind of 1 lemon
1 tablespoon chopped fresh parsley
2 teaspoons garlic purée
1 tablespoon chopped fresh rosemary
salt and freshly ground black pepper
8-bone rack of lamb
8 small onions, peeled
1 tablespoon olive oil
8 fl oz/1 cup lamb or vegetable stock
3 tablespoons red wine vinegar
2 tablespoons superfine sugar
rosemary sprig, to garnish

Preheat oven to 400F (200C). In a small bowl, mix together the lemon rind, parsley, garlic purée, rosemary and salt and pepper.

Put the lamb, fat side up, in a flameproof dish. Spread the lemon and herb mixture over the lamb. Place the onions in the dish and brush with the oil. Roast for 20 minutes. Turn off the heat and leave the lamb and onions in the oven for 20 minutes. Remove from the dish and keep warm.

Add the stock, vinegar and sugar to the dish. Season with plenty of black pepper. Bring to the boil and boil, stirring, until the liquid has reduced by half and thickened. Return the onions to the dish, turn in the sauce and simmer for 5 minutes. Cut the lamb into individual chops, garnish and serve with the onions and sauce.

Serves 4.

Note: If you prefer, roast the lamb for an extra 5-10 minutes, according to taste.

4 lb boned leg of lamb, plus the bones
salt and freshly ground black pepper
1 onion, quartered
7 tablespoons olive oil
3 rosemary sprigs
5 fl oz/⅔ cup dry white wine
juice of 2 lemons
STUFFING;
2 oz/¼ cup couscous
2 tablespoons olive oil
1 small onion, finely chopped
1 clove garlic, crushed
1 teaspoon ground cinnamon
1 teaspoon ground cumin
4 oz/1 cup ready-to-eat dried apricots, chopped
2 oz/⅔ cup pine nuts

To make the stuffing, place the couscous in a bowl and cover with boiling water; leave to stand until absorbed and fluff up with a fork. Heat the oil, add the onion and garlic and cook for 10 minutes. Leave to cool. Stir into the couscous with the cinnamon, cumin, apricots, pine nuts, salt and pepper. Place 5 pieces of string in parallel lines on the work surface. Place the lamb, skin side down, across them and season with salt and pepper. Spoon the stuffing on to the meat. Roll up firmly and tie to make a neat shape. Preheat the oven to 475F (240C).

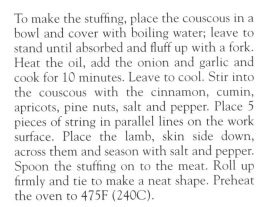

Roast the lamb bones and onion in a tin with 3 tablespoons of the oil for 15 minutes. Add the rosemary and lamb. Pour in the wine and lemon juice, spoon over remaining olive oil and season. Roast for 15 minutes, then reduce heat to 400F (220C) and cook for 1 hour, basting occasionally. Remove the lamb and leave to stand for 15 minutes. Add 20 fl oz/2½ cups water to the tin, and boil until reduced. Serve with the lamb. Serve with a mixed salad.

Serves 6-8.

SPICED RACK OF LAMB

1 tablespoon all-purpose flour
salt and freshly ground black pepper
2 racks of lamb
1 clove garlic, finely chopped
2 tablespoons olive oil
1 lb tomatoes, roughly chopped
½ lemon, chopped
1 stick cinnamon
3 cloves
1 small red chili, seeded and chopped
4 fl oz/½ cup dry white wine
2 tablespoons tomato paste
lemon slices, to garnish

Preheat oven to 350F (180C). Mix together flour, salt and pepper. Rub over lamb. Press garlic into gaps between bones. In a roasting tin, heat oil. Put lamb, skin side down, in oil to brown. Remove lamb. Add tomatoes, lemon, cinnamon, cloves and chili to roasting pan. Return lamb, skin side up, to pan.

In a bowl, mix together wine, 4 fl oz/½ cup water and tomato paste. Pour over lamb. Cover pan loosely with foil. Cook in the oven for 1 hour. Remove foil and cook for a further 30 minutes until lamb is cooked. Cut the lamb into individual chops and keep warm. Place roasting pan on heat and boil liquid to reduce to a thick sauce. Pour over meat. Garnish with lemon slices.

Serves 6.

LAMB BOULANGÈRE

4½ lb leg of lamb
4 cloves garlic
salt and freshly ground black pepper
2 lb potatoes, fairly thickly sliced
1 Spanish onion, thinly sliced
1 bay leaf
2 sprigs of thyme
about 10 fl oz/1¼ cups veal or vegetable stock or
    water
1½ oz/3 tablespoons butter
olive oil for greasing
salt and freshly ground black pepper
flat-leaf parsley, to garnish

Cut small incisions in lamb. Thinly slice 2 garlic cloves and insert into incisions.

Season lamb and set aside. Preheat oven to 325F (170C). Grease a shallow ovenproof dish with ½ oz/1 tablespoon butter. Crush remaining garlic. Arrange layers of potatoes, onion, garlic, herbs and salt and pepper in the buttered dish. Add enough stock or water to just cover, dot with remaining butter, cover with foil and bake in the oven for 1 hour.

Grease a heavy skillet with a little oil, add lamb and cook quickly until lightly browned all over. Put lamb on top of potatoes and cover with foil. Increase oven temperature to 375F (190C) and bake lamb and potatoes for 1¼-1½ hours, uncovered 15 minutes before end of cooking time, to brown. Carve lamb, garnish with flat-leaf parsley and serve with potatoes.

Serves 6.

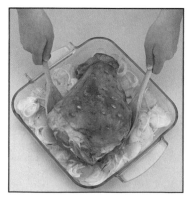

LAMB & FLAGEOLET BEANS

4 x 8 oz lamb shanks
4 cloves garlic, thinly sliced
2 tablespoons olive oil
1 onion, finely chopped
12 oz/1½ cups flageolet beans, soaked overnight
1¼ lb tomatoes, peeled, seeded and chopped
1 tablespoon tomato paste
5 fl oz/⅔ cup red wine
bouquet garni
salt and freshly ground black pepper
1 small bunch of parsley, chopped
flat-leaf parsley and bay leaves, to garnish

LAMB WITH ROSEMARY

4½ lb leg of young lamb
3 sprigs of rosemary
2-3 cloves garlic, cut into slivers
salt and freshly ground black pepper
2 oz/¼ cup butter
5 fl oz/⅔ cup red or white wine

Cut 4 incisions in each lamb shank. Insert a slice of garlic in each incision.

Preheat oven to 450F (230C). Cut small incisions in lamb with the point of a sharp knife.

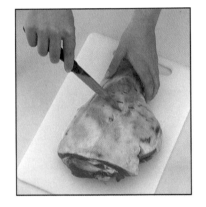

Heat oil in a heavy flameproof casserole, add shanks and cook until browned all over. Remove and set aside. Add onion and remaining garlic to casserole and cook, stirring occasionally, for 5 minutes, until soft but not browned.

Remove leaves from one rosemary sprig. Insert leaves and garlic slivers into incisions. Season lamb, put the remaining rosemary sprigs on top and dot with butter. Put in a roasting pan and roast for 15 minutes. Lower oven temperature to 350F (180C) and roast for a further 40-60 minutes.

Drain and rinse beans and add to casserole with tomatoes, tomato paste, wine, bouquet garni and salt and pepper. Return lamb to casserole, cover tightly and cook gently for 1-2 hours, until lamb and flageolet beans are tender. Discard bouquet garni and stir in parsley. Garnish and serve with béarnaise sauce (see page 97)

Serves 4.

Leave lamb in oven, with door propped open, for 15 minutes, to rest. Remove lamb from roasting pan and transfer to a serving plate. Tilt roasting pan and spoon off most of fat. Add wine, stirring to dislodge sediment. Bring to the boil and simmer briefly. Season with salt and pepper. Carve lamb, garnish with rosemary sprigs and serve with sauce.

Serves 6.

RED-COOKED LAMB FILLET

1 lb lean lamb fillet
3 tablespoons dry sherry
½ in. piece fresh root ginger, peeled and finely chopped
2 cloves garlic, thinly sliced
1 teaspoon five-spice powder
3 tablespoons dark soy sauce
10 fl oz/1¼ cups Chinese chicken stock (see page 57)
2 teaspoons superfine sugar
2 teaspoons cornstarch mixed with 4 teaspoons water
salt and freshly ground black pepper
shredded scallions, to garnish

BAKED LAMB WITH VEGETABLES

1 leg of lamb, weighing about 4½ lb
3 cloves garlic, cut into slivers
salt and freshly ground black pepper
1 eggplant
1½ lb potatoes, peeled
1 large onion, thinly sliced
1 lb tomatoes, sliced
2 fl oz/¼ cup white wine
1 tablespoon chopped fresh oregano

Preheat oven to 425F (220C). Cut slits in meat and insert slivers of garlic. Rub generously with salt and pepper. Place lamb in a large roasting pan and put in oven.

Trim any excess fat and silver skin from lamb and cut into ¾ in. cubes.

Blanch the lamb in a saucepan of boiling water for 3 minutes. Drain well. Heat a non-stick or well seasoned wok and add the lamb with the sherry, ginger, garlic, five-spice powder and soy sauce. Bring to the boil, reduce heat and simmer for 2 minutes, stirring. Pour in stock, return to the boil and simmer for 25 minutes.

Reduce heat to 350F (180C) and roast for 1½ hours for slightly pink meat or 2 hours for medium-well done. Meanwhile, slice eggplant into ¼ in. slices, place in a colander and sprinkle with salt. Leave for 30 minutes, then rinse and pat dry with absorbent kitchen paper.

Add sugar, cornstarch mixture and seasoning and stir until thickened. Simmer gently for 5 minutes. Garnish with shredded scallions and serve on a bed of rice.

Serves 4.

One hour before end of cooking time remove any fat from roasting pan and add vegetables. Pour the wine over, season with salt and pepper and sprinkle with oregano. Return to the oven. Turn vegetables over during the cooking time to cook them evenly in juices. Carve lamb into slices, adding any meat juices to vegetables. Serve lamb with the vegetables and meat juices.

Serves 6.

TARRAGON LAMB NOISETTES

SOUVLAKIA

1 tablespoon olive oil
2 oz/¼ cup butter
8 lamb noisettes, about 1 in. thick
salt and freshly ground black pepper
4 tablespoons brandy
3 tablespoons thick cream
2 tablespoons chopped fresh tarragon
tarragon sprigs and flat-leaf parsley, to garnish

Heat oil and half the butter in a heavy skillet until sizzling.

2 cloves garlic, crushed
2 fl oz/¼ cup lemon juice
2 tablespoons olive oil
4 tablespoons chopped fresh oregano
salt and freshly ground black pepper
1 lb lean lamb fillet, cubed
6 fresh bay leaves, halved
oregano sprigs, to garnish
TOMATO AND OLIVE SALSA:
6 oz mixed green and black olives, pitted and finely
    chopped
1 small red onion, finely chopped
4 plum tomatoes, finely chopped
2 tablespoons olive oil

Add lamb and cook for 2½-3 minutes on each side, until well-browned but still pink in the center. Remove with a slotted spoon, transfer to warmed serving plates, season with salt and pepper and keep warm.

In a shallow dish, mix together the garlic, lemon juice, olive oil, oregano and salt and pepper. Add the lamb and mix well. Leave in a cool place for 2 hours. To make the salsa, put the olives, onion, tomatoes, olive oil and salt and pepper in a bowl and mix together. Chill until required.

Add remaining butter to pan. When melted, add brandy, stirring to dislodge sediment, and bring to the boil. Stir in cream and tarragon and boil until thickened. Season, pour over lamb, garnish with tarragon sprigs and flat-leaf parsley and serve.

Serves 4.

Remove the lamb from the marinade and thread on to skewers, adding the bay leaves to the skewers at regular intervals. Cook over a barbecue or under a hot broiler, turning occasionally, for 10 minutes or until the lamb is brown and crisp on the outside and pink and juicy inside. Garnish with oregano sprigs and serve with the tomato and olive salsa.

Serves 4.

LAMB EN PAPILLOTTE

4 × 6 oz lamb leg steaks
1 tablespoon Dijon mustard
4 scallions, sliced
1 teaspoon chopped fresh rosemary
salt and freshly ground black pepper
1 lb sweet potatoes, cut into chunks
1 lb zucchini, thickly sliced
1 tablespoon olive oil
rosemary sprigs, to garnish

Preheat oven to 400F (200C). Cut 4 large squares of foil and place a lamb steak on each one. Spread the lamb with the mustard and sprinkle with the scallions and rosemary. Season with salt and pepper.

Bring the foil up over the steaks to make a parcel and twist the edges together to seal. Put the parcels in an ovenproof dish. Arrange the sweet potatoes and zucchini around the parcels.

Drizzle with oil and season with salt and pepper. Cook in the oven for 1 hour, basting and turning the vegetables at least twice. Remove the lamb from the parcels, garnish with rosemary and serve with the vegetables.

Serves 4.

LAMB WITH STAR ANISE

4 × 5 oz lean lamb loin chops
2 teaspoons sunflower oil
1 clove garlic, thinly sliced
4 star anise
1 tablespoon light soy sauce
4 tablespoons dry sherry
1 teaspoon superfine sugar
salt and freshly ground white pepper
1 teaspoon cornstarch mixed with 2 tablespoons water
2 scallions, shredded, to garnish

Trim any rind, fat and bone from the lamb. Using string, tie the lamb into round steaks.

Heat oil in a non-stick or well seasoned wok, add the garlic and lamb and fry for 2 minutes on each side until browned. Drain on kitchen paper and wipe out wok. Return lamb and garlic to wok. Add star anise, soy sauce, sherry, sugar and salt and pepper.

Bring to the boil, reduce heat and simmer for 4 minutes, turning lamb halfway through. Add cornstarch mixture and cook, stirring, until thickened. Simmer for 2 minutes. Discard star anise and remove string from lamb before serving. Garnish with scallions and serve with rice and vegetables.

Serves 4.

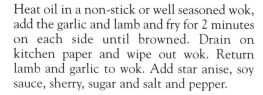

LAMB PARCELS

12 vine leaves, preserved in brine
2 fl oz/¼ cup olive oil
juice ½ lemon
2 cloves garlic, crushed
1 tablespoon chopped fresh marjoram
salt and freshly ground black pepper
6 sheets filo pastry
2 oz/¼ cup butter, melted
6 thin lamb steaks or pieces of lamb fillet
shredded nasturtium flowers and mint, to garnish

Soak vine leaves in water for 1 hour. In a saucepan of boiling water, cook vine leaves for 5 minutes. Drain and dry on a tea towel.

In a bowl, mix together olive oil, lemon juice, garlic, marjoram, salt and pepper. Place lamb in a dish, pour marinade over and leave in a cool place for 1 hour.

Preheat oven to 375F (190C). Brush each sheet of filo pastry with butter. Lay a vine leaf in middle of 1 end of each sheet. Place a lamb steak on top, then cover with another vine leaf. Fold sides of pastry over lamb and roll up to form neat parcels. Place on a baking sheet. Bake in the oven for 20-30 minutes until pastry is golden and crisp. Serve garnished with shredded nasturtium flowers and mint.

Serves 6.

NOISETTES WITH CALVADOS

2 tablespoons oil
1 onion, finely chopped
2 dessert apples, peeled, cored and sliced
1 lb shelled peas
1 bay leaf
salt and freshly ground black pepper
8 fl oz/1 cup medium-dry (alcoholic) cider
4 sprigs mint
8 thick lamb noisettes
4 tablespoons Calvados or brandy
1 small Cos lettuce, coarsely shredded
mint sprigs, to garnish

Heat half the oil in a skillet. Add the onion and cook for 5 minutes, then mix in the apples, peas, bay leaf and seasoning. Turn the mixture into the soaked clay pot and pour in the cider. Top with the mint sprigs.

Heat the remaining oil in the skillet. Quickly brown the noisettes on all sides. Pour the Calvados or brandy over the lamb, set it alight and allow to burn out. Then arrange the noisettes on top of the vegetables in the pot. Season well. Cover the pot and place in the cold oven. Set at 425F (220C). Cook for 40 minutes. Uncover the pot, add the lettuce and cook for a further 10 minutes. Serve garnished with mint.

Serves 4.

LAMB WITH BLACK OLIVES

4 tablespoons olive oil
1½ lb lean lamb, cut into small cubes
4 oz piece belly pork, cut into small strips
2 cloves garlic, sliced
½-1 teaspoon chopped fresh oregano
6 fl oz/¾ cup full-bodied white wine
1 fresh chili, seeded and finely chopped
12-15 black olives, pitted

Heat oil in a wide, shallow flameproof casserole. Add lamb, pork and garlic and cook over high heat to seal and brown meat.

In a small saucepan, boil oregano and wine for 2-3 minutes. Stir into casserole, cover and cook gently for 30 minutes.

Stir chili and olives into casserole. Cover again and cook for about 30 minutes until lamb is tender. If necessary, uncover casserole towards end of cooking time so liquid can evaporate to make a light sauce.

Serves 4.

STIR-FRIED SESAME LAMB

12 oz lean lamb fillet
1 tablespoon sunflower oil
4 oz shallots, sliced
1 red bell pepper, sliced
1 green bell pepper, sliced
1 clove garlic, finely chopped
1 tablespoon light soy sauce
1 teaspoon white rice vinegar
1 teaspoon superfine sugar
freshly ground black pepper
2 tablespoons sesame seeds

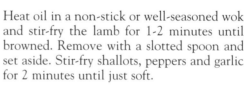

Trim any fat and silver skin from the lamb fillet. Cut into ¼ in. cubes.

Heat oil in a non-stick or well-seasoned wok and stir-fry the lamb for 1-2 minutes until browned. Remove with a slotted spoon and set aside. Stir-fry shallots, peppers and garlic for 2 minutes until just soft.

Return lamb to wok with all the remaining ingredients except the sesame seeds. Stir-fry for 2 minutes. Sprinkle with sesame seeds and serve with rice and vegetables.

Serves 4.

FLORENTINE ROAST PORK

2¼ lb pork loin, boned
2 tablespoons chopped fresh rosemary leaves
2 cloves garlic, chopped
salt and freshly ground black pepper
3 tablespoons olive oil
5 fl oz/⅔ cup dry white wine

Preheat oven to 325F (170C). Using a flat skewer, make deep incisions all over the meat. Mix rosemary and garlic together with plenty of salt and pepper. Push the rosemary mixture into the incisions. Rub any remaining mixture into flap where the bones have been removed.

Season very well and tie up neatly with string. Rub meat all over with olive oil and place in a roasting pan. Pour in white wine and roast in oven for 1½ hours, basting frequently and turning the joint each time. If you have a spit or rotisserie, roast it on the spit, basting frequently.

Transfer pork to a serving dish and keep warm. Skim fat off pan, and add a little water to the juices. Scrape up sediment and bring to the boil, taste and season. Carve the pork into thick slices, garnish with rosemary sprigs and serve with the sauce, carrots and brown lentils.

Serves 6.

CARAWAY POT ROAST

1 tablespoon olive oil
2¼ lb hand of pork, boned
2 large onions, chopped
1 lb parsnips, cut into chunks
1 oz caraway seeds
½ teaspoon freshly grated nutmeg
salt and freshly ground black pepper
8 fl oz/1 cup chicken stock
8 fl oz/1 cup red wine
thyme sprigs, to garnish

Preheat oven to 350F (180C). Heat the oil in a large flameproof casserole. Add the pork and cook until browned all over.

Remove the meat from the casserole. Add the onions and parsnips and cook, stirring occasionally, for 7 minutes, until golden. Lay the pork on top of the vegetables. Mix together the caraway seeds and nutmeg and sprinkle on top of the pork. Season with salt and pepper. Pour the stock and wine around the pork. Cover tightly and cook in the oven for 2 hours, or until the pork is cooked through and tender. Remove the pork from the casserole and keep warm.

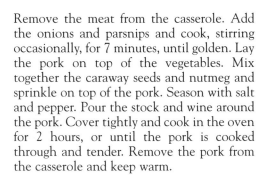

Remove the vegetables from the casserole with a slotted spoon. Bring the sauce to the boil and boil until reduced and thickened. Season with salt and pepper. Slice the meat, garnish with thyme sprigs and serve with the vegetables and sauce.

Serves 6-8.

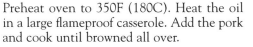

STUFFED PORK SHOULDER

ROAST PORK WITH HONEY

3 lb shoulder of pork, boned and skinned
1 lb potatoes, cut into chunks
1 lb rutabaga, cut into chunks
1 lb parsnips, cut into chunks
1 tablespoon olive oil
salt and freshly ground black pepper
1 tablespoon cornstarch
18 fl oz/2¼ cups vegetable stock
1 tablespoon mango and lime chutney
sage leaves, to garnish
STUFFING:
6 oz can corned beef, finely chopped
4 oz/2 cups fresh white breadcrumbs
1 onion, finely chopped
1 teaspoon dried sage
1 tablespoon mango and lime chutney

1 lb piece lean pork fillet
4 tablespoons chopped fresh cilantro
GLAZE:
1 teaspoon Szechuan peppercorns, toasted and
    ground
1 tablespoon clear honey
2 teaspoons brown sugar
1 tablespoon dark soy sauce
1 in. piece fresh root ginger, peeled and finely
    chopped
1 clove garlic, finely chopped

Preheat oven to 375F (190C). Trim any fat and silver skin from pork and place on a rack in a roasting pan.

Preheat oven to 350F (180C). Open out the shoulder of pork and flatten. To make the stuffing, mix together the corned beef, breadcrumbs, onion and sage. Add the chutney and bind the mixture together. Spread the stuffing along the center of the inside of the pork. Roll the pork into a round shape and tie securely with string. Season with salt and pepper. Put in a flameproof dish, cover with a lid or piece of foil and cook in the oven for 2 hours, basting the meat every 45 minutes. Increase the oven temperature to 400F (200C).

Pour in enough water to cover base of pan. Mix together all the glaze ingredients and brush generously over the pork. Roast for 1 hour until cooked through, brushing occasionally with glaze and adding more water to the pan if it dries out.

Place the potatoes, rutabaga and parsnips around the meat. Drizzle the vegetables with oil and season. Cook, uncovered, for 45-55 minutes, turning meat and vegetables occasionally, until tender. Remove the meat and vegetables and keep warm. Add the cornstarch and stir into the cooking juices. Gradually add the stock and bring to the boil, stirring. Add the chutney and simmer for 3-4 minutes. Slice the pork, garnish and serve with the vegetables and sauce.

Remove cooked pork from rack and sprinkle with chopped cilantro until coated all over. Slice and serve with rice and vegetables.

Serves 4.

Serves 6-8.

SPICED PORK LOIN

1 tablespoon paprika
3 cloves garlic, finely chopped
1 teaspoon chopped fresh oregano
½ teaspoon finely crushed cumin seeds
1 bay leaf, crushed
salt
3 tablespoons virgin olive oil
1½ lb boned and rolled loin of pork
olive oil for frying
4 tablespoons full-bodied dry white wine
pitted green olives, to serve

In a small bowl, mix together paprika, garlic, oregano, cumin seeds, bay leaf and salt, then stir in olive oil.

Place pork in a non-metallic dish, spoon the marinade mixture over the top, cover and leave in refrigerator for 2-3 days. Return pork to room temperature 30 minutes before cooking.

Cut pork into 4 slices. Heat oil in a skillet over fairly high heat. Add pork, brown quickly on both sides, then cook more gently for 4-5 minutes a side until cooked through. Transfer slices to a warm serving plate. Stir wine into cooking juices, boil for 2-3 minutes, then pour over pork. Scatter green olives over the top.

Serves 4.

PORK IN CIDER & ORANGE

3 tablespoons olive oil
flour for coating
salt and freshly ground black pepper
1½ lb boned and rolled loin of pork
1 small Spanish onion, sliced
10 fl oz/1¼ cups well-flavored dry (alcoholic) cider
juice 1 large juicy orange
rind ¼ orange, cut into fine strips
pinch ground cinnamon
pinch superfine sugar
thin orange slices, parsley springs and flaked toasted almonds, to garnish

Heat oil in a heavy flameproof casserole. Put flour on a plate and season with salt and pepper. Roll pork in seasoned flour to coat evenly and lightly. Add to casserole and brown evenly for about 10 minutes. Remove and keep warm. Stir onion into casserole and cook over a low heat for about 20 minutes, stirring occasionally, until very soft and lightly browned. Stir in cider, orange juice and rind strips and cinnamon. Bring to the boil and simmer for 2-3 minutes.

Return pork to casserole, turn it in sauce, cover and cook gently for about 45 minutes until pork is tender. Transfer pork to a serving dish and boil sauce, if necessary, to thicken lightly. Adjust seasoning and level of cinnamon, and add a pinch of superfine sugar, if desired. Pour sauce over pork and garnish with orange slices, parsley sprigs and toasted flaked almonds.

Serves 4.

PORK WITH MELON & MANGO

1 small Galia or ½ honeydew melon, cut into
   julienne strips
1 slightly under-ripe mango, peeled and cut into
   julienne strips
salt and freshly ground black pepper
1 tablespoon sugar
juice of 1 lime or lemon
2 tablespoons sesame oil
8 oz pork fillet, cut into shreds
4-6 scallions, thinly sliced
2 cloves garlic, finely chopped
5 tablespoons nam pla (fish sauce)
1 tablespoon cider vinegar
½ teaspoon crushed chilies
chopped peanuts and chopped cilantro, to garnish

PORK WITH PEARS

2 tablespoons olive oil
2 onions, chopped
2 ¼ lb boned lean pork, cut into cubes
8 fl oz/1 cup red wine
grated rind ½ orange
½ cinnamon stick
salt and freshly ground black pepper
2 pears
2 teaspoons clear honey
chopped fresh cilantro leaves, orange rind strips and
   pitta bread, to garnish

In a flameproof casserole, heat oil. Add
onions; cook until soft. Push to side of pan,
turn up heat and brown meat in batches.

In a medium bowl, toss melon and mango
strips with the salt and pepper to taste, sugar
and lime or lemon juice. Set aside. Heat the
wok until very hot. Add oil and swirl to coat,
add shredded pork and stir-fry for 2-3
minutes until golden. With a slotted spoon,
remove to absorbent kitchen paper and
drain.

Add wine, orange rind, cinnamon stick, salt,
pepper and 10 fl oz/1¼ cups water. Bring to
simmering point, then cover casserole and
cook for 1 hour.

To the oil remaining in the wok, add scallions and garlic and stir-fry for 1 minute. Stir
in the nam pla (fish sauce), vinegar and
chilies and salt and pepper if necessary. Add
the reserved pork and melon and mango,
together with any juices. Toss to mix ingredients and heat through. Spoon on to a shallow serving dish and sprinkle with chopped
peanuts and cilantro. Serve hot or warm
with noodles or shredded Chinese cabbage.

Serves 2.

Peel, core and slice pears and place on top of
meat. Drizzle honey over pears. Cover pan
and simmer gently for 30-40 minutes until
meat is tender. Garnish with chopped
cilantro leaves, strips of orange rind and
pieces of pitta bread.

Serves 6.

Note: This recipe is traditionally made with
quinces. If quinces are available, use them
instead of pears.

PORK ESCALOPES NORMAND

AFELIA

4 pork escalopes about 1¼ lb, 1½ in. thick
2 tablespoons vegetable oil
1 oz/2 tablespoons butter
1 clove garlic, chopped
2 dessert apples, halved lengthwise, cored and thinly
   sliced
½ teaspoon dried thyme
3 tablespoons Calvados or brandy
4 fl oz/½ cup thick or whipping cream
salt and freshly ground black pepper
apple slices and parsley sprigs, to garnish

2 teaspoons coriander seeds
1 teaspoon black peppercorns
2 teaspoons soft brown sugar
4 pork chops
1 tablespoon olive oil
10 fl oz/1¼ cups dry white wine
1 oz/2 tablespoons butter, diced
salt
2 teaspoons chopped fresh cilantro
cilantro sprigs, to garnish

Place pork escalopes between 2 sheets of greaseproof paper and pound to a ¼ in. thickness. Cut into thin strips.

In a pestle and mortar, lightly crush the coriander seeds and peppercorns. Stir in the brown sugar. Rub the mixture into both sides of the chops.

Heat the wok until very hot. Add oil and swirl to coat wok. Add half the pork strips and stir-fry for 2-3 minutes until golden on all sides. Remove to a plate, keep warm, and cook the remaining strips in the same way. Pour off any oil from the wok. Add butter to the wok and allow to melt. Add garlic, apple slices and thyme and stir-fry for 1-2 minutes until apple slices are golden.

Put the chops in a shallow dish and leave in a cool place for 1-4 hours. Heat the oil in a large skillet. Add the chops and cook until browned on both sides. Pour in the wine and let it bubble for 1 minute. Reduce the heat and simmer for 20-30 minutes, turning occasionally, until the chops are cooked through.

Add Calvados or brandy to the wok and stir to deglaze. Add cream and bring to the boil. Add salt and pepper to taste. Cook for 1 minute, stirring constantly, until sauce thickens slightly and apples are tender. Arrange pork strips on 4 dinner plates and spoon over apples and sauce. Garnish with apple slices and parsley strips. Serve with buttered egg noodles or sautéed potatoes.

Serves 4.

Transfer the chops to a warmed serving dish. If the sauce if too thin, boil for 1-2 minutes until reduced and thickened to a syrupy sauce. Stir in the butter, season with salt and pepper and the cilantro. Garnish with cilantro sprigs and serve.

Serves 4.

MARINATED SPICED PORK

THAI PORK CURRY

1 tablespoon olive oil
3½ lb leg or pork, skin and fat removed
4 oz brown cap or shiitake mushrooms, sliced
thyme sprigs and celery leaves, to garnish
MARINADE:
2 tablespoons olive oil
1 onion, finely chopped
1 carrot, finely chopped
1 stick celery, chopped
16 fl oz/2 cups full-bodied red wine
6 juniper berries, crushed
8 peppercorns, crushed
¼ teaspoon ground allspice
bouquet garni
salt

4 fl oz/½ cup coconut cream
1 onion chopped
1 clove garlic, finely crushed
2 tablespoons fragrant curry paste
2 teaspoons fish sauce
½ teaspoon crushed palm sugar
12 oz lean pork, diced
3 kaffir lime leaves, shredded
25 Thai holy basil leaves
1 long fresh red chili, seeded and cut into strips, and
  Thai holy basil sprig, to garnish

To make marinade, heat the oil in a heavy skillet, add onion and carrot and cook, stirring occasionally, for 5 minutes. Add celery and cook, stirring occasionally, until vegetables are browned. Add wine, juniper berries, peppercorns, allspice, bouquet garni and salt. Leave to cool. Put pork in a non-metallic dish, pour over marinade, cover and leave in a cool place for 24 hours, turning pork occasionally. Preheat oven to 350F (180C). Remove pork and vegetables with a slotted spoon and drain pork on kitchen paper. Strain marinade and set aside.

In a wok, heat 3 fl oz/⅓ cup coconut cream until oil begins to separate. Stir in onion and garlic and cook, stirring occasionally, until lightly browned. Stir in curry paste and continue to stir for about 2 minutes. Stir in fish sauce and sugar, then pork to coat. Cook for 3-4 minutes.

Heat oil in a heavy flameproof casserole just large enough to hold pork, add pork and cook until browned all over. Remove and set aside. Add mushrooms and cook for 5 minutes. Add reserved vegetables and put pork on top. Pour over marinade. Heat to almost simmering, cover and cook in oven, turning occasionally, for 2-2½ hours. Transfer to a warmed plate. Skim excess fat from sauce then boil to thicken. Season. Carve pork, garnish and serve with sauce.

Add lime and basil leaves and cook for 1 more minute. If necessary, add a little water, but final dish could be dry. Serve garnished with a trail of remaining coconut cream, chili strips and basil sprig.

Serves 3.

Serves 4-6.

PORK WITH CIDER

1 oz/2 tablespoons butter
4 pork chops
1 onion, finely chopped
2 teaspoons Calvados or brandy
10 fl oz/1¼ cups dry cider
1 bay leaf
salt and freshly ground black pepper
2 small cooking apples, peeled, cored and sliced
1 tablespoon lemon juice
2 tablespoons crème fraîche or thick sour cream
salt and freshly ground black pepper
thyme sprigs and leaves, to garnish

Heat butter in a heavy flameproof casserole, add chops and cook quickly until browned on both sides. Remove and set aside.

Preheat oven to 350F (180C). Add onion to casserole and cook, stirring occasionally, for 5 minutes, until soft. Add Calvados or brandy and set alight. When flames die down, stir in cider and bring to the boil. Return chops to casserole, add bay leaf and salt and pepper, cover tightly and cook in oven for 20 minutes.

Toss apples in lemon juice. Add to casserole, cover again and cook for 10-15 minutes. Remove pork and apples from casserole with a slotted spoon, transfer to warmed serving plates and keep warm. Boil cooking liquid until lightly syrupy. Stir in crème fraîche or thick sour cream, pour over pork and apples, garnish with thyme and serve.

Serves 4

PORK WITH PRUNES

5 oz large prunes
20 fl oz/2½ cups dry white wine
1½ oz/3 tablespoons butter
4 pork chops
8 oz mixed chopped onion, carrot and celery
8 fl oz/1 cup veal or pork stock
bouquet garni
salt and freshly ground black pepper
squeeze of lemon juice

Put prunes in a bowl, pour over half the wine and leave to soak overnight.

Heat 1 oz/2 tablespoons butter in a heavy flameproof casserole, add chops and cook quickly until browned on both sides. Remove and set aside. Add vegetables to casserole and cook, stirring occasionally, for 5-7 minutes, until lightly browned. Stir in remaining wine, bring to the boil and boil for 2-3 minutes. Add stock and bring to the boil. Return chops to casserole, add bouquet garni and salt and pepper, cover tightly and cook gently for 45 minutes.

Add prunes and soaking liquid to casserole, bring to boil, cover and cook for 30 minutes. Transfer pork and prunes to warmed serving plates and keep warm. Discard bouquet garni and boil sauce to thicken slightly. Reduce heat and gradually stir in remaining butter. Add lemon juice to taste, pour over pork and prunes and serve.

Serves 4.

PORK & CLAMS

2¼ lb loin of pork, cubed
3 tablespoons olive oil
1 onion, chopped
2 teaspoons tomato paste
salt and freshly ground black pepper
2¼ lb clams or cockles, cleaned
cilantro leaves and lemon wedges, to garnish
MARINADE:
2 teaspoons balsamic vinegar
10 fl oz/1¼ cups dry white wine
2 cloves garlic, crushed
1 fresh bay leaf
pinch of saffron strands
sprig of cilantro

To make the marinade, mix together the vinegar, wine, garlic, bay leaf, saffron and cilantro. Add the pork and mix well to coat with the marinade. Cover and leave in a cool place overnight. Remove the pork with a slotted spoon and dry on kitchen paper. Reserve the marinade.

Heat the oil in a flameproof casserole. Add the onion and cook gently for 5 minutes until soft. Add the pork and cook over a high heat for 10 minutes or until cooked through. Add the strained marinade, the tomato paste, salt and pepper and the clams or cockles. Cover tightly and cook over a medium heat for 5 minutes until all the clams or cockles have opened. Discard any that remain closed. Garnish with cilantro leaves and lemon wedges and serve.

Serves 4-6.

PORK WITH WALNUTS

1 lb lean pork fillet
1 tablespoon rice wine
1 tablespoon light soy sauce
1 teaspoon cornstarch
1 bunch scallions
2 teaspoons sunflower oil
1 teaspoon superfine sugar
salt and freshly ground black pepper
1 oz/¼ cup walnut pieces

Trim any fat and silver skin from pork and cut into ¼ in. strips. Place in a bowl and add rice wine, soy sauce and cornstarch. Mix well, cover and chill for 30 minutes.

Trim the scallions, discarding any damaged outer leaves. Cut the scallions into 2 in. pieces.

Heat oil in a non-stick or well-seasoned wok and stir-fry pork mixture for 2-3 minutes until browned. Add scallions, sugar and seasoning and stir-fry for 3 minutes. Sprinkle with walnut pieces and serve with noodles.

Serves 4.

PORK SATAY

12 oz lean pork, cubes
juice 1 lime
1 stalk lemon grass, finely chopped
1 clove garlic, chopped
2 tablespoons vegetable oil
SAUCE:
4 tablespoons vegetable oil
3 oz/½ cup raw shelled peanuts
2 stalks lemon grass, chopped
2 fresh red chilies, seeded and sliced
3 shallots, chopped
2 cloves garlic, chopped
1 teaspoon fish paste
2 teaspoons crushed palm sugar
10 fl oz/1¼ cups coconut milk
juice ½ lime

Meanwhile, make sauce. Over a high heat, heat 1 tablespoon oil in a wok, add nuts and cook, stirring constantly, for 2 minutes. Using a slotted spoon, transfer to absorbent kitchen paper to drain. Using a pestle and mortar or small blender, grind to a paste. Remove and set aside.

Divide pork between 4 skewers and lay them in a shallow dish. In a bowl, mix together lime juice, lemon grass, garlic and oil. Pour over pork, turn to coat, cover and set aside in a cool place for 1 hour, turning occasionally.

Using a pestle and mortar or small blender, pound or mix lemon grass, chilies (chilies), shallots, garlic and fish paste to a smooth paste.

Preheat broiler. Remove pork from dish, allowing excess liquid to drain off. Broil, turning frequently and basting, for 8-10 minutes.

Heat remaining oil in wok, add spice mixture and cook, stirring, for 2 minutes. Stir in peanut paste, sugar and coconut milk. Bring to boil, stirring, then adjust heat so sauce simmers. Add lime juice and simmer, stirring, for 5-10 minutes until thickened. Serve in a warmed bowl to accompany pork. Garnish with carrot flowers and lettuce leaves.

Serves 4.

BROILED CITRUS PORK STEAKS

4 × 4 oz lean pork steaks, trimmed
grated rind and juice of 1 lime, 1 small lemon and 1
   small orange
1 teaspoon sesame oil
2 tablespoons dry sherry
2 tablespoons light soy sauce
1 tablespoon superfine sugar
large pinch of ground white pepper
1 teaspoon cornstarch mixed with 2 teaspoons water
lime, lemon and orange slices and strips of rind, to
   garnish

Score the steaks in a criss-cross pattern. Place in a shallow dish, sprinkle with citrus rinds and pour over juices.

Cover and chill for 30 minutes. Drain steaks well, reserving juices. Preheat broiler. Place steaks on broiler rack and brush lightly with sesame oil. Broil for 3-4 minutes on each side until cooked through. Drain on kitchen paper and keep warm. Place reserved juices in a small saucepan with the remaining ingredients except the garnish. Bring to the boil, stirring until thickened.

Slice pork steaks and arrange on serving plates with lime, lemon and orange slices. Pour over the sauce, garnish with strips of citrus rind and serve with a crisp salad.

Serves 4.

SPICY PORK & LEMON GRASS

1 clove garlic, chopped
2 shallots, chopped
3 tablespoons chopped lemon grass
1 tablespoon sugar
1 tablespoon fish sauce
salt and freshly ground black pepper
12 oz pork fillet, cut into small, thin slices
2-3 tablespoons vegetable oil
2-3 sticks celery, thinly sliced
4 oz straw mushrooms, halved lengthways
4 small red chilies, seeded and shredded
2 scallions shredded
1 tablespoon soy sauce
about 2 fl oz/¼ cup stock or water
2 teaspoons cornstarch
cilantro sprigs, to garnish

Using a pestle and mortar, pound the garlic, shallots and lemon grass to a paste. Transfer to a mixing bowl and add the sugar, fish sauce, salt and pepper. Blend well, then add the pork slices, turning to coat them with the mixture, and leave to marinate for 25-30 minutes.

Heat oil in a wok or skillet and stir-fry pork slices for 2 minutes. Add the celery, straw mushrooms, chilies, scallions and soy sauce and stir-fry for 2-3 minutes. Use the stock to rinse out the marinade bowl and add to the pork. Bring to the boil. Mix cornstarch with 1 tablespoon water and add to sauce to thicken it. Garnish with cilantro sprigs and serve at once with a mixture of rice and wild rice.

Serves 4.

SINGAPORE STEAMBOAT

6 oz fillet of beef, well chilled
6 oz pork fillet (tenderloin), well chilled
6 oz lamb fillet, well chilled
6 oz boneless, skinless chicken breast, well chilled
12 oz thin rice noodles
4 oz each snow peas, French beans, baby sweetcorn,
  oyster mushrooms, shiitake mushrooms, asparagus
  spears, cut into bite-size pieces

Thinly slice beef, pork, lamb and chicken. Cover with cling film and set aside. Cook noodles according to instructions on packet. Drain, refresh under running cold water. Drain again, cover and set aside.

SHRIMP BALLS
12 oz raw, peeled shrimp
1½-2½ teaspoons cornstarch
2 small scallions, finely chopped
1 small egg white, lightly beaten

Put shrimp and 1½ teaspoons cornstarch into blender and mix until smooth. Mix in scallion. Stir in egg white and more cornstarch if necessary to bind mixture. With wet hands, roll mixture into walnut-size balls. Refrigerate.

CHILI VINEGAR
3 tablespoons rice vinegar
1½ tablespoons water
2 teaspoons sugar
½-1 fresh red chili, cored, seeded and finely sliced

In a bowl, mix all the ingredients together.

DIPPING SAUCE
2 tablespoons tomato paste
2 tablespoons water
1 teaspoon soy sauce
1 teaspoon toasted sesame oil
1 fresh red chili, cored, seeded and finely chopped

In a bowl, mix all the ingredients together.

COCONUT SAUCE
2 teaspoons groundnut oil
1 small onion, finely chopped
2 in. lemon grass stalk, bruised and thinly sliced
¼ teaspoon crushed coriander seeds
3 oz piece of coconut cream
about 3 tablespoons stock

In a skillet or saucepan, heat oil. Add onion, lemon grass and coriander seeds and fry until the onion has softened. Stir in coconut cream until melted. Add enough stock to make a dipping sauce.

STOCK
35 fl oz/scant 4¼ cups chicken or vegetable stock
1½ tablespoons chopped cilantro
2 in. thick end of lemon grass stalk, thinly sliced
2 scallions, thinly sliced

In a saucepan, bring stock ingredients to the boil, then pour into a warm fondue pot or heavy flameproof casserole set over a burner. To serve, dip the meat, shrimp balls and vegetables into the stock to cook, then transfer them to plates to eat with the sauces and chili vinegar.

When all the meat, fish and vegetables have been eaten, either warm the noodles in the hotpot, or dunk them in a bowl or saucepan of boiling water, then drain and divide them among bowls. Ladle remaining stock, which will have become concentrated, into the bowls.

Serves 6.

To serve: Use fondue forks, chopsticks, Chinese wire mesh baskets or long wooden skewers.

PORK WITH HERB SAUCE

COCONUT PORK WITH LIME

1 oz/½ cup fresh white breadcrumbs
2 tablespoons white wine vinegar
2 cloves garlic
2 canned anchovy fillets, drained
½ oz/¼ cup chopped fresh parsley
2 teaspoons capers
1 hard-cooked egg yolk
8 fl oz/1 cup extra virgin olive oil
salt and freshly ground black pepper
4 loin chops, about 1 in. thick

In a small bowl, soak the breadcrumbs in the white wine vinegar.

6 pork escalopes, about 4 oz each
½ in. piece fresh root ginger, peeled and grated
2 teaspoons ground cumin
1 teaspoon ground coriander
1 teaspoon chili powder (to taste)
1 teaspoon paprika
½ teaspoon salt
2-3 tablespoons vegetable oil
1 onion, cut lengthwise in half and thinly sliced
3-4 cloves garlic, finely chopped
10 fl oz/1¼ cups unsweetened coconut milk
grated rind and juice of 1 large lime
1 small Chinese cabbage, shredded
lime slices and cilantro leaves, to garnish

Meanwhile, using a pestle and mortar, crush garlic with anchovy fillets, parsley, capers and egg yolk. Squeeze vinegar from breadcrumbs, then mix breadcrumbs into mortar. Stir in oil in a slow trickle to make a creamy sauce. Add black pepper, and salt if necessary. Set aside.

Place escalopes between 2 sheets of baking parchment. Pound to a ¼ in. thickness. Cut into strips. In a large, shallow dish, combine ginger, cumin, coriander, chili powder, paprika and salt. Stir in pork strips and leave to stand for 15 minutes. Heat wok until very hot. Add half the oil and swirl to coat wok. Add half the pork and stir-fry for 2-3 minutes. Remove to a plate and keep warm. Cook remaining strips using remaining oil. Keep warm. Pour off all but 1 tablespoon oil from the wok.

Preheat broiler. Broil chops for about 12 minutes on each side until lightly browned and cooked through but still juicy in center. Season chops and spoon on some of sauce. Serve remaining sauce separately.

Serves 4.

Add onion and garlic to wok; stir-fry for 2-3 minutes until onion is softened. Slowly add coconut milk. Bring to simmering point but do not boil. Stir in lime rind and juice and shredded cabbage. Simmer gently for 5-7 minutes, stirring frequently, until cabbage is tender and sauce slightly thickened. Add pork and cook, covered, for 1-2 minutes until heated through. Arrange pork and cabbage on plates and garnish with lime slices and cilantro. Serve with noodles.

Serves 6.

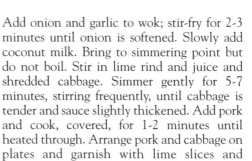

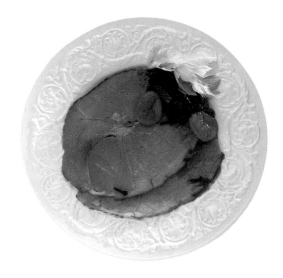

FRUITY GAMMON STEAKS

½ in. piece fresh root ginger, peeled and grated
2 tablespoons tomato catsup
1 tablespoon soft brown sugar
1 tablespoon light soy sauce
1 tablespoon malt vinegar
1 tablespoon lemon juice
2 tablespoons olive oil
4 × 6 oz gammon steaks
1 green bell pepper, chopped
1 red bell pepper, chopped
1 onion, chopped
8 oz can pineapple pieces, drained, with 2
  tablespoons juice reserved
1 tablespoon cornstarch
watercress, to garnish

In a bowl, mix together the ginger, tomato catsup, brown sugar, soy sauce, vinegar and lemon juice. Set aside. Heat the oil in a flameproof dish. Add the gammon steaks and cook for 5 minutes on each side.

Remove the steaks from the dish and keep warm. Add the peppers and onion to the dish and cook, stirring occasionally, for 5 minutes, until soft. Stir in the tomato catsup mixture and the pineapple pieces. Blend the reserved pineapple juice with the cornstarch. Add to the dish and bring to the boil, stirring. Return the steaks to the dish and simmer for 5 minutes. Garnish and serve.

Serves 4.

GLAZED HAM

3 lb boned and rolled gammon joint
1 onion, quartered
1 carrot, sliced
4 tablespoons orange marmalade
1 tablespoon dry mustard
2 tablespoons soft brown sugar
1 tablespoon sherry
1 tablespoon cloves
12 ready-to-eat prunes
12 ready-to-eat dried apricots
4 fl oz/½ cup red wine

Place the gammon in a large saucepan with the onion and carrot. Cover with cold water, bring to the boil and skim any scum from the surface. Cover and simmer for 1 hour. Drain, remove the rind and score the fat in diamond shapes. Melt the marinade in a small saucepan, then mix with the mustard, sugar and sherry. Coat the gammon with this mixture and stud with cloves.

Place the gammon in the soaked clay pot. Add the prunes and apricots and pour the wine over the fruit. Cover the pot and place in the cold oven. Set the oven at 425F (220C). Cook for 1 hour, basting occasionally with the cooking juices. Serve the glazed prunes and apricots with the ham.

Serves 6-8.

CHICKEN & WILD MUSHROOMS

4 tablespoons olive oil
2 cloves garlic, crushed
4 boneless corn-fed chicken breasts
5 fl oz/⅔ cup dry white vermouth
salt and freshly ground black pepper
1 lb mixed wild mushrooms or a mixture of
   cultivated mushrooms, such as brown cap, shiitake
   and oyster
2 tablespoons chopped fresh oregano
oregano sprigs, to garnish

Heat half the oil in a sauté pan. Add garlic and cook for 2 minutes until golden. Add chicken breasts, skin-side down and brown well on all sides.

Pour in the vermouth and season well with salt and pepper. Bring to the boil, cover and simmer for 20-30 minutes until tender.

Meanwhile, halve or slice the mushrooms, if large. Heat remaining oil, add mushrooms and sauté for 3-5 minutes until brown and tender, but still firm. Gently stir mushrooms and any cooking juices into the chicken with the chopped oregano. Garnish with oregano sprigs and serve at once with rice.

Serves 4.

LEMON & CHILI CHICKEN

3¼-3½ lb corn-fed or free-range chicken, jointed into
   8
4 ripe juicy lemons
8 cloves garlic
1 small red chili, split, seeds removed, and chopped
1 tablespoon honey
4 tablespoons chopped fresh parsley
salt and freshly ground black pepper

Place chicken joints in a shallow ovenproof baking dish. Squeeze juice from the lemons and pour into a small bowl. Reserve the lemon halves.

Remove skin from 2 of the garlic cloves, crush them and add to lemon juice with the chili and honey. Stir well and pour mixture over the chicken, tucking the lemon halves around joints. Cover and leave to marinate for at least 2 hours, turning once or twice.

Preheat oven to 400F (200C). Turn the chicken skin side up and place lemon halves cut side down around the joints with the remaining whole garlic. Roast in oven for 45 minutes or until golden brown and tender. Stir in the parsley, taste and season. Garnish with the roasted lemon halves and serve with puréed potatoes.

Serves 4.

GARLIC ROASTED CHICKEN

2 tablespoons olive oil
6 cloves garlic, thinly sliced
8 chicken thighs
4 oz fennel, cut into wide strips
1 carrot, cut into wide strips
1 parsnip, cut into wide strips
1 large potato, diced
1 red bell pepper, diced
1 green bell pepper, diced

LEMON CHICKEN

2 oz/¼ cup butter
grated rind and juice 1 lemon
3 teaspoons chopped fresh oregano
4 lb chicken
4 fl oz/½ cup chicken stock
salt and freshly ground black pepper
lemon slices and parsley sprigs, to garnish
SAUCE:
3 eggs
juice ½ lemon

Preheat oven to 350F (180C). Place half butter, the lemon rind and most of oregano inside chicken.

Preheat oven to 425F (220C). Heat the oil in a shallow flameproof dish. Add the garlic and cook for 2-3 minutes. Add the chicken and vegetables and turn to coat.

Heat remaining butter in a large flameproof casserole, put in chicken and brown all over. Pour in lemon juice, stock, salt, pepper and remaining oregano. Cover casserole and cook in the oven for 1¼-1½ hours until chicken is cooked and juices run clear when the thickest part is pierced. Transfer chicken to a heated dish. Measure 8 fl oz/1 cup of the cooking liquid.

Roast for 55-60 minutes, until chicken is cooked through and golden. Serve.

Serves 4.

To make the sauce, in a bowl whisk together eggs and lemon juice. Gradually whisk in hot cooking liquid. Place bowl over a pan of simmering water and heat gently, stirring, until sauce is thick and smooth. Add salt and pepper. Carve chicken and arrange on a hot serving plate. Pour the sauce over the chicken. Garnish with slices of lemon and parsley sprigs.

Serves 6.

ROQUEFORT VERONIQUE

1 oz/2 tablespoons butter
1 tablespoon oil
4 skinned and boned chicken breasts
1 leek, trimmed and chopped
2 teaspoons all-purpose flour
6 fl oz/¾ cup milk
2½ oz Roquefort cheese
3 fl oz/⅓ cup light cream
5 oz seedless green grapes, skinned
chopped fresh parsley, to garnish

In a skillet, heat the butter and oil and cook the chicken on all sides until golden.

Reduce the heat, stir in the chopped leek, cover and continue cooking for 30 minutes until the juices of the chicken run clear when pierced. Remove the chicken from the pan and set aside on a warmed serving plate.

Sprinkle the flour into the pan and cook for 1 minute, remove from the heat and gradually add the milk. Return to the heat and stirring bring to the boil and cook for 2 minutes until thickened. Add the cheese, cream and grapes and cook for a further 5 minutes, stirring all the time. Pour over the chicken and garnish with chopped fresh parsley.

Serves 4.

CHICKEN WITH SHERRY

4 tablespoons raisins
8 fl oz/1 cup oloroso sherry
3 tablespoons olive oil
3½ lb chicken, cut into 8 pieces
1 Spanish onion, finely chopped
1 clove garlic, finely chopped
8 fl oz/1 cup chicken stock
salt and freshly ground black pepper
4 tablespoons pine nuts

In a small bowl, soak raisins in sherry for 30 minutes

In a flameproof casserole, heat 2 tablespoons oil, add chicken and cook gently until lightly and evenly browned, about 10 minutes. Transfer to absorbent kitchen paper to drain. Add onion and garlic to casserole and cook gently, stirring occasionally, until softened and lightly colored, about 7 minutes. Strain raisins and set aside.

Stir sherry into casserole. Simmer until reduced by half. Add stock, chicken and seasoning, bring to boil, then simmer gently until chicken is cooked, about 35 minutes. In a small pan, fry nuts in remaining oil until lightly colored. Drain on absorbent kitchen paper, then stir into casserole with raisins. Transfer chicken to a warm serving dish. Boil liquid in casserole to concentrate slightly. Pour over chicken.

Serves 4.

CHICKEN WITH SALSA VERDE

4 small skinless chicken breasts
8 tablespoons chopped fresh parsley
1 clove garlic, finely chopped
4 tablespoons chopped fresh mint
1 tablespoon finely chopped capers
1 tablespoon finely chopped gherkins
finely grated rind and juice of 1 lemon
3½ fl oz/⅓ cup olive oil
salt and freshly ground black pepper

Place chicken breasts in a sauté pan. Cover with water and bring to the boil. Simmer very gently for 15-20 minutes until cooked. Allow to cool completely in the water.

In a bowl, mix together the parsley, garlic, mint, capers, gherkins, lemon juice and rind. Gradually beat in olive oil and season to taste. Do not do this in a food processor or the texture will be ruined.

Thickly slice each chicken breast crosswise and arrange on a plate, spoon a little salsa verde over it and serve the rest separately. Serve with salad.

Serves 4.

STUFFED CHICKEN PARCELS

4 skinned and boned chicken breasts
4 oz duck liver pâté
1 teaspoon finely grated orange rind
1 tablespoon orange juice
5 sprigs of thyme
salt and freshly ground black pepper
1 oz butter
2 teaspoons olive oil
12 oz ready-made puff pastry
1 large egg, beaten
1 teaspoon poppy seeds

Preheat the oven to 400F (200C). Cut a small incision in each chicken breast to make a pocket.

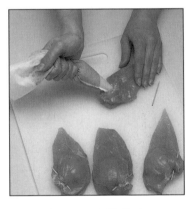

Mix together pâté, orange rind and juice, 1 sprig finely chopped thyme and seasoning. Transfer mixture to a piping bag fitted with a plain tip and pipe a quarter of the mixture into each pocket. Seal with a wooden tooth pick. In a skillet, heat butter and oil and seal chicken quickly on both sides until well browned. Remove from heat, drain and cook, then chill. Thinly roll out pastry and cut into long 1½ in. strips. Discard tooth-picks and top each breast with a thyme sprig.

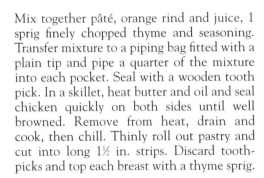

Brush the pastry strips with egg and wind the strips, egg-side in, around the breasts, over-lapping very slightly to enclose the chicken completely place on a lightly dampened baking sheet, brush with remaining egg and sprinkle with poppy seeds. Make a small hole in the top of each one and bake in the oven for 35-40 minutes until golden. Serve with buttered new potatoes and an orange salad.

Serves 4.

CHICKEN WITH TARRAGON

POULET AU VINAIGRE

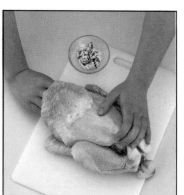

2 tablespoons finely chopped fresh tarragon
2 oz/¼ cup butter, softened
3½ lb chicken
salt and freshly ground black pepper
4 fl oz/½ cup dry white wine
2 fl oz/¼ cup thick cream
tarragon sprigs, to garnish

Preheat oven to 400F (200C). Beat tarragon into butter then push butter between chicken breast and skin.

1 tablespoon oil
½ oz/1 tablespoon butter
4 chicken legs
1 onion, finely chopped
bouquet garni
4 ripe tomatoes, peeled, seeded and chopped
10 fl oz/1¼ cups red wine vinegar
2 teaspoons tomato paste
10 fl oz/1¼ cups chicken stock
salt and freshly ground black pepper
chopped fresh parsley, to garnish

Heat oil and butter in a heavy flameproof casserole. Add chicken and cook until lightly browned all over.

Season chicken with salt and pepper and put in a heavy flameproof casserole. Pour over wine. Cover tightly and cook in oven for 30 minutes. Lower oven temperature to 350F (180C) and cook for 1¼-1½ hours, until chicken is tender.

Remove chicken and set aside. Add onion to casserole and cook, stirring occasionally, for 5 minutes, until soft. Return chicken to casserole, add bouquet garni, cover and cook gently for 20 minutes, turning occasionally.

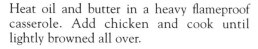

Transfer chicken to a warmed plate and keep warm. Tilt casserole and spoon off the fat, leaving behind cooking juices. Boil cooking juices to thicken to a light sauce. Reduce heat, stir in cream and simmer to thicken slightly. Carve the chicken, garnish with tarragon sprigs and serve with sauce.

Serves 4.

Add tomatoes to casserole, and cook, uncovered, until liquid has evaporated. Combine tomato paste and vinegar and add to casserole. Simmer until most of liquid has evaporated. Add stock and salt and pepper and simmer until reduced by half. Sprinkle with parsley and serve.

Serves 4.

SATAY-STYLE CHICKEN

lettuce leaves and cucumber sticks for serving
3 tablespoons peanut oil
1 in. piece fresh root ginger, peeled and finely
  chopped
1 clove garlic, finely chopped
1¼ lb skinned and boned chicken thighs, cut into
  small pieces
1 teaspoon chili powder
2 tablespoons crunchy or smooth peanut butter
2 tablespoons Chinese chili sauce
4-6 scallions, thinly sliced
10 fl oz/1¼ cups unsweetened coconut milk
1 teaspoon sugar
½ teaspoon salt
chopped peanuts and fresh cilantro leaves, to garnish

Arrange lettuce leaves and cucumber sticks on a shallow serving dish and set aside. Heat the wok until hot. Add oil and swirl to coat wok. Add ginger and garlic and stir-fry for 1 minute, until fragrant; do not brown. Add chicken and stir-fry for 3-4 minutes until just golden and pieces feel slightly firm to the touch.

Stir in chili powder, peanut butter, chili sauce and the scallions. Slowly add coconut milk, stirring until sauce is smooth. Add sugar and salt and simmer for 3-5 minutes until sauce is thickened. Spoon on to a serving dish and sprinkle with chopped peanuts and cilantro leaves. Serve with rice.

Serves 4.

BURGUNDY CHICKEN

1 oz/2 tablespoons butter
4 chicken legs
1 shallot, finely chopped
2 tablespoons Marc de Bourgogne or brandy
8 fl oz/1 cup white Burgundy or other Chardonnay
  wine
2 sprigs of thyme
salt and freshly ground black pepper
6 oz seedless green grapes, halved
4 tablespoons crème fraîche or thick cream
flat-leaf parsley and thyme sprigs, to garnish

Heat butter in a heavy flameproof casserole, add chicken and cook until browned all over. Remove and drain on kitchen paper.

Add shallot to casserole and cook, stirring occasionally, for 2-3 minutes, until soft. Return chicken to casserole. Pour over Marc de Bourgogne or brandy and set alight. When flames have died down, add wine, thyme and salt and pepper.

Bring to the boil, cover and simmer very gently, turning chicken 2 or 3 times, for 50-60 minutes. Transfer chicken to warmed serving plates and keep warm. Add grapes to casserole and boil until sauce is thickened slightly. Stir in crème fraîche or cream and simmer to thicken slightly. Pour over chicken, garnish with flat-leaf parsley and thyme and serve.

Serves 4.

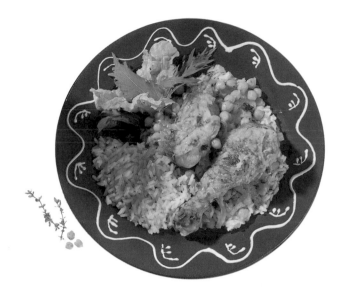

SAFFRON CHICKEN CASSEROLE

COQ AU VIN

4 oz/¾ cup garbanzos
½ teaspoon paprika
½ teaspoon each ground cumin and ground coriander
salt and freshly ground black pepper
4½ lb chicken, cut into serving pieces
2 oz/¼ cup butter
1 tablespoon vegetable oil
2 large mild onions, thinly sliced
½ teaspoon saffron threads
about 35 fl oz/4½ cups chicken stock
1 sprig thyme
4 tablespoons chopped fresh parsley
8 oz/1½ cups rice, to serve

Place garbanzos in a bowl. Cover with cold water and leave overnight to soak.

1 oz/2 tablespoons butter
4 oz thick-cut smoked streaky bacon, chopped
18 button onions
8 oz button mushrooms
olive oil for frying (optional)
6 chicken legs
1 onion, chopped
1 carrot, diced
2 cloves garlic, crushed
1½ tablespoons all-purpose flour
20 fl oz/2½ cups red Burgandy wine
6 fl oz/¾ cup chicken stock
bouquet garni
salt and freshly ground black pepper
chopped fresh parsley, to garnish

Drain the garbanzos and place in a saucepan, cover with water and bring to the boil. Boil for 1 hour. In a bowl, mix together the paprika, cumin, coriander, salt and pepper. Toss the chicken pieces in the mixture. Heat the butter and oil in a large flameproof casserole. Add the chicken pieces and sauté until browned. Transfer to a plate. Add the onions to the casserole and cook for 10 minutes until soft. Return the chicken pieces to the casserole and add the garbanzos. Add the saffron threads to the stock.

Heat butter in a heavy flameproof casserole, add bacon and cook until crisp. Remove with a slotted spoon and drain on kitchen paper. Add button onions to casserole and cook, stirring occasionally, until golden. Remove with a slotted spoon and drain on kitchen paper. Add mushrooms to casserole, adding oil if necessary, and cook until lightly browned. Remove with a slotted spoon and drain on kitchen paper. Add chicken to casserole and cook over a moderately high heat until browned all over. Remove and drain on kitchen paper.

Pour over enough stock to cover the chicken and bring to the boil. Add the thyme. Cover and simmer gently for about 1 hour or until the chicken is tender. Stir in the chopped parsley and check the seasoning. Meanwhile, cook the rice in boiling salted water. To serve, drain the rice and arrange half of it on a heated serving dish. Place the chicken and onions on top and pour over as much saffron sauce as desired. Add the remaining rice and serve with salad.

Add chopped onion and carrot to casserole and cook until lightly browned, adding garlic towards end. Sprinkle over flour and cook, stirring, for 2 minutes. Stir in wine and stock and bring to boil. Return all ingredients to casserole, add bouquet garni and salt and pepper, cover and cook very gently for 50-60 minutes. Remove chicken and vegetables, discard bouquet garni and boil sauce to thicken. Return chicken and vegetables to casserole. Garnish with parsley and serve.

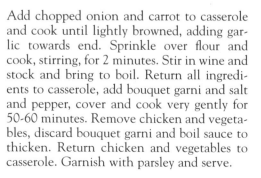

Serves 6.

Serves 6.

MALAY CHICKEN

8 boneless chicken thighs, total weight about 1½ lb
1 bunch of scallions, white parts finely chopped
2 tablespoons chopped fresh cilantro
2 oz creamed coconut, chopped
1 clove garlic, crushed and finely chopped
½ red chili, cored, seeded and chopped
2 teaspoons sunflower oil
1 teaspoon sesame oil
2 tablespoons lime juice
2 teaspoons each ground roasted cumin seeds and
    coriander seeds
salt
lime slices
cilantro sprigs, to garnish

Open out the chicken thighs. Mix together the scallions and cilantro and spoon an equal quantity on each opened chicken thigh. Reform the thighs. Put in a single layer in a non-reactive dish. Put coconut in a bowl and stir in 7 fl oz/scant 1 cup boiling water until dissolved. Stir in garlic, chili, oils, lime juice, spices and salt. Pour over chicken, turn to coat in marinade then cover and refrigerate overnight.

Preheat broiler or barbecue. Transfer chicken to room temperature. Soak bamboo skewers in water for 20-30 minutes. Remove chicken from marinade (reserve marinade) and thread 1 or 2 chicken thighs on to each skewer with a lime slice. Broil or barbecue for about 20 minutes, basting with remaining marinade, until chicken juices run clear when tested with the point of a sharp knife. Garnish with cilantro sprigs.

Serves 4.

CHICKEN WITH WALNUT SAUCE

6 chicken breasts
salt and freshly ground black pepper
juice 1 orange
4 oz/1¼ cups walnut halves
2 cloves garlic, chopped
3 fl oz/⅓ cup walnut oil
3 fl oz/⅓ cup olive oil
squeeze lemon juice
chopped fresh parsley or chives and lemon slices, to
    garnish

Preheat oven to 400F (200C). Season chicken breasts and pour the orange juice over them; set aside.

Spread walnuts on a baking sheet and place in oven until lightly browned, about 5-10 minutes. Transfer to a food processor or blender with garlic, 2 tablespoons water and a pinch of salt. Mix to a paste. With motor running, slowly pour in walnut and olive oils to make a smooth, mayonnaise-like sauce. Add lemon juice and pepper to taste; set aside.

Preheat broiler. Broil chicken for 5-7 minutes each side until juices run clear when thickest part is pierced with a sharp knife. Garnish with chopped parsley or chives and lemon slices, then serve with the sauce.

Serves 6.

CILANTRO CHICKEN

CHICKEN IN BALSAMIC VINEGAR

2 teaspoons sunflower oil
1 clove garlic, finely chopped
1 shallot, finely chopped
12 oz lean cooked skinless chicken, diced
1 teaspoon ground coriander
2 teaspoons dark soy sauce
freshly ground black pepper
2 tablespoons chopped fresh cilantro
4 oz bean sprouts
4 oz grated carrot
1 oz fresh cilantro leaves
2 nectarines, sliced
2 bananas, halved, sliced and tossed in the juice of 1
    small lemon

mixed salad leaves for serving
2 tablespoons olive oil
1 onion, finely chopped
2 cloves garlic, finely minced or crushed
1½ lb skinned and boned chicken breasts, cut into
    1 in. strips
3 tablespoons balsamic vinegar
1 tablespoon Dijon mustard
freshly ground black pepper
2 tablespoons shredded fresh basil
fresh basil leaves, to garnish

Arrange salad leaves on 4 dinner plates and
set aside.

Heat oil in a non-stick or well-seasoned wok
and stir-fry garlic and shallot for 1 minute.
Add chicken, ground coriander, soy sauce
and black pepper and stir-fry for 2-3 minutes
until chicken is lightly browned. Remove
from heat and stir in chopped cilantro.

Heat the wok. Add olive oil and swirl to coat
wok. Add onion and garlic and stir-fry for
1-2 minutes until onion begins to soften.
Add chicken strips, working in 2 batches,
and stir-fry for 3-4 minutes until golden and
chicken feels firm to the touch. Return all
chicken to the wok.

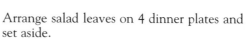

Mix together the bean spouts, grated carrot
and cilantro leaves. Place on serving plates
and top with warm chicken mixture.
Arrange nectarine and banana slices around
the edge of each salad and serve immediately.

Serves 4.

Stir in vinegar and mustard and stir-fry for
2-3 minutes until chicken is cooked through
and well coated with vinegar and mustard.
Season with pepper and sprinkle with
shredded basil. Spoon on to salad-lined
plates and garnish with additional basil
leaves. Serve with sautéed potatoes.

Serves 4.

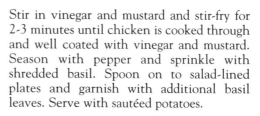

CHICKEN WITH LEMON GRASS

3 lb chicken, cut into 8 pieces
4 thick stalks lemon grass
4 scallions, chopped
4 black peppercorns, cracked
2 tablespoons vegetable oil
1 fresh green chili, seeded and thinly sliced
2 teaspoons fish sauce
fresh red chili, cut into thin slivers, to garnish

With the point of a sharp knife, cut slashes in each chicken piece; place in a shallow dish.

Bruise top parts of each lemon grass stalk and reserve. Chop lower parts, then pound with scallions and peppercorns using a pestle and mortar. Spread over chicken and into slashes. Cover and set aside for 2 hours.

In a wok, heat oil, add chicken and cook, turning occasionally, for about 5 minutes until lightly browned. Add green chili, bruised lemon stalks and 4 tablespoons water. Cover wok and cook slowly for 25-30 minutes until chicken is cooked through. Stir in fish sauce. Transfer chicken pieces to a warmed serving dish, spoon over cooking juices and sprinkle with red chili.

Serves 4-6.

CHICKEN STROGANOFF

1 lb skinned and boned chicken breasts
2 oz/¼ cup butter
1 tablespoon olive oil
2 onions, thinly sliced
6 oz button mushrooms, sliced
2 teaspoons Dijon mustard
2 oz gherkins, sliced
7 fl oz/¾ cup thick sour cream
salt and freshly ground black pepper
noodles or rice, to serve
chopped fresh parsley and paprika, to garnish

Place the chicken between 2 sheets of cling film. Use a rolling pin to flatten. Slice into 1 × 1½ in. strips.

In a skillet heat half the butter and oil and cook the onions until softened. Add the mushrooms and cook for a further 5 minutes. Remove from the pan and set aside.

Heat the remaining butter and oil in the pan and fry the chicken over a high heat, turning frequently, for 6-8 minutes until cooked. Return the onions and mushrooms to the pan, stir in the mustard, gherkins, cream and seasonings and heat through gently for 3-4 minutes. Serve on a bed of noodles or rice and garnish with chopped parsley and paprika.

Serves 4.

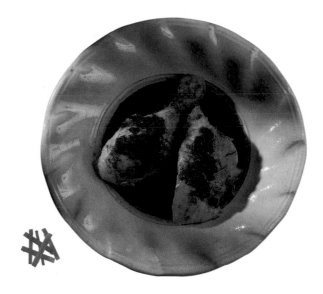

CHICKEN ROLLED ASPARAGUS

4 chicken breast fillets
2 fl oz/¼ cup sake or white wine
salt and freshly ground black pepper
12 asparagus tips or 32-40 stalks French beans,
  trimmed
vegetable oil for frying
8 fl oz/1 cup dashi or chicken stock
9 oz spinach, trimmed
MUSTARD SAUCE:
2 teaspoons mustard
3 tablespoons shoyu

Cut chicken fillets in half along natural line and slice thickest half horizontally in two.

By making a few slits on thick parts, even out thickness to make 3 thin flat pieces, about ¼ in. thick, per chicken breast. Sprinkle with a little of the sake and salt and pepper. Parboil asparagus, or French beans, in lightly salted water and drain. Place an asparagus stalk (or 4-5 French beans) on a chicken piece, roll up and secure with wooden toothpicks. If necessary trim asparagus to length of chicken. Repeat with rest of chicken and asparagus or beans. Heat oil in a skillet and fry chicken rolls until light golden.

Add rest of sake and dashi or stock, bring to boil, then simmer for 15 minutes. Cook spinach in boiling salted water for 1 minute, drain and chop into bite-sized lengths. Dissolve mustard with shoyu and add 2-3 tablespoons of cooking juices to make a sauce. Cut the chicken rolls into bite-size pieces. Divide the spinach between 4 individual serving plates, heaping it into a nest, pour the sauce over the top, then arrange chicken pieces, cut-side-up, on top.

Serves 4.

GINGER & SOY ROAST CHICKEN

1½ in. piece of fresh root ginger, coarsely chopped
1 onion, coarsely chopped
3 cloves garlic, coarsely chopped
3½ lb chicken
5 tablespoons vegetable oil
3 tablespoons dark soy sauce
3 tablespoons rice vinegar
2½ tablespoons light brown sugar

Put ginger, onion and garlic in a blender. Mix to a paste, adding just enough water so the blender blades work.

Put chicken in a roasting pan. Rub inside and outside of chicken with half of ginger mixture. Cover and leave for 1 hour. Put remaining ginger paste in a bowl and stir in oil, soy sauce, rice vinegar, sugar and 6 tablespoons water.

Preheat oven to 350F (180C). Prop up tail end of chicken. Pour as much soy sauce mixture as possible into cavity of chicken. Roast chicken for 25 minutes, basting occasionally with remaining soy mixture. Pour remaining soy mixture around chicken and cook for a further 50 minutes, basting occasionally, until chicken juices run clear. Stir a little water into pan if sauce begins to dry out too much.

Serves 4.

CHICKEN WITH CHEESE SAUCE

3 tablespoons vegetable oil
1 small onion, finely chopped
12 oz chicken breast, sliced
5 oz chestnut mushrooms
¼ oz all-purpose flour
5 fl oz/⅔ cup dry white wine
5 fl oz/⅔ cup chicken stock or water
2 × 2¼ oz Boursin cheeses with herbs and garlic
2 tablespoons chopped fresh parsley
salt and freshly ground black pepper
1 lb fresh pasta

Heat 2 tablespoons oil and cook the onion until soft. Add the chicken and fry for 2 minutes. Add the mushrooms.

Fry for a further 2 minutes or until the chicken is cooked. Sprinkle over the flour and stir until all the fat is absorbed. Remove from the heat and slowly add the white wine and stock or water. Return the pan to the heat and bring to the boil, stirring, then reduce the heat and cook for 2 minutes, stirring until the sauce thickens.

Cut the cheese into cubes and add to the sauce, stirring until it has melted. Add the chopped parsley and season with a little salt and pepper. Cook the pasta in plenty of boiling salted water to which you have added the remaining tablespoon of oil (this prevents the pasta sticking together as it cooks) until just tender (*al dente*). Drain the pasta well and serve with the chicken sauce.

Serves 4.

CHICKEN & PINEAPPLE CURRY

5 shallots, chopped
3 large fresh red chilies, cored, seeded and chopped
3 cloves garlic, crushed
2 in. piece galangal, chopped
1 stalk lemon grass, chopped
2 tablespoons vegetable oil
1½ lb boneless, skinless chicken breast, cut into strips
2 tablespoons light brown sugar
2 × 14 fl oz/1¾ cups canned coconut milk
2 teaspoons tamarind paste
2 tablespoons fish sauce
4 kaffir lime leaves
1 small pineapple, about 1 lb, thinly sliced
grated rind and juice of 1 lime, or to taste
small handful cilantro leaves, chopped

Put shallots, chilies, garlic, galangal and lemon grass in a small blender. Mix to a paste; add 1 tablespoon of the oil, if necessary. In a wok or sauté pan, heat remaining oil. Add chicken and stir-fry until just turning pale golden brown. Remove and set aside.

Stir chili paste into pan and stir-fry for 3-4 minutes until fragrant. Stir in sugar, coconut milk, tamarind, fish sauce and kaffir lime leaves. Bring to a boil, and boil for 4-5 minutes until reduced by half and lightly thickened. Return chicken to pan. Add pineapple and simmer for 3-4 minutes until chicken juices run clear. Add the lime rind, and lime juice to taste. Stir in cilantro.

Serves 6.

TUNISIAN SPICED POUSSIN

2 poussins
1 oz/2 tablespoons butter
2 teaspoons paprika
2 teaspoons each clear honey and tomato paste
4 tablespoons lemon juice
5 fl oz/⅔ cup chicken stock
1 teaspoon harissa
STUFFING:
1 oz/2 tablespoons butter
1 onion, chopped
2 cloves garlic, crushed
1 teaspoon each ground cinnamon and ground cumin
1 oz/2 tablespoons almonds, finely chopped
6 oz mixed ready-to-eat dried fruit, chopped
salt and freshly ground black pepper

To make the stuffing, melt the butter in a saucepan. Add the onion and garlic and cook gently for 10 minutes until soft. Add the cinnamon and cumin and cook, stirring, for 2 minutes. Add the almonds and fruit, season with salt and pepper and cook for 2 minutes. Leave to cool. Preheat the oven to 400F (200C). Stuff the neck end of the poussins with the stuffing. Set aside any excess. In a small saucepan, melt the butter with the paprika; brush over the poussins. Place in a roasting pan and roast for 45-60 minutes, basting occasionally, until cooked.

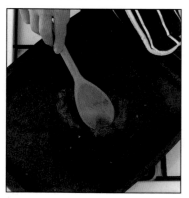

Transfer the poussins to a carving board. Pour any excess fat from the roasting pan. Stir the honey, tomato paste, lemon juice, stock and harissa into the juices in the pan. Add salt to taste. Bring to the boil and simmer for 2 minutes. Reheat any excess stuffing. Serve the poussins with the stuffing and sauce, and with parsley rice.

Serves 4.

FLEMISH BRAISED CHICKEN

2 oz/¼ cup butter
4 lb chicken
1 lb leeks, sliced
8 oz carrots, sliced
½ head celery, chopped
4 oz button mushrooms, halved
20 fl oz/2½ cups chicken stock
2 bay leaves
12 small new potatoes
8 fl oz/1 cup dry white wine
2½ fl oz/⅓ cup thick cream
2 egg yolks
flat-leaf parsley sprigs and chopped parsley, to garnish

Melt the butter in a flameproof casserole. Add the chicken and brown all over.

Remove from the casserole. Preheat oven to 400F (200C). Add the leeks, carrots, celery and mushrooms to the casserole and stir well. Cover and cook for 5-10 minutes, until soft. Add the stock and bay leaves. Bring to the boil and add the chicken. Cover and cook in the oven for 30 minutes. Add the potatoes and cook for 30 minutes. Lift out the chicken and remove the vegetables with a slotted spoon. Keep warm.

Add the wine to the casserole and bring to the boil. Reduce to a simmer. In a large bowl, mix together the cream and the egg yolks. Pour the simmering stock on to the cream mixture, and heat gently. Do not boil. Return the vegetables to the casserole. Carve the chicken, garnish with flat-leaf parsley sprigs and chopped parsley and serve with the vegetables and sauce.

Serves 6.

CHICKEN MOUSSELINE

FOR THE MOUSSE:
3 oz watercress leaves
3 oz chicken breast
salt and freshly ground black pepper
5 fl oz/⅔ cup thick cream
8 chicken thighs, skinned and boned
FOR THE SAUCE:
1 tablespoon vegetable oil
1 shallot, finely chopped
5 fl oz/⅔ cup dry white wine
5 fl oz/⅔ cup chicken stock
2 fl oz/¼ cup thick cream
1 teaspoon chopped fresh tarragon or basil
1 teaspoon lemon juice

Preheat the oven to 375F (190C). Lay the chicken thighs on a board, season the insides with salt and pepper and add spoonfuls of the mousse. Roll the flesh around the mousse to enclose it and wrap each thigh in a square of oiled kitchen foil, sealing each one well. Place on a baking sheet and cook in the oven for 20-35 minutes or until the chicken is cooked and the mousse is firm.

To make the mousse, blanch the watercress in boiling, salted water for 15 seconds, drain and refresh under cold water. Drain again and squeeze as dry as possible.

Meanwhile, make the sauce. In a saucepan heat the oil and gently fry the shallot until softened. Increase the heat, add the wine and boil rapidly until the quantity is reduced by half. Add the chicken stock and continue to boil to reduce the liquid until just under 5 fl oz/⅔ cup of stock remains.

Put the watercress into a food processor, add the chicken breast and season with a little salt and pepper. Process the mixture until very smooth. Gradually pour in the cream while the processor is still running, taking care not to over-beat the mousse or the cream will separate and spoil the texture.

With the stock at boiling point, add the cream and simmer for 3-4 minutes, stirring all the time, until the sauce starts to thicken. Add the tarragon and lemon juice and season with salt and pepper. Remove the chicken thighs from the foil and spoon over the sauce.

Serves 4.

AROMATIC DUCK

2 half or 4 quarter portions of duck (2 breasts and 2 legs)
salt and freshly ground black pepper
1 tablespoon five-spice powder
4-5 small pieces fresh root ginger
3-4 scallions, cut into short sections
3-4 tablespoons Chinese rice wine or dry sherry
12 sheets dried rice paper, halved if large
fresh mint, basil and cilantro leaves
Sherry Dip (see page 98)

Rub the salt, pepper and five-spice powder all over the duck portions.

In a shallow dish, mix ginger, scallions, and rice wine or sherry, add duck portions and leave to marinate for at least 3-4 hours, turning the duck pieces now and then. Steam the duck portions with marinade in a hot steamer for 2-3 hours. Remove the duck portions from the liquid and leave to cool (the duck can be cook up to this stage in advanced, if wished).

Preheat oven to 450F (230C) and bake the duck pieces, skin-side up, for 10-15 minutes, then pull the meat off the bone. Meanwhile, soften dried rice paper in warm water. Place about 2 tablespoons of meat in each half sheet of rice paper, add a few mint, basil and cilantro leaves, roll into a neat bundle, then dip the roll in the dip before eating it.

Serves 4-6.

CIDER APPLE CHICKEN

pared rind of 1 lemon plus 1 teaspoon juice
½ cinnamon stick
1 onion, quartered
3¼-3½ lb chicken
salt and freshly ground black pepper
3 oz/⅓ cup butter
1 tablespoon oil
3 tablespoons brandy
1 lb dessert apples, peeled and cored
5 fl oz/⅔ cup dry (alcoholic) cider
10 fl oz/1¼ cups crème fraîche
1 tablespoon each chopped fresh chives and parsley

Place rind, cinnamon stick and onion in the chicken. Season well.

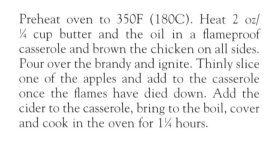

Preheat oven to 350F (180C). Heat 2 oz/¼ cup butter and the oil in a flameproof casserole and brown the chicken on all sides. Pour over the brandy and ignite. Thinly slice one of the apples and add to the casserole once the flames have died down. Add the cider to the casserole, bring to the boil, cover and cook in the oven for 1¼ hours.

Melt remaining butter in a pan, cut the remaining apples into thick slices and sauté until just cooked. Remove the chicken from the casserole and place on a warmed serving platter and surround with the sautéed apples. Add the crème fraîche and lemon juice to the casserole, stir well and boil to reduce slightly. Season well and pour over the chicken. Sprinkle with the chopped herbs and serve at once.

Serves 4-6.

POUSSINS WITH WATERCRESS

VIETNAMESE ROAST DUCK

4 small oven-ready poussins
watercress sprigs, to garnish
STUFFING:
4 oz/2 cups fresh wholemeal breadcrumbs
2 oz ready-to-eat dried apricots, chopped
1 small bunch watercress, chopped
2 oz/½ cup hazelnuts, chopped
salt and freshly ground black pepper
1 egg yolk
WATERCRESS SAUCE:
1 onion, finely chopped
1 bunch watercress, chopped
4 fl oz/½ cup dry white wine
1 tablespoon chopped fresh tarragon
1 teaspoon lemon juice
2 fl oz/¼ cup Greek yogurt

1 teaspoon minced garlic
2-3 shallots, finely chopped
2 teaspoons five-spice powder
2 tablespoons sugar
2 fl oz/¼ cup red rice vinegar
1 tablespoon fish sauce
1 tablespoon soy sauce
4 quarter portions duck (2 breasts and 2 legs)
8 fl oz/1 cup coconut milk
salt and freshly ground black pepper
watercress, to serve
cilantro sprigs, to garnish

In a bowl, mix garlic, shallots, five-spice powder, sugar, vinegar, fish and soy sauces.

Preheat oven to 400F (200C). To make the stuffing, mix together the breadcrumbs, apricots, watercress, hazelnuts and salt and pepper. Bind together with the egg yolk. Use to stuff the cavity of each poussin. Place the poussins in a shallow flameproof dish and roast for 50-60 minutes, until cooked through. To test, pierce the thigh with a skewer: if the juices run clear the poussins are cooked. Remove the poussins from the dish and keep warm.

Add duck pieces and leave to marinate for at least 2-3 hours, or overnight in the refrigerator, turning occasionally. Preheat oven to 425F (220C). Remove duck portions from marinade and place, skin-side up, on a rack in a baking pan and cook in the oven for 45 minutes, without turning or basting.

To make the watercress sauce, add the onion to the cooking juices in the dish and cook gently, stirring occasionally, for 5 minutes, until soft. Add the chopped watercress and stir well. Add the white wine, tarragon and lemon juice and heat gently. Stir in the Greek yogurt and season with salt and pepper. Heat gently to warm through. Pour the sauce on to warmed serving plates and place the poussins on top. Garnish with watercress and serve.

Serves 4.

Remove duck and keep warm. Heat the marinade with the drippings in the baking pan, add the coconut milk, bring to the boil and simmer for 5 minutes. Season, then pour into a serving bowl. Serve duck portions on a bed of watercress, garnished with cilantro sprigs.

Serves 4-6.

Note: The duck portions can be chopped through the bone into bite-size pieces for serving, if wished.

DUCK WITH KIWI FRUIT

2 × 8 oz boneless duck breasts
½ in. piece fresh root ginger, peeled and finely
  chopped
1 clove garlic, finely chopped
2 tablespoons dry sherry
2 kiwi fruit
1 teaspoon sesame oil
SAUCE:
4 tablespoons dry sherry
2 tablespoons light soy sauce
4 teaspoons clear honey

Skin and trim duck breasts. With a sharp knife, score flesh in diagonal lines. Beat with a meat tenderizer until ½ in. thick.

Place duck breasts in a shallow dish and add ginger, garlic and sherry. Cover and chill for 1 hour. Peel and thinly slice kiwi fruit and halve widthwise. Cover and chill until required. Preheat broiler. Drain duck breasts and place on broiler rack. Brush with sesame oil and cook for 8 minutes. Turn and brush again with oil. Cook for 8-10 minutes until tender and cooked through.

Meanwhile, put the sauce ingredients in a saucepan, bring to the boil and simmer for 5 minutes until syrupy. Drain duck breasts on kitchen paper and slice thinly. Arrange duck slices and kiwi fruit on serving plates. Pour over sauce and serve with rice and vegetables.

Serves 4.

ROAST STUFFED POUSSIN

2 poussins weighing about 1¾ lb each
1 oz/2 tablespoons butter for spreading
salt and freshly ground black pepper
STUFFING:
1 oz dried chestnuts
2 oz/¼ cup long-grain rice
1 oz/¼ cup shelled pistachio nuts
1 oz/¼ cup currants
salt and freshly ground black pepper
½ teaspoon ground cinnamon
2oz/¼ cup butter

Make the stuffing. Put chestnuts in a bowl; cover with cold water and leave to soak for several hours.

Drain chestnuts, put in a saucepan and cover with cold water. Bring to the boil. Cover and simmer for 20-30 minutes or until chestnuts are tender. Drain and leave to cool. Bring a pan of water to the boil. Add rice and cook for 8-10 minutes until just tender. Drain and rinse with cold water. Preheat oven to 375F (190C). Chop chestnuts and pistachio nuts finely. Put in a bowl with rice, currants, salt, pepper and cinnamon. Mix well.

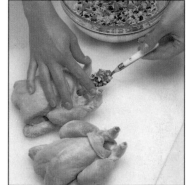

In a skillet, melt butter. Add stuffing mixture. Cook, stirring, until thoroughly combined. Allow to cook. Stuff poussins with stuffing. Spread a little butter over each bird. Season with salt and pepper. Place in a roasting pan and roast, basting from time to time, for 45 minutes until thoroughly cooked and golden brown. Cut each poussin in half. Serve with the stuffing and pan juices.

Serves 4.

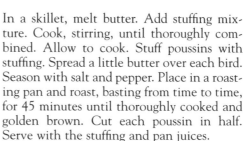

DUCK WITH PEARS

2 tablespoons olive oil
1 duck, cut into 8 serving pieces
2 Spanish onions, finely chopped
1 carrot, chopped
2 beefsteak tomatoes, peeled, seeded and chopped
1 cinnamon stick
1 teaspoon chopped fresh thyme
8 fl oz/1 cup chicken stock
4 tablespoons Spanish brandy
4 firm pears, peeled, cored and halved
1 clove garlic
10 almonds, toasted
salt and freshly ground black pepper
herbs, to garnish (optional)

Heat oil in a skillet, add duck in batches, skin-side down, and cook over a fairly high heat for about 10 minutes until browned. Turn over and cook for about 8 minutes until underside is lightly browned. Using tongs, transfer duck to absorbent kitchen paper to drain.

Remove excess oil from pan, leaving about 2 tablespoons. Add onions, carrot, tomatoes, cinnamon and thyme and cook for about 5 minutes, stirring occasionally, until onions have softened but not browned. Add stock and simmer for 20 minutes.

Discard cinnamon and purée contents of pan in a food processor or blender, or rub through a sieve. Return this sauce to pan, add brandy and boil for 1-2 minutes. Add duck and heat through gently for 5-10 minutes.

Meanwhile, put pears in a saucepan into which they just fit. Cover pears with water and simmer gently until tender.

Using pestle and mortar, pound garlic and almonds to a paste. Mix in a little of the pear cooking liquid, then stir into sauce. Adjust consistency of sauce, if necessary, with more pear cooking liquid. Season to taste. Transfer duck to a warmed serving plate and pour the sauce over the top. Arrange pears around duck. Garnish with herbs, if desired.

Serves 4.

SPICY BROILED QUAIL

1 clove garlic
salt
1 teaspoon each ground cumin and coriander
½ small onion
1 tablespoon chopped fresh cilantro
pinch cayenne pepper
2 fl oz/¼ cup olive oil
8 quail
vine leaves, parsley and lemon slices, to garnish

Put all the ingredients except quail and garnish in a food processor.

Process to make a paste. Spread paste over quail. Cover and leave to marinate in a cool place for 2 hours.

Broil quail for 10-15 minutes, turning frequently, until cooked and slightly charred on the outside. Serve quail on vine leaves, garnished with parsley and lemon slices.

Serves 4.

Variation: Poussins or chicken portions can be cooked in this way.

Note: The broiled quail are particularly good cooked on a barbecue.

DUCK WITH ORANGE

2 × 6 oz boneless duck breasts
salt and freshly ground black pepper
1½ teaspoons chopped fresh thyme
2 oranges
1 teaspoon cornstarch
juice of 1 lemon
4 tablespoons Cointreau
½ oz/1 tablespoon unsalted butter
orange twists and thyme sprigs, to garnish

Using a sharp knife, score skin and fat on duck breasts in a criss-cross pattern, taking care not to cut through flesh. Season with salt and pepper and rub with thyme.

Heat a heavy skillet, add duck, skin side down, and cook over a moderate to high heat for 10-12 minutes, lowering heat a little if skin becomes too brown. Turn duck over and cook for 5 minutes, or to taste. Transfer duck to a warmed plate and keep warm.

Meanwhile, pare enough rind from oranges to give 1½ tablespoons. Add to a small pan of boiling water and blanch for 2 minutes. Drain, rinse in cold water and set aside. Squeeze juice from oranges. Pour most of fat from skillet. Stir cornstarch into pan then add orange and lemon juice and orange rind. Bring to the boil, stirring, then add Cointreau and salt and pepper. Reduce heat and whisk in butter. Slice duck, arrange on serving plates, pour over sauce, garnish and serve.

Serves 2.

QUAIL WITH GRAPES

2 in. fresh root ginger, peeled and finely chopped
8 quails
2 oz butter
salt and freshly ground black pepper
6 oz seedless white grapes, halved
9 fl oz/1 cup unsweetened white grape juice
1 teaspoon cornstarch
fresh flat-leaf parsley, to garnish

Preheat the oven to 425F (220C). Place some chopped ginger inside each quail. In a roasting dish, heat the butter. Add the quail and turn in the butter until browned all over. Season with salt and pepper.

Roast in the oven for 20 minutes, basting occasionally, until quail are browned and cooked through. Tilt the birds to let the pan juices run back into the pan. Transfer to a heated serving dish and keep warm.

Pour any fat away from the roasting dish. Add the grapes and grape juice and place over the heat. Simmer for a few minutes, scraping up the sediment, until the grapes are warm. In a bowl, blend the cornstarch with a little cold water and stir into the sauce. Simmer until thickened. Season with salt and pepper. Arrange the grapes round the quail and pour the sauce round. Serve with bulgar wheat or rice, garnished with flat leaf parsley.

Serves 4.

SOY-ROAST DUCK

5 lb duck, giblets removed
4 tablespoons dark soy sauce
2 tablespoons brown sugar
2 cloves garlic, finely chopped
DIP:
1 tablespoon sunflower oil
4 scallions, finely chopped
1 clove garlic, finely chopped
3 tablespoons dark soy sauce
2 teaspoons brown sugar
2 tablespoons dry sherry

Preheat oven to 375F (190C). Wash duck and pat dry. Place on a wire rack in a roasting pan. Prick all over with a fork.

Sprinkle over soy sauce, brown sugar and garlic. Bake for 2 hours 15 minutes until juices run clear and skin is well browned. Make the dip. Heat the oil in a non-stick or well seasoned wok and stir-fry scallions and garlic for 1 minute. Drain on kitchen paper and mix with remaining ingredients.

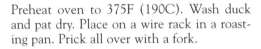

To serve, remove all skin and fat from duckling and shred flesh away from bone. Serve with the dip, soft pancakes and shredded scallions and cucumber.

Serves 4.

Note: Soft pancakes can be bought ready-made from Chinese supermarkets.

PHEASANT IN PARSLEY SAUCE

2oz/¼ cup butter
2 pheasants
3 oz fresh parsley
3 onions, thinly sliced
1 oz/¼ cup all-purpose flour
10 fl oz/1¼ cups chicken stock
5 fl oz/⅔ cup crème fraîche
salt and freshly ground black pepper
flat-leaf parsley sprigs, to garnish

Preheat oven to 350F (180C). Melt the butter in a large flameproof dish. Add the pheasants and cook until browned all over. Remove and keep warm.

Separate the thick parsley stalks from the leaves and tie the stalks together with string. Chop the leaves and set aside. Add the onions to the dish and cook, stirring occasionally, for 7 minutes, until soft and lightly colored. Add the flour and cook, stirring, for 1 minute. Gradually add the chicken stock, stirring constantly until smooth. Bring to the boil and add the bundle of parsley stalks. Add the pheasants, cover and cook in the oven for 1 hour.

Remove the pheasants from the dish and keep warm. Remove and discard the parsley stalks. Add the chopped parsley and crème fraîche to the sauce and season with salt and pepper. Heat gently to warm through. Cut the pheasants in half with kitchen scissors. Garnish with flat-leaf parsley sprigs and serve with the parsley sauce.

Serves 4.

PAN-FRIED CORNISH GAME HEN

1 tablespoon olive oil
2 Cornish game hens
4 oz streaky bacon, chopped
6 oz button mushrooms
6 oz shallots
2 tablespoons brandy
8 fl oz/1 cup red wine
20 fl oz/2½ cups chicken stock
3 tablespoons redcurrant jelly
salt and freshly ground black pepper
marjoram sprigs, to garnish

Preheat oven to 350F (180C). Heat the oil in an ovenproof dish. Add the game hens and brown all over.

Cover and cook in the oven for 35-40 minutes. Remove and keep warm. Add the bacon, mushrooms and shallots to the dish and cook, stirring, for 4-5 minutes, until golden brown. Remove with a slotted spoon and keep warm. Add the brandy, wine, stock and redcurrant jelly to the cooking juices and stir well. Bring to the boil, stirring, and boil for 20-25 minutes, stirring occasionally, until the sauce is reduced and thickened.

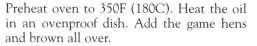

Return the game hens, bacon, mushrooms and shallots to the casserole and season well. Bring to the boil and simmer for 4-5 minutes to warm through. Cut the game hens in half with kitchen scissors or a sharp knife. Garnish with marjoram sprigs and serve.

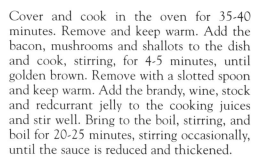

Serves 4.

SPANISH PARTRIDGE

2 partridges, halved along backbone
2 tablespoons brandy
salt and freshly ground black pepper
3 tablespoons olive oil
1 Spanish onion, chopped
3 cloves garlic, finely chopped
2 tablespoons all-purpose flour
4 tablespoons red wine vinegar
8 fl oz/1 cup red wine
8 fl oz/1 cup chicken stock
6 black peppercorns
2 cloves
1 bay leaf
2 carrots, cut into short lengths
8 shallots
1 oz/1 square dark chocolate, grated

Rub partridges with brandy, salt and pepper and set aside for 30 minutes. Heat oil in heavy flameproof casserole into which the birds fit snugly. Add onion and fry, stirring occasionally, for 3 minutes. Stir in garlic and cook for 2 minutes.

Sprinkle birds lightly with flour, then fry in casserole for 5 minutes each side. Remove and set aside.

Stir vinegar into casserole and boil for 1-2 minutes. Add wine and boil for 1-2 minutes, then add stock, peppercorns, cloves, bay leaf and partridges. Heat to simmering point, cover tightly and cook gently for 40 minutes. Add carrots and shallots, cover again, and continue to cook gently for 20 minutes.

Transfer partridges, shallots and carrots to a warm dish. If necessary, boil the cooking juices until reduced to 10 fl oz/1¼ cups, then purée in a blender or food processor.

Return juices to casserole, heat gently and stir in chocolate until melted. Return partridges and vegetables to casserole and turn them over in the sauces so they are well coated.

Serves 4.

RABBIT WITH MUSTARD

VENISON RAGOÛT

3 oz/⅓ cup butter
3½ lb boneless rabbit portions
salt and freshly ground black pepper
olive oil for greasing
2 oz Dijon mustard
2 oz/1 cup fresh breadcrumbs
1 tablespoon chopped fresh tarragon
tarragon sprigs, to garnish

Heat 2 oz/4 tablespoons butter in a skillet.
Add rabbit and cook until lightly browned
all over.

1 tablespoon all-purpose flour
salt and freshly ground black pepper
2lb stewing venison, cubed
1 tablespoon olive oil
1 clove garlic, chopped
10 fl oz/1¼ cups beef stock
1 tablespoon balsamic vinegar
8 juniper berries
8 black peppercorns
4 cloves
14 oz can chopped tomatoes
8 oz baby carrots, trimmed
4 oz button mushrooms
1 tablespoon chopped fresh parsley

Season with salt and pepper. Remove with a
slotted spoon, transfer to a wire rack and
leave for 10 minutes. Preheat oven to 475F
(240C). Oil a roasting pan. Spread mustard
over rabbit portions then coat in breadcrumbs. Put in roasting pan in a single layer
and bake for 20 minutes.

Preheat oven to 350F (180C). Season the
flour with salt and pepper and use to coat the
venison. Heat the oil in a large flameproof
casserole. Add the venison, the remaining
seasoned flour and garlic and cook, stirring,
for 4-5 minutes.

Transfer rabbit portions to a warmed dish
and keep warm. Melt remaining butter and
pour over rabbit. Sprinkle with chopped tarragon, garnish with tarragon and serve.

Serves 4.

Add the stock, vinegar, juniper berries, peppercorns, cloves, tomatoes and carrots. Bring
to the boil, cover and cook in the oven for
1 hour. Add the mushrooms and cook for 15
minutes. Sprinkle with chopped parsley and
serve.

Serves 6-8.

SOLE WITH MINT & CUCUMBER

SOLE WITH CHIVE SAUCE

cucumber, halved lengthwise, seeded and cut into
  2 in. fingers
salt and white pepper
4 sole fillets, about 6-7 oz, each, skinned
1 small shallot, finely chopped
6 fl oz/¾ cup fish stock
4 fl oz/½ cup medium-bodied dry white wine
6 fl oz/¾ cup crème fraîche or heavy cream plus a
  squeeze of lemon juice
5 mint leaves, torn
1 oz/2 tablespoons unsalted butter, diced
mint leaves, to garnish
snow peas, to serve

4 oz/½ cup firm cottage cheese, drained and sieved
grated rind and juice 1 lemon
salt and freshly ground black pepper
3½ oz cooked peeled shrimp, finely chopped
8 sole or plaice fillets, skinned
8 fl oz/1 cup fish stock
1 small shallot, finely chopped
1 tablespoon dry white vermouth
6 tablespoons dry white wine
6 fl oz/¾ cup heavy cream or fromage frais or soft
  cheese
1½ tablespoons finely chopped fresh chives
shrimp and chopped fresh chives, to garnish

Place cucumber in a colander, sprinkle with
salt and leave to drain for 30 minutes. Rinse
and dry well with absorbent kitchen paper.
Fold fillets in half, skinned side in, and place
in a skillet with shallot. Add stock and wine
and heat to just on simmering point. Poach
for about 4-5 minutes, then transfer fish to a
warm plate and cover to keep warm.

Preheat oven to 350F (180C). Oil a shallow
baking dish. Beat together cheese, lemon
rind and juice and season with salt and pepper. Mix in shrimp. Spread on skinned side
of fillets and roll up neatly. Secure with
wooden toothpicks. Place fish in a single
layer in dish, pour in stock to come halfway
up the rolls and add chopped shallot. Cover
dish and cook in the oven for about 20
minutes. Meanwhile, in a small saucepan,
boil vermouth and wine until reduced by
half.

Add cucumber to pan, increase heat and boil
until liquid is reduced by three quarters. Add
crème fraîche and boil until beginning to
thicken. Add mint, salt and pepper and
juices collected on plate with fish. Simmer
gently for 3 minutes. Remove pan from heat
and gradually swirl in butter. Spoon sauce
over fish and serve garnished with mint
leaves, accompanied by snow peas.

Transfer sole to a warm plate and keep warm.
Add stock and shallot to wines and boil hard
until reduced by three quarters. Stir in
cream, if using, and simmer to a light creamy
consistency. If using fromage frais or soft
cheese, stir in and heat without boiling.
Quickly pour into a blender and mix until
frothy. Add chives and season. Pour some
sauce over fish and serve rest in a warm jug.
Garnish rolls with shrimp and chives and
serve with broccoli.

Serves 4.

Serves 4.

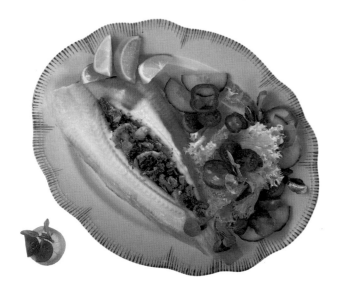

STUFFED SOLE

4 small sole, cleaned and dark skin removed
salt and freshly ground black pepper
1 tablespoon olive oil
1 small onion, finely chopped
2 cloves garlic, finely crushed
5 oz mixed mushrooms, such as oyster, shiitake and
    button, finely sliced
2 oz sun-dried tomatoes, thinly sliced
2 oz/1 cup fresh brown breadcrumbs
1 tablespoon chopped fresh parsley
1 teaspoon chopped fresh marjoram
1-2 teaspoons anchovy paste or few drops
    Worcestershire sauce
mixed salad, to serve
lemon and lime wedges, to garnish

Insert knife point under 1 end of broken backbone and ease away from the under fillets. Lift up bone with the attached ribs and remove from the fish. Season fish inside and out with salt and pepper and place in baking dish.

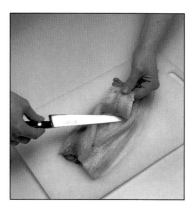

Preheat oven to 400F (200C). Butter 1 or 2 baking dishes large enough to hold fish in a single layer. Place fish skinned side uppermost with tail pointing towards you. Run point of filleting knife along line of backbone then, keeping knife blade firmly against rib bones, slice carefully lifting fillet as it is freed, until outer edge is almost reached – take care not to pierce right through edge.

In a non-stick skillet, heat oil, add onion and garlic and cook over fairly low heat until softened but not colored. Add mushrooms and tomatoes and cook over a higher heat to drive off most of the moisture. Stir in breadcrumbs and herbs and anchovy paste or Worcestershire sauce and seasoning to taste.

Repeat with fillet on other side of the backbone. Using sharp small scissors, cut through the top and tail end of backbone and snip the bones around the edges of the fish, taking care not to pierce the underskin.

Divide mushroom mixture between pockets in fish, cover with foil and bake in the oven for 10-20 minutes until flesh flakes. Serve with mixed salad, garnished with lemon and lime wedges.

Serves 4.

SWORDFISH KABOBS

1½ lbs skinless, boneless swordfish steaks
CHERMOULA:
4 cloves garlic
1 teaspoon salt
juice 2 lemons
1 tablespoon ground cumin
2 teaspoons paprika
1 fresh red chili, cored, seeded and roughly chopped
½ oz fresh cilantro
½ oz fresh parsley
2 fl oz/¼ cup olive oil

To make the chermoula, in a mortar and pestle, crush the garlic with the salt. Place in a blender or food processor.

Add the lemon juice to the food processor with the cumin, paprika, red chili, cilantro and parsley. Process briefly then gradually add the olive oil and reduce to a coarse purée. Transfer to a bowl. Cut the swordfish into 1 in. cubes and add to the chermoula mixture. Mix well to coat, cover and leave in a cool place for 1 hour.

Thread the fish on to skewers and place on a rack over a broiler pan. Spoon the marinade over the fish. Cook under the preheated broiler, close to the heat, for 3-4 minutes on each side, until the fish is lightly browned and flakes easily when tested with a knife. Serve with tomato, olive and caper salad and warm pitta bread.

Serves 4.

Variation: Monkfish, or raw jumbo shrimp may be used.

TURBOT PARCELS

2 cloves garlic, unpeeled
2 large red bell peppers
2 teaspoons balsamic vinegar
1½ teaspoons olive oil
salt and freshly ground black pepper
8 spinach leaves, stalks removed
4 pieces turbot fillet, about 5½ oz each
stir-fried mixed bell peppers, to serve

Preheat broiler. Wrap garlic in foil and broil for 5-7 minutes to soften. Broil peppers, turning frequently, until evenly charred and blistered.

Leave peppers until cool enough to handle, then remove skins. Halve peppers and remove seeds and white membrane. Peel garlic and purée with peppers, vinegar and oil in a food processor or blender. Season with salt and pepper. Add spinach leaves to a saucepan of boiling water and cook for 30 seconds. Drain, refresh under cold running water, then spread out on absorbent kitchen paper to dry.

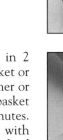

Season turbot, then wrap each piece in 2 spinach leaves. Place in a steaming basket or colander and cover. Bring base of steamer or a saucepan of water to the boil, place basket or steamer on it and steam for 5-6 minutes. Heat pepper sauce gently and serve it with the turbot parcels, accompanied by stir-fried mixed peppers.

Serves 4.

ROAST MONKFISH & GARLIC

SEA BASS ROASTED WITH FENNEL

2 lb monkfish tail or two 1 lb pieces, skinned
2 heads plump garlic, divided into cloves
2 tablespoons olive oil
salt and freshly ground black pepper
¼ teaspoon fresh thyme leaves
¼ teaspoon fennel seeds
juice 1 lemon
1 bay leaf
1 large red bell pepper, peeled, seeded and cut into strips

2½ lb sea bass without head, scaled and gutted
4 rosemary sprigs and 4 oregano sprigs
3 large fennel bulbs
salt and freshly ground black pepper
3 tablespoons olive oil
juice of 1 lemon
4 tablespoons chopped fresh oregano and parsley
5 fl oz/⅔ cup dry white wine
8 large green olives, pitted

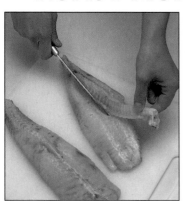

Preheat oven to 425F (220C). Make sure membrane has been removed from fish. Cut out bone, then tie fish back into shape.

Preheat oven to 425F (220C). Wash fish inside and out and pat dry on absorbent kitchen paper. Lay it in an oval ovenproof dish. Fill cavity with sprigs of rosemary.

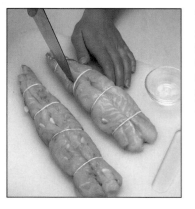

Using the point of a sharp knife, make some incisions in fish. Cut 2 garlic cloves into thin slices and push into incisions. Heat 1 tablespoon oil in a skillet, add fish and brown on all sides for about 5 minutes. Remove and season with salt, pepper, thyme, fennel and lemon juice.

Cut fennel bulbs in half lengthwise, cut out core and slice the bulbs thickly. Blanch in boiling salted water for 5 minutes. Drain. Whisk oil, lemon juice, chopped herbs, salt and pepper together in a medium bowl. Stir in the fennel, turning until coated. Spoon the fennel over and around the fish, and pour over any remaining marinade. Spoon the wine over top and scatter with olives.

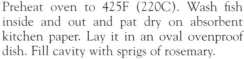

Place fish on bay leaf in roasting pan. Arrange remaining garlic around fish. Bake for 15 minutes. Add pepper strips and cook for about 5 minutes until fish flakes when pierced with a knife. Arrange fish, garlic, pepper and cooking juices on a plate. Carve fish in thin slices.

Serves 4.

Bake in oven for 15 minutes, then spoon the cooking juices over the fish and gently stir the fennel around. Bake for a further 15 minutes. Turn off the oven and leave fish for 5 minutes before serving. Garnish with oregano sprigs and serve with mixed rice.

Serves 4.

MONKFISH ON RATATOUILLE

2 eggplants, halved lengthwise
3 zucchini, sliced
salt and freshly ground black pepper
2 monkfish tails, total weight about 2½ lb
6 cloves garlic
5 tablespoons olive oil
1 Spanish onion, very thinly sliced
2 large bell peppers, thinly sliced
4 large tomatoes, skinned, seeded and chopped
leaves from a few sprigs of thyme, marjoram and
   oregano
about 2 tablespoons each chopped parsley and torn
   basil

In a heavy flameproof casserole, heat 2 table-spoons oil, add eggplant slices and sauté for a few minutes. Add another tablespoon oil and the onion and garlic and sauté for a few more minutes. Add peppers and cook for 1 minute, stirring occasionally.

Cut eggplants into 1 in. slices. Put in a colander with zucchini slices, sprinkle with salt and leave for 1 hour. Rinse well, then dry thoroughly with absorbent kitchen paper.

Add 2 more tablespoons oil and the zuc-chini. Stir occasionally for a few minutes, then add tomatoes, snip in herb leaves and season lightly. Cover and cook very gently for 30-40 minutes, stirring occasionally until fairly dry.

Meanwhile, remove fine skin from monkfish and cut slits in flesh. Cut 3 garlic cloves into thin slivers and insert into slits. Season with salt and pepper and set aside. Chop remain-ing garlic.

Preheat oven to 400F (200C). Stir parsley into ratatouille and tip into a baking dish. Lay monkfish on top and cook for 30-40 minutes, turning fish occasionally. Sprinkle with basil just before end of cooking.

Serves 4-6.

TUNA & GINGER VINAIGRETTE

MONKFISH IN CITRUS SAUCE

1 in. piece fresh ginger, finely chopped
2 large scallions, white and some green parts, thinly
    sliced
8 fl oz/1 cup olive oil
juice 2 limes
2 tablespoons soy sauce
2 tablespoons sesame oil
1 bunch cilantro, finely chopped
pepper
6 tuna steaks, about 5-6 oz each
leek and red bell pepper stir-fry with sesame seeds
cilantro sprigs, to garnish

1¾ lb trimmed monkfish, cut into chunks
2 tablespoons seasoned flour
2 tablespoons olive oil
finely grated rind and juice of 1 lemon and 1 orange
2½ fl oz/⅓ cup dry white wine
2 tablespoons chopped fresh parsley
salt and freshly ground black pepper

Toss monkfish in the seasoned flour and
shake off the excess.

Preheat broiler. To make vinaigrette, stir
together ginger, scallions, olive oil, lime
juice and soy sauce, then whisk in sesame oil.
Add chopped cilantro and season with pepper; set aside.

Heat oil in a non-stick skillet, add fish and
fry until golden all over. Add the citrus rinds
and juices and wine, then cook over high
heat to evaporate the alcohol. Turn down
heat and simmer gently for 3 minutes.

Broil tuna under a high heat for 3½-4
minutes each side, or a little longer for well-
done fish. Spoon some dressing on to 6 plates
and add the fish. Serve with leek and red
pepper stir-fry, garnished with sprigs of
cilantro. Serve any remaining dressing separately.

Serves 6.

Add chopped parsley and salt and pepper to
taste. Lift the fish out and place on a serving
dish. Reduce the sauce a little more and pour
it over the fish. Serve at once, with new
potatoes and sugar snap peas.

Serves 4.

WARM TUNA NIÇOISE

1½ lb small new potatoes
1 lb green beans
2 tablespoons olive oil
4 tuna steaks, about 5 oz each and ½ in. thick
2 tomatoes, chopped
Niçoise or small black oil-cured olives, to garnish
DRESSING:
2 teaspoons wholegrain mustard
1 tablespoon anchovy paste
1 clove garlic, finely chopped
3 tablespoons red wine vinegar
4 tablespoons olive oil
2 teaspoons capers
freshly ground black pepper

Meanwhile, cut beans into 1 in. lengths. Heat a large, heavy skillet, add 1 tablespoon oil, then the beans (be careful they do not splutter). Stir-fry for about 5 minutes until tender but still crisp. Transfer beans to a bowl and stir in 1 tablespoon dressing.

To make dressing, whisk mustard, anchovy paste, garlic and vinegar together in a bowl or jug, then slowly pour in oil, whisking constantly. Whisk in capers and set aside.

Add remaining oil to pan. Season both sides of tuna with pepper, then add to pan and cook over a moderately high heat for about 4 minutes, turning once, until brown outside and still slightly rare in the middle.

Boil potatoes in their skins until tender, drain and then cut into ¾ in. pieces and put into a bowl. Add pepper to dressing and lightly stir 3 tablespoons of dressing into potatoes.

Transfer tuna to a warm serving dish. Add tomatoes and trickle 1 tablespoon dressing over the top; trickle remainder over the tuna. Add beans and potatoes and scatter olives over them. Serve immediately.

Serves 4.

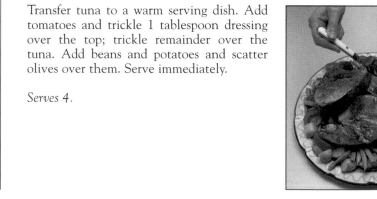

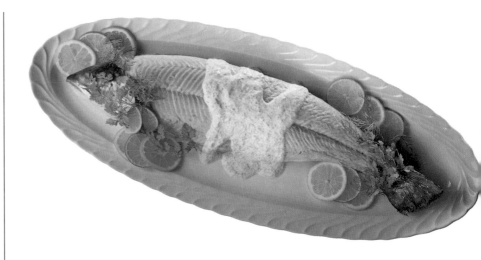

STUFFED RED MULLET

2 oz oyster mushrooms
2 oz cooked, peeled shrimp, thawed and dried, if
   frozen
grated rind of 1 small lemon
2 tablespoons oyster sauce
4 × 8 oz red mullet or red snapper, cleaned and
   scaled
4 tablespoons dry sherry
1 large carrot, cut into thin strips
1 mooli, peeled and cut into thin strips
8 oz small broccoli flowerets
lemon rind and chopped scallions, to garnish

Finely chop the mushrooms and shrimp. Place in a small bowl and mix in lemon rind. Bind together with oyster sauce and set aside. Wash the fish and pat dry with kitchen paper. Divide stuffing into 4 and press into cavity of each fish. Place stuffed fish in a shallow dish and spoon over sherry. Cover and chill for 30 minutes.

Bring a wok or large saucepan of water to the boil. Arrange the vegetables on baking parchment in 2 steamers, lay fish on top and spoon over sherry marinade. Place over the water, cover and steam for 10 minutes. Carefully turn fish over and steam for a further 8-10 minutes or until cooked through. Garnish and serve.

Serves 4.

SALMON WITH HERB SAUCE

½ onion, chopped
1 carrot, chopped
1 stick celery, chopped
1 lemon, sliced
3½ lb salmon
bouquet garni of 2 bay leaves and sprig each
   rosemary, sage and parsley
6 fl oz/¾ cup dry white wine
salt and freshly ground black pepper
bunch watercress, roughly chopped
3 tablespoons chopped fresh parsley
2 tablespoons chopped fresh chervil
1 tablespoon chopped fresh dill
8 oz/1 cup ricotta or low fat soft cheese
lime and lemon slices and herb sprigs, to garnish

Preheat oven to 425F (220C). Place a large piece of foil on a large baking sheet. Make a bed of vegetables and half the lemon slices on the foil. Put salmon on vegetables and add bouquet garni and remaining lemon slices. Fold up foil, pour in wine, season with pepper, then seal edges of foil tightly. Bake in the oven for 1 hour. Remove baking sheet from oven and leave fish to cool completely in foil.

Strain cooking liquid, then boil it until reduced to about 3 fl oz/⅓ cup. Add watercress and herbs and boil until softened. Tip into a blender, add cheese and purée. Season with salt and pepper, pour into a serving bowl or jug and refrigerate. Lift fish on to a rack. Carefully remove skin, fins and fatty line that runs along spine. Transfer to a large serving plate, garnish with lime and lemon slices and sprigs or herbs and serve with sauce.

Serves 6.

BAKED SADDLE OF SALMON

2 oz/¼ cup butter, softened
1 clove garlic, crushed
juice of ½ lemon
2 tablespoons chopped fresh parsley
1½ lb saddle of salmon, filleted
1 tablespoon olive oil, plus extra for greasing
6 shallots, chopped
5 fl oz/⅔ cup fish stock
6 fl oz/¾ cup red wine
8 fl oz/1 cup veal stock
salt and freshly ground black pepper

In a small bowl, mix the butter with the garlic, lemon juice and 1 tablespoon of the chopped parsley.

Spread one of the halves of salmon with the butter mixture and sandwich the pieces back together. Wrap tightly in cling film and put in the freezer for about 1 hour, to set. Do not freeze. Preheat oven to 400F (200C). Lightly oil a large piece of foil. Take the salmon out of the cling film and wrap tightly in the foil. Place in a shallow ovenproof dish and cook in the oven for 30-35 minutes. Remove from dish and keep warm.

Heat the oil in the dish, add the shallots and cook gently, stirring, for 3 minutes, until soft. Add the fish stock and red wine and boil until reduced and syrupy. Add the veal stock and boil to reduce slightly. Add the remaining parsley and season with salt and pepper. Divide the sauce among warmed serving plates. Slice the salmon, place on top of the sauce and serve.

Serves 4.

CAJUN-STYLE RED SNAPPER

2 red snapper, about 1¼-1½ lb each
1 oz/2 tablespoons unsalted butter
2 tablespoons olive oil
SPICE MIX:
1 plump clove garlic
½ onion
1 teaspoon salt
1 teaspoon paprika
½ teaspoon cayenne pepper
½ teaspoon ground cumin
½ teaspoon mustard powder
1 teaspoon each dried thyme and dried oregano
½ teaspoon freshly ground black pepper

With the point of a sharp knife, cut 3 slashes on each side of both fish.

To make spice mix, crush together garlic and onion with salt in a pestle and mortar or in a bowl using the end of a rolling pin. Stir in remaining spice mix ingredients. Spread some spice mix over each fish, making sure it goes into the slashes. Lay the fish in a shallow dish, cover and leave in a cool place for 1 hour.

In a large skillet, heat butter and oil until sizzling. Add fish and fry for about 4 minutes on each side until fish is cooked and spice coating has blackened.

Serves 2.

Note: Serve with a colorful selection of tomato, lemon and lime slices with thyme and parsley sprigs.

BREAM DUGLÉRÉ

4 bream fillets, about 6 oz each
salt and freshly ground black pepper
9 fl oz/generous 1 cup fish stock
6 tablespoons medium-bodied dry white wine
5 fl oz/⅔ cup heavy cream
1 large sun-ripened beefsteak tomato, peeled, seeded
   and cut into ½ in. strips
basil or parsley sprigs, to garnish

Season fish, then place in a single layer in a well buttered skillet. Add stock and wine and bring just to the boil. Reduce heat, cover pan and poach fish for 4-6 minutes.

Using a fish slice, transfer fish to a warm plate, cover and keep warm. Boil cooking liquid rapidly until reduced to a quarter. Stir cream into pan and simmer for 2-3 minutes.

Add tomato strips and heat gently for 1 minute. Season sauce, then pour it over the fish. Serve garnished with basil or parsley sprigs.

Serves 4.

BAKED BREAM WITH FENNEL

2 fennel bulbs, thinly sliced
1 red onion, thinly sliced
3 cloves garlic, sliced
1 lemon, peeled and thinly sliced
3 small sprigs rosemary
2 sea bream, about 1¼ lb each, cleaned and scaled
1 tablespoon fennel seeds, cracked
salt and freshly ground black pepper
5 tablespoons olive oil
rosemary sprigs, to garnish

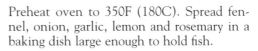

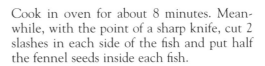

Preheat oven to 350F (180C). Spread fennel, onion, garlic, lemon and rosemary in a baking dish large enough to hold fish.

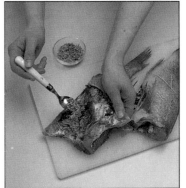

Cook in oven for about 8 minutes. Meanwhile, with the point of a sharp knife, cut 2 slashes in each side of the fish and put half the fennel seeds inside each fish.

Place fish on vegetables, season with salt and pepper and pour oil over them. Bake for 20-25 minutes, turning fish halfway through, until vegetables and fish are tender. Serve garnished with rosemary sprigs.

Serves 4-6.

FISH WITH LEMON GRASS

HOT FISH LOAF

2 tablespoons vegetable oil
1 flat fish, such as pomfret, plump lemon sole or
  plaice, gutted and cleaned
4 cloves garlic, finely chopped
2 fresh red chilies, seeded and finely chopped
1 red shallot, chopped
4½ tablespoons lime juice
½ teaspoon crushed palm sugar
1½ tablespoons finely chopped lemon grass
2 teaspoons fish sauce
chili flowers, to garnish

1½ oz/3 tablespoons butter
2 cloves garlic, crushed
¼ tablespoon all-purpose flour
15 fl oz/scant 2 cups milk
1¼ lb white fish fillets, such as hake or haddock,
  skinned and chopped
5 fl oz/⅔ cup heavy cream
2 teaspoons anchovy sauce
3 eggs and 1 egg yolk
lemon juice
salt and cayenne pepper
4 oz cooked peeled shrimp
2 tablespoons chopped fresh basil
lemon wedges and cilantro sprigs, to garnish
cheese, tomato or broccoli sauce, to serve (optional)

In a wok, heat oil, add fish, skin-side down first, and cook for 3-5 minutes a side until lightly browned and lightly cooked. Using a fish slice, transfer to a warmed serving plate, cover and keep warm. Add garlic to wok and fry, stirring occasionally, until browned.

Preheat oven to 300F (150C). Butter and line base of a 2¾ pint/6½ cup terrine or loaf pan. In a saucepan, melt butter, add garlic and cook for 1 minute. Stir in flour and cook, stirring, for 1 minute, then gradually stir in milk. Bring to the boil, stirring, and simmer for about 3 minutes, stirring occasionally. Pour into a blender, add fish, cream, anchovy essence, eggs and egg yolk. Purée, add lemon juice and season with salt and cayenne pepper.

Stir in chilies, shallot, lime juice, sugar, lemon grass and fish sauce. Allow to simmer gently for 1-2 minutes. Pour over fish and garnish with chili flowers.

Serves 2.

Spoon half of fish mixture into terrine or loaf pan. Finely chop shrimp, then sprinkle them evenly over the fish with the basil. Spoon remaining fish over the top. Cover terrine or loaf pan tightly with baking parchment, place in a roasting pan and pour in enough boiling water to come halfway up sides. Bake for about 1¼ hours. Invert terrine or pan on to a serving plate. Garnish with lemon and cilantro and serve with sauce, if wished.

Serves 4-6.

ZARZUELA

16 mussels
12 oz squid
3 tablespoons olive oil
1 lb uncooked shrimp in their shells
1¼ lb monkfish, cut into 4 slices
salt and freshly ground black pepper
4 tablespoons Spanish brandy
1 large Spanish onion, finely chopped
1 teaspoon paprika
2 beefsteak tomatoes, peeled, seeded and chopped
1 bay leaf
4 fl oz/½ cup dry white wine
4 fl oz/½ cup fish stock
3 saffron threads, crushed
3 cloves garlic
3 tablespoons chopped fresh parsley

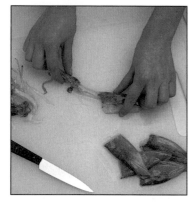

Clean and cook mussels, remove from shells and set aside. Clean squid, chop tentacles and slice bodies into rings; set aside.

Heat 3 tablespoons oil in a large flameproof casserole. Add shrimp and fry until pink. Transfer to a plate. Season monkfish, add to oil and fry over medium heat until light brown. Add squid rings and tentacles and fry briefly. Pour in brandy, then set brandy alight. When flames die down, tip contents of casserole into a bowl and set aside.

Add onion to casserole and cook gently for about 4 minutes until soft. Stir in paprika and cook for 30-60 seconds.

Stir tomatoes into casserole with bay leaf and simmer for 2-3 minutes. Stir in wine and boil until reduced by a third. Stir in stock and simmer for 3-4 minutes.

Pound saffron, garlic and parsley together, mix in a little hot stock, then return to casserole. Boil for 1 minute. Add contents of bowl, the mussels and shrimp and cook gently for about 5 minutes.

Serves 4.

MOROCCAN SHRIMP

1 lb raw peeled large shrimp
2 cloves garlic, crushed
1 teaspoon paprika
1 teaspoon ground cumin
½ teaspoon ground coriander
¼ teaspoon cayenne pepper
2 tablespoons olive oil
½ bunch scallions, finely chopped
2 tablespoons chopped fresh cilantro
AVOCADO & MELON SALSA:
1 ripe avocado
juice 1 lime
8 oz melon, seeded and cut into small dice
½ bunch scallions, finely chopped
1 fresh red chili, cored, seeded and finely chopped
salt

To make the salsa, cut the avocado in half, remove the pit and peel off the skin. Dice the flesh finely and place in a bowl. Add the lime juice and mix well. Add the diced melon, scallions, chili and salt to taste. Cover and leave to stand for 30 minutes.

If necessary, remove the heads and tails from the shrimp and de-vein. Rinse and pat dry with kitchen paper. In a bowl, mix together the garlic, salt, paprika, cumin, ground coriander and cayenne. Add the shrimp and mix well. In a large skillet, heat the oil. Add the shrimp and scallions and stir fry for 5 minutes or until the shrimp are pink and cooked through. Stir in the chopped cilantro. Serve with the salsa and with rice.

Serves 4.

SHRIMP WITH LEMON GRASS

2 cloves garlic, chopped
1 tablespoon chopped cilantro
2 tablespoons chopped lemon grass
½ teaspoon black or white peppercorns
3 tablespoons vegetable oil
12-14 oz raw peeled shrimp, cut in half lengthwise if large
2 shallots or 1 small onion, sliced
2-3 small fresh chilies, seeded and chopped
2-3 tomatoes, cut into wedges
1 tablespoon fish sauce
1 tablespoon oyster sauce
2-3 tablespoons chicken stock or water
cilantro sprigs, to garnish

Using a pestle and mortar, pound the garlic, cilantro, lemon grass and peppercorns to a paste. Heat oil in a wok or skillet and stir-fry the spicy paste for 15-20 seconds until fragrant. Add shrimp, shallots or onion, chilies and tomatoes and stir-fry for 2-3 minutes.

Add fish sauce, oyster sauce and stock, bring to the boil and simmer for 2-3 minutes. Serve garnished with cilantro sprigs.

Serves 4.

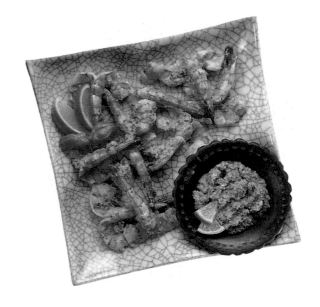

MUSSELS WITH WATERCRESS

36-40 large mussels
2 tablespoons olive oil
1 onion, finely chopped
2 cloves garlic
8 fl oz/1 cup light fish or chicken stock
1 small red bell pepper, thinly sliced
5 fl oz/⅔ cup whipping cream
2 bunches watercress or rocket, washed, dried and
    chopped
salt and freshly ground black pepper
1 lb tagliatelle

With a stiff brush, scrub mussels. Discard any that are not tightly closed. Using a small knife, remove beards and barnacles.

Heat the wok until hot. Add the olive oil and swirl to coat wok. Add the onion and garlic and stir-fry for 1-2 minutes, until onion begins to soften. Stir in the fish or chicken stock and the mussels. Bring to the boil, cover and simmer for 3-4 minutes until mussels open. Using a Chinese strainer, scoop out the mussels into a large bowl; discard any unopened mussels. If you like, remove and discard half the mussel shells.

Add the red pepper and boil the cooking liquid until reduced to about 8 fl oz/1 cup. Add cream and simmer for a further 3 minutes until slightly thickened. Stir in the watercress or rocket and season with salt and pepper. Return the mussels to the sauce, stirring to heat through. In a large saucepan of boiling water, cook the tagliatelle according to the packet directions. Drain and divide among 4 soup places. Top with equal amounts of mussels and sauce.

Serves 4.

SHRIMP WITH ASIAN SAUCE

1½ lb raw jumbo shrimp
lime wedges and basil sprigs, to garnish
MARINADE:
handful Thai or ordinary fresh basil, finely chopped
2 tablespoons finely chopped garlic
2 tablespoons finely chopped fresh ginger
2 tablespoons finely chopped green chilies
2 teaspoons rice wine or medium dry sherry
2½ tablespoons groundnut oil
1 teaspoon Chinese sesame oil
salt and freshly ground black pepper

To make marinade, pound ingredients together in a pestle and mortar or using the end of a rolling pin in a bowl.

Discard legs and heads from shrimp, then using strong scissors, cut shrimp lengthwise in half leaving tail end intact. Remove dark intestinal vein. Rub marinade over shrimp, spoon any remaining marinade over them, cover and leave in a cool place for 1 hour.

Preheat broiler or barbecue. Cook shrimp in a single layer for about 3 minutes until curled, or 'butterflied', and bright pink. Garnish with lime wedges and sprigs of basil. Serve any remaining marinade separately.

Serves 4-6.

CRAB SOUFFLÉ

1½ oz/3 tablespoons butter
1 tablespoon grated onion
1½ oz/5 tablespoons all-purpose flour
6 fl oz/¾ cup milk
5 oz/⅔ cup soft cheese
3 tablespoons chopped fresh parsley
1½ teaspoons anchovy essence
2-3 teaspoons lemon juice
5 eggs, separated
1 egg white
8 oz mixed white and brown crabmeat
salt and freshly ground black pepper
2 tablespoons freshly grated Parmesan cheese
orange and fennel salad, to serve
marjoram sprigs, to garnish

Preheat oven to 400F (200C). Put a baking sheet to heat on lowest shelf. Butter a 4 pint/2½ quart soufflé dish. In a saucepan, melt butter, add onion and cook for 2-3 minutes. Stir in flour, cook for 1 minute, then gradually stir in milk. Bring to boil, stirring, then simmer gently for 4 minutes, stirring occasionally. Remove pan from heat and stir in soft cheese, chopped parsley, anchovy essence, lemon juice, egg yolks and crab and season with salt and pepper.

Whisk all the egg whites until stiff but not dry. Stir in 2 tablespoons crab mixture, then fold egg whites into remaining crab mixture in 3 batches. Transfer to soufflé dish, sprinkle Parmesan cheese over top and place dish on baking sheet. Bake for 40-45 minutes until lightly set in the center. Serve immediately with orange and fennel salad, garnished with sprigs of marjoram.

Serves 4-6.

OYSTER WOK STEW

olive oil for frying
1 small loaf French or Italian bread, cut into ½ in. cubes
freshly ground black pepper
Parmesan cheese for sprinkling
½ oz/1 tablespoon butter
1 small onion, finely chopped
1 clove garlic, finely minced
2 tablespoons flour
14 oz can chopped tomatoes, drained
½ teaspoon chili powder or hot pepper sauce to taste
½ teaspoon paprika
24-30 shucked oysters, liquid reserved
16 fl oz/2 cups whipping cream
8 fl oz/1 cup milk
2 tablespoons chopped fresh parsley

Heat 2 in. oil in the wok until very hot, but not smoking. Add bread cubes and, working in batches, deep-fry for 1 minute until golden. Drain on absorbent kitchen paper, then sprinkle with pepper and Parmesan cheese, tossing to coat. Pour off all but 1 tablespoon oil and return wok to heat. Add the butter, onion and garlic and stir-fry for 1-2 minutes until onion begins to soften. Add flour and cook for 1 minute. Add tomatoes, chili powder or hot pepper sauce and paprika and cook for 3-4 minutes until thickened, stirring frequently.

Through a cheesecloth lined strainer, pour in the reserved oyster liquid. Stir in the whipping cream and milk and slowly bring to simmering point. Cook for 4-5 minutes until sauce thickens and reduces slightly. Season with black pepper. Add oysters to liquid and simmer gently for 1-2 minutes until edges of the oysters begin to curl. Stir in chopped parsley and pour into soup plates. If you like sprinkle with extra Parmesan and pass croûtons separately.

Serves 4-6.

LOBSTER WITH BASIL DRESSING

CRAB & BLACK BEAN SAUCE

4 lobsters, about 1-1¼ lb each, cooked (see Note)
lamb's lettuce salad and lemon wedges, to serve
DRESSING:
2 oz sun-dried tomatoes in olive oil, drained and
  chopped
1 small bunch basil, chopped
4 tablespoons walnut oil
2 tablespoons Spanish sherry vinegar
freshly ground black pepper

To make dressing, chop tomatoes and basil
together. Whisk together oil and vinegar
then stir in tomatoes and basil. Season with
black pepper.

Using a large heavy knife and working from
head to tail along the back, split lobsters in
half. Remove and discard intestine that runs
through center to tail, the stomach from
near the head, and the spongy gills.

Brush cut side of lobsters generously with
dressing and set aside for 15 minutes. Broil
lobster for about 3 minutes. Meanwhile,
gently warm remaining dressing in a small
saucepan. Brush lobster with dressing and
serve with lamb's lettuce and lemon wedges.
Serve remaining dressing separately.

Serves 4.

Note: If possible, order the lobsters from your
fishmonger and ask for them to be only three
quarters cooked. Use them the same day.

1½ lb fresh whole crab, cooked (see Note)
1¼ tablespoons groundnut oil
2-3 cloves garlic, crushed
3 whole scallions, cut into 2 in. pieces
three ¼ in. slices fresh ginger, chopped
2 tablespoons fermented black beans
2 fresh red chilies, seeded and thinly sliced
1¼ tablespoons light soy sauce
2 tablespoons rice wine or medium sherry
4 fl oz/½ cup fish stock, preferably made from shrimp
  shells and heads
cilantro sprigs, to garnish

Detach claws and legs from crab and divide
claws at joints. Using nutcrackers or a sharp
heavy knife, lightly crack claws and legs so as
not to damage the flesh within. Place crab on
its back with tail flap towards you. Holding
shell, press body section upwards from under
tail flap and ease out with thumbs. Pull off
inedible grey gills and discard. Using the
knife, cut crab body into quarters. Using a
spoon, remove stomach bag and mouth from
back shell. Scrape out brown meat. Heat a
wok or large skillet, then add oil.

When it is hot, add garlic, scallions and ginger and stir-fry until fragrant. Add black
beans, chilies and crab, stir-fry for 2 minutes,
then add soy sauce, rice wine and stock. Tip
contents of wok or skillet into a flameproof
casserole. Cover and cook for 5 minutes.
Serve garnished with cilantro sprigs.

Serves 4.

Note: If possible, order a crab from your fish-
mongers and ask for it to be only three
quarters cooked. Use it the same day.

PASTA & SQUASH TRIANGLES

6 oz all-purpose flour
1 teaspoon salt
6 sage leaves, chopped
2 eggs
1 egg yolk
3 tablespoons olive oil
shavings of Parmesan cheese, to serve
FILLING:
8 oz peeled butternut squash, cubed
1 small clove garlic, crushed
3 oz/⅓ cup ricotta cheese
2 oz/½ cup freshly grated Parmesan cheese
pinch of grated nutmeg
salt and freshly ground black pepper

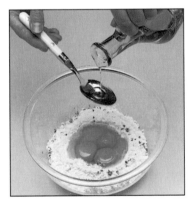

In a large bowl, mix the flour, salt and sage. Make a well in the center and work in the eggs, egg yolk and 1 tablespoon oil to form a stiff dough. Knead on a lightly floured surface for 5 minutes until smooth and elastic. Wrap in cling film and leave to rest for 30 minutes.

Prepare the filling. Steam the squash for 10-15 minutes until soft. Mash with a fork until smooth, transfer to a clean pan and heat gently until completely dry. Place in a bowl and leave until cold. Beat in the garlic, ricotta and Parmesan cheeses, nutmeg and seasoning to taste.

Divide the pasta dough into 4 pieces and roll out each piece on a lightly floured surface as thinly and evenly as possible. Cut into 3 in. squares.

Place a teaspoon of the squash filling in the middle of each square, dampen the edges and fold in half, diagonally, to form triangles. Transfer the triangles to a floured tray, or tea-towel, to prevent them sticking together.

Bring a large pan of salted water to a rolling boil, add 1 tablespoon of the remaining olive oil and cook the triangles in batches for 3-5 minutes until cooked. Drain and toss with extra olive oil and serve with shavings of Parmesan and black pepper.

Serves 4-6.

Note: The pasta dough can be made in a food processor using a dough blade. If you have a pasta machine, roll the dough out to the thinnest setting.

CHICORY-ASPARAGUS GRATIN

20 asparagus spears
4 small heads chicory
4 fl oz/½ cup virgin olive oil
1 clove garlic, crushed
grated zest and juice ½ lemon
1 tablespoon chopped fresh basil
1½ oz/⅓ cup freshly grated Parmesan or Cheddar
  cheese
salt and freshly ground black pepper

Trim the asparagus spears, removing the woody ends, and peel almost to the tips. Steam the spears for 2 minutes until bright green.

Lightly oil 4 small gratin dishes. Preheat broiler. Halve and trim the chicory and place 2 halves into each dish. Arrange the asparagus between the chicory.

Mix together the oil, garlic, lemon zest and juice and basil and pour over the vegetables. Place under a hot broiler and cook for 3-4 minutes. Sprinkle over the cheese and return to the broiler for 2-3 minutes until golden. Season and serve at once.

Serves 4.

WATERCRESS CUSTARDS

2 red bell peppers
2 tablespoons olive oil
4 fl oz/½ cup vegetable stock
½ oz/1 tablespoon butter
4 oz watercress leaves
3 eggs
7 fl oz/¼ cup thick cream
1 oz/¼ cup finely grated Cheddar cheese
1 teaspoon Dijon mustard
salt and freshly ground black pepper

Preheat oven to 400F (200C) and roast the peppers for 20-25 minutes until skins are lightly charred. Transfer to a plastic bag and leave to cool for 30 minutes. Peel the peppers, discard the seeds, reserving any juices. Purée the peppers and juices with the oil and stock to form a smooth sauce. Pass through a sieve into a small pan. Reduce oven temperature to 350F (180C) and grease 6 dariole molds.

Melt the butter and fry the watercress leaves for 1 minute until just wilted. Purée in a blender or food processor and gradually add the eggs, cream, cheese, mustard and salt and pepper until smooth. Pour into the molds. Place in a roasting pan and pour in enough boiling water to come two-thirds the way up the sides of the molds. Bake for 25 minutes until firm in the center. Leave to rest for 5 minutes, then unmold and serve warm with the reheated pepper sauce.

Serves 6.

VEGETABLE FILO PARCELS

4 small new potatoes, halved
8 baby carrots, trimmed
8 baby zucchini, halved
8 asparagus tips, trimmed
1 baby leek, trimmed and sliced into 8
2 oz/¼ cup butter, softened
1 tablespoon chopped fresh mint
¼ teaspoon ground cumin
pinch of cayenne pepper
salt and freshly ground black pepper
4 large sheets filo pastry
3 fl oz/⅓ cup olive oil

Preheat oven to 375F (190C) and place a baking sheet on the middle shelf.

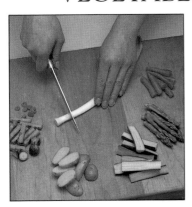

Cook the potatoes in boiling water for 6-8 minutes until almost cooked. Blanch the remaining vegetables for 2-3 minutes, depending on the size, until almost tender. Drain all the vegetables, plunge into cold water, allow to cool, then drain and dry thoroughly. Cream together the butter, mint, spices and salt and pepper. Take 1 large sheet of pastry and using a 10 in. plate or saucepan lid as a template, carefully cut out a circle; repeat to make 4 in total. Brush liberally with oil.

Take a quarter of the vegetables and place a small pile on one side of the pastry circle. Dot with the mint butter and fold the other side of pastry over the filling, pressing the edges together well. Brush a little oil along the edge and turn over a bit at a time to ensure filling is totally enclosed. Repeat to make 4 parcels and transfer to the heated baking sheet. Carefully brush over remaining oil and bake for 12-15 minutes until pastry is golden. Serve immediately.

Serves 4.

GOATS' CHEESE & FIG TART

7 oz/1¼ cups all-purpose flour
pinch of salt
4 oz/½ cup butter
1 egg yolk
2 tablespoons iced water
1 tablespoon olive oil
1 large onion, thinly sliced
2 teaspoons chopped fresh thyme
½ teaspoon fennel seeds
4 fresh figs
4 oz/½ cup soft goats' cheese
1 oz/¼ cup freshly grated Parmesan cheese
5 fl oz/⅔ cup thick sour cream
1 large egg, lightly beaten

Preheat oven to 400F (200C). Sift the flour and salt into a bowl and rub in the butter until mixture resembles fine breadcrumbs. Make a well in the center and work in the egg yolk and water to form a soft dough. Knead on a floured surface, wrap and chill for 30 minutes. Roll out thinly and use to line a 9 in. tart pan. Prick the base and chill for 20 minutes. Line with foil and baking beans and bake blind for 10 minutes; remove foil and beans and bake for a further 10-12 minutes until crisp and golden.

Heat the oil and fry the onions, thyme and fennel for 10 minutes. Chop 2 figs, add to the pan and remove from the heat. Beat the goats' cheese, Parmesan, cream and egg together until smooth. Spread the onion mixture into tart case and spoon in the cheese mixture. Slice the remaining figs and arrange around the outside of the tart. Bake for 25 minutes until risen and set. Leave to cool and serve warm or cold.

Serves 8.

STUFFED EGGPLANTS

2 eggplants, each about 8 oz
2 cloves garlic, finely chopped
2 stalks lemon grass, chopped
2 tablespoons vegetable oil
1 small onion, finely chopped
6 oz chicken breast meat, finely chopped
2 teaspoons fish sauce
25 Thai holy basil leaves
freshly ground black pepper
Thai holy basil leaves, to garnish

Preheat broiler. Place eggplants under broiler and cook, turning as necessary, for about 20 minutes until evenly charred.

Meanwhile, using a pestle and mortar, pound together garlic and lemon grass; set aside. Heat oil in a wok, add onion and cook, stirring occasionally, until lightly browned. Stir in garlic mixture, cook for 1-2 minutes, then add chicken. Stir-fry for 2 minutes. Stir in fish sauce, basil leaves and plenty of black pepper.

Using a sharp knife, slice each charred eggplant in half lengthwise. Using a teaspoon, carefully scoop eggplant flesh into a bowl; keep skins warm. Using kitchen scissors, chop flesh. Add to wok and stir ingredients together for about 1 minute. Place eggplant skins on a large warmed plate and divide chicken mixture between them. Garnish with basil leaves.

Serves 4.

OLIVE & MOZZARELLA PUFFS

2 oz/½ cup pitted green olives
1 oz Mozzarella cheese
2 teaspoons chopped fresh parsley
½ teaspoon chopped fresh sage
pinch of chili powder
8 oz bought puff pastry, thawed if frozen
1 egg
salt

Preheat oven to 425F (220C) and lightly oil a baking sheet. Very finely chop the olives and cheese and mix with the herbs and chili powder to form a paste. Set aside.

Roll out the pastry thinly and stamp out 8 rounds, using a 4 in. fluted cookie cutter. Place a heaped teaspoon of olive mixture in the center of each round. Lightly dampen the edges of pastry, fold in half to form semicircles, pressing edges together well to seal. Transfer to the baking sheet.

Beat the egg with a little salt and brush over pastries. Cut 2 small slashes in each one and bake for 12-15 minutes until puffed up and golden. Serve warm or cold with a salad garnish.

Serves 8.

Note: These make ideal buffet party nibbles. Make up double quantity of the filling and cut pastry into small rounds to make bite-sized appetizers.

BAKED BUTTERNUT SQUASH

2 small butternut squash
4 tablespoons melted butter
1 tablespoon lemon juice
salt and freshly ground black pepper
4 tablespoons walnut oil
4 tablespoons dry sherry
4 tablespoons chopped fresh parsley
2 tablespoons snipped fresh chives
2 tablespoons chopped walnuts
2 tablespoons fresh breadcrumbs
2 tablespoons grated Parmesan cheese
parsley sprigs, to garnish

Cut the squash in half lengthwise. Scoop any small amount of fibre from the central hole, then place the squash halves in the soaked clay pot. Trickle the butter and lemon juice over the cut surface of each half, then season lightly. Cover the pot and place in the cold oven. Set the oven at 425F (220C). Cook for 45 minutes.

Mix the walnut oil and sherry with the parsley and chives. Spoon this over the squash halves. Sprinkle with the walnuts, breadcrumbs and Parmesan and cook, uncovered, for a further 15 minutes, or until the topping is crisp and golden and the squash is tender. Serve garnished with parsley.

Serves 4.

NOODLES WITH PEANUT SAUCE

8 oz fresh thin Chinese egg noodles
2 tablespoons sesame oil
1 oz plus 1 tablespoon unsalted roast peanuts
1 clove garlic, crushed
1 tablespoon light soy sauce
2 teaspoons Chinese black vinegar
1 teaspoon light brown sugar
1 tablespoon groundnut oil
few drops hot chili oil
white part of scallion, thinly sliced and fresh red chili,
   very thinly sliced, to garnish

Bring a large saucepan of water to the boil. Add noodles, return to boil, stir then cover pan and boil until just tender.

Drain well and tip into a serving bowl. Toss with 1 tablespoon sesame oil. Set aside. In a blender or a spice grinder, crush the 1 tablespoon peanuts. Set aside. Put remaining peanuts and sesame oil, garlic, soy sauce, vinegar, sugar and groundnut oil in a blender. Add 2 fl oz/¼ cup water. Mix to a smooth sauce. Add chili oil to taste.

To serve, pour peanut sauce over noodles. Toss to mix. Sprinkle the crushed peanuts on top, and garnish with scallion and chili slices.

Serves 3-4 as a side dish.

RICH VEGETABLE RAGOÛT

knob of butter
4 leeks, sliced
2 celery sticks, sliced
2 large potatoes, cut in large dice
2 carrots, halved and sliced
2 parsnips, halved and sliced
½ cauliflower, broken into florets
15 oz can garbanzos, drained
2 tablespoons tomato paste
8 fl oz/1 cup dry (alcoholic) cider
1 tablespoon sugar
salt and freshly ground black pepper
1 bay leaf
4 oz/1 cup cheese, grated
4 tablespoons fresh breadcrumbs
2 tablespoons sesame seeds

PISTO MANCHEGO

2 tablespoons olive oil
2 oz/2 slices bacon, chopped
2 large Spanish onions, chopped
1 clove garlic, chopped
2 zucchini, chopped
4 red bell peppers, peeled and chopped
1 lb beefsteak tomatoes, peeled, seeded and chopped
bunch of mint, parsley and basil, chopped
salt and freshly ground black pepper
4 poached or fried eggs, to serve (optional)

Melt the butter in a large saucepan. Add the leeks and celery, and cook for 5 minutes, until the leeks are softened and reduced in volume. Turn the leek mixture into the soaked clay pot. Add all the remaining vegetable and the garbanzos. Mix the ingredients together well. Stir the tomato paste, cider and sugar together, then add a generous sprinkling of seasoning and pour the mixture over the vegetables. Tuck the bay leaf into the ingredients.

In a large skillet, heat oil, add bacon, onions and garlic and cook gently for about 15 minutes, stirring occasionally, until onions are very soft and lightly colored.

Cover the pot and place in the cold oven. Set the oven at 425F (220C). Cook for 1 hour. Stir well and taste for seasoning. Mix together the cheese, breadcrumbs and sesame seeds. Sprinkle this topping over the ragoût and cook, uncovered, for a further 15 minutes, or until the topping is golden and the vegetables are tender.

Serves 4-6.

Add zucchini and peppers to pan and fry for about 4 minutes until soft. Stir in tomatoes and herbs and cook for 20-30 minutes until thickened. Season to taste. Serve topped by poached or fried eggs, if desired.

Serves 4.

BULGAR & VERMICELLI PILAFF

2 tablespoons olive oil
1 onion, thinly sliced
1 green bell pepper, seeded and sliced
1 oz cut vermicelli
8 oz/1¼ cups bulgar wheat
12 fl oz/1½ cups vegetable stock
2 tomatoes, roughly chopped
salt and freshly ground black pepper
2 tablespoons chopped fresh flat leafed parsley
fried onions, to garnish

Heat the olive oil in a large saucepan. Add the onion and cook for 5 minutes then add the sliced pepper and cook until the onion is soft.

Add the vermicelli and stir to coat with oil. Put the bulgar wheat in a colander and rinse in cold water, then add to the pan. Pour in the vegetable stock and bring to the boil. Cover the pan and simmer for 5 minutes.

Add the tomatoes and simmer for a further 5-10 minutes until the bulgar wheat is tender and the stock is absorbed. Add more stock if necessary. Season with salt and pepper and stir in the parsley. Serve, garnished with fried onions.

Serves 6.

SPICED RICE & BELL PEPPERS

4 tablespoons olive oil
8 oz long-grain rice
2 cloves garlic
salt
1 teaspoon each cumin and coriander seeds
3 tablespoons tomato paste
2 teaspoons paprika
1 teaspoon chili powder
pinch saffron threads, crushed and dissolved in 2 tablespoons boiling water
20 fl oz/2½ cups boiling chicken or vegetable stock or water
3-4 red bell peppers, peeled, halved lengthwise and seeded
extra virgin olive oil, to serve (optional)
chopped fresh herbs, to garnish

Heat oil in a paella pan or wide, heavy-based shallow saucepan. Stir in rice, then stir-fry for 2-3 minutes. Meanwhile, using a pestle and mortar, grind together garlic, salt, cumin and coriander seeds, then stir in tomato paste, paprika, chili and saffron liquid. Stir into rice. Stir in stock or water. Bring to boil, then cover and simmer for about 7 minutes.

Arrange peppers around sides of pan. Simmer for 7-10 minutes until rice is tender and plump, and liquid absorbed. Remove from heat and leave for 5 minutes. Trickle extra virgin olive oil over peppers, if desired, and garnish with chopped herbs.

Serves 4.

DESSERTS AND BAKING

MELON & CHILLED BERRIES

12 oz mixed fresh berries (raspberries, strawberries, blackberries, blueberries)
4 fl oz/½ cup Muscat dessert wine
1 teaspoon chopped preserved stem ginger
2 teaspoons stem ginger syrup (from jar)
1 teaspoon shredded fresh mint
2 small Cantaloupe or Charentais melons
mint leaves, to decorate

Wash and dry the berries and hull and halve as necessary. Place in a bowl and pour over the wine, ginger, ginger syrup and mint. Stir well, cover and chill for 2 hours.

With a sharp knife, cut the melons in half, cutting the flesh in a zig-zag pattern all the way around the center of each fruit to form attractive edges. Carefully scoop out and discard the seeds and fill each hollow with a large spoonful of the chilled berries. Pour in the juices, decorate with mint leaves and serve with crème fraîche or mascarpone cheese.

Serves 4.

PINEAPPLE WITH COCONUT

3½ oz superfine sugar
1½ in piece fresh root ginger, grated
3½ oz light brown sugar
12 thin slices fresh pineapple
3-4 tablespoons toasted coconut flakes

Put superfine sugar, ginger and light brown sugar in a heavy based saucepan. Stir in 13 fl oz/1⅔ cups water. Heat gently, stirring with a wooden spoon, until sugars have melted. Bring to the boil. Simmer until reduced by about ⅓.

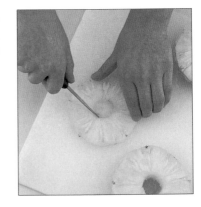

Remove cores from slices of pineapple using a small sharp knife or a small cookie cutter. Strain syrup over pineapple rings and leave to cool. Cover and chill.

To serve, lay 2 pineapple rings on each plate. Spoon some of the syrup over and scatter the toasted coconut flakes on top.

Serves 6.

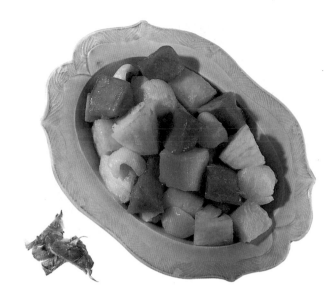

MALAYSIAN FRUIT SALAD

2 oz light brown sugar
grated rind and juice of 1 lime
1 small pineapple, peeled, cored and cubed
1½ lb lychees, peeled, halved and pitted
 3 ripe mangoes, peeled, pitted and chopped
1 papaya, peeled, seeded and chopped

Put sugar, lime rind and juice and 5 fl oz/⅔ cup water in a saucepan. Heat gently, stirring with a wooden spoon, until sugar has dissolved.

Heat syrup to boiling point then simmer for 1 minute. Remove from heat and leave to cool.

Put pineapple, lychees, mangoes and papaya in a serving dish. Pour over cool syrup. Cover dish with cling film and put in the refrigerator to chill.

Serves 4.

FLAMBÉED FRUIT

2oz/¼ cup butter
2oz/½ cup superfine sugar
2 oranges, peeled and segmented
12 oz can pineapple pieces in natural juice
4 bananas, thickly sliced
1 tablespoon orange liqueur or brandy
mint sprigs, to decorate

Put the butter and sugar in a flameproof dish and cook over a gentle heat until they melt and turn a caramel color.

Add the oranges, pineapple pieces and their juice and bananas. Bring to the boil and boil for 5 minutes, until sauce thickens.

Put the liqueur or brandy in a ladle and warm gently. Set alight and pour over the fruit. Cook for 1 minute, until the flames die down. Decorate with mint and serve warm.

Serves 4.

CLEMENTINE & DATE SALAD

FIGS WITH CINNAMON CREAM

8 clementines
2 teaspoons orange-flower water
4 oz/¼ cup fresh dates
1 oz/¼ cup pistachio nuts
clementine leaves, to decorate

Peel the clementines. Cut them into slices, reserving any juice.

9 large ripe figs
2oz/¼ cup sweet butter
4 teaspoons brandy
½ oz/3 teaspoons brown sugar
almond flakes, to decorate
CINNAMON CREAM:
5 fl oz/⅔ cup thick cream
1 teaspoon ground cinnamon
1 tablespoon brandy
2 teaspoons clear honey

Prepare the cinnamon cream. Combine all the ingredients in a small bowl, cover and refrigerate for 30 minutes to allow time for flavors to develop.

Arrange the clementine slices on serving plates. Pour over the reserved juice and sprinkle with the orange-flower water.

Preheat broiler. Halve the figs and thread on to 6 skewers. Melt the butter in a small pan and stir in the brandy.

Remove the pits from the dates. Chopped the dates. Roughly chop the pistachio nuts. Scatter the dates and nuts over the clementines. Decorate with clementine leaves and serve.

Serve 4-6.

Brush the figs with the brandy butter and sprinkle with a little sugar. Place under a hot broiler for 4-5 minutes until bubbling and golden. Whip the cinnamon cream until just holding its shape, decorate with almond flakes, and serve with the broiled figs.

Serves 6.

GREEN TEA FRUIT SALAD

4 teaspoons jasmine tea leaves
2 tablespoons dry sherry
2 tablespoons superfine sugar
1 lime
2 kiwi fruit
8 oz fresh lychees
¼ honeydew melon
4 oz seedless green grapes
lime slices, to decorate

Place tea leaves in a small bowl or jug and pour over 10 fl oz/1¼ cups boiling water. Leave to steep for 5 minutes. Strain through a sieve into a saucepan.

Stir in sherry and sugar. Using a vegetable peeler, pare the rind from the lime and add to the pan. Squeeze the juice from the lime and add the juice to the pan. Bring to the boil, reduce heat and simmer for 5 minutes. Leave to cook, then discard lime rind.

Peel and thinly slice kiwi fruit. Peel, halve and pit the lychees. Peel melon and slice thinly. Arrange prepared fruits and grapes in small clusters on serving plates. Pour over cooled tea syrup, decorate and serve.

Serves 4.

FRUIT & ELDERFLOWER CREAM

4 fl oz/½ cup thick cream
4 fl oz/½ cup fromage frais
2 tablespoons elderflower syrup
1 small ripe mango
1 small ripe papaya
1 large ripe peach
1 large apple
4 oz strawberries
4 oz bunch seedless grapes
freshly grated nutmeg and fresh lemon balm or mint, to decorate

Whip the thick cream and gently fold in the fromage frais and elderflower syrup, cover and chill until required.

Peel the mango, cut down either side of the pit and cut the flesh into thin slices. Peel and halve the papaya, scoop out and discard the seeds and cut flesh into thin strips. Halve and pit the peach and cut into thin wedges. Quarter and core the apple and cut into thin wedges. Hull and halve the strawberries.

Arrange all the prepared fruit and the grapes on a large platter and place the bowl of elderflower dip in the center. Sprinkle over a little nutmeg and serve the fruit decorated with the lemon balm or mint.

Serves 8.

Note: Use any fruit liqueur such as crème fraîche or crème de pêche as an alternative to elderflower syrup, if wished. Sprinkle lemon juice over the fruit if not serving immediately.

STUFFED RAMBUTANS

1 small banana, chopped
grated rind and juice of 1 lime
16 rambutans
3 oz pitted dates, chopped
1 papaya, peeled, seeded and chopped
strips of lime rind, to decorate

Mix the banana with the lime rind and juice and set aside. Slice the top off the rambutans, exposing the tip of the stone. Using a sharp, small-bladed knife, carefully slice down around the stone, loosening the flesh away from the pit.

Peel away the skin, and slice lengthwise through flesh at quarterly intervals. Gently pull down the flesh to expose the pit and carefully cut away the pit. The flesh should now resemble a four-petalled flower.

In a food processor or blender, blend banana and dates until smooth. Place a teaspoon of filling in the center of each rambutan and bring up the sides to enclose the filling. Cover and chill for 30 minutes. Blend the papaya in a food processor or blender until smooth, pass through a sieve and spoon on to four serving plates. Top with rambutans, decorate with strips of lime rind and serve.

Serves 4.

FRUIT PLATTER

1 small melon
2 peaches
4 figs
6 oz seedless green grapes
orange flower water
2 pomegranates

Halve melon and remove seeds. Cut into thin slices and remove skin. Arrange slices on 4 plates.

Put peaches in a bowl and pour boiling water over them. Leave for 30 seconds, then plunge into cold water for 30 seconds. Peel off skins. Cut peaches in half and remove pits. Cut into slices and arrange on the plates. Cut figs into slices and add to the plates. Arrange grapes on the plates.

Sprinkle the fruit with orange flower water. Cut pomegranates in half and scoop out seeds, removing any pith. Scatter the seeds over the fruit on the plates.

Serves 4.

PEACHES IN WHITE WINE

4 ripe peaches
4 raspberries, strawberries or small pieces of almond
    paste
1-2 tablespoons confectioners' or superfine sugar,
    preferably vanilla flavored
10 fl oz/1¼ cups fruity white wine, chilled
lemon twists, raspberries and raspberry leaves, to
    decorate

Put peaches in a large bowl, cover with boiling water and leave for about 20 seconds. Remove peaches from water, peel, then cut in half and remove pits.

Put a raspberry, strawberry or piece of almond paste in cavity of each peach and reassemble peaches. Put peaches in four serving dishes, sprinkle with sugar and pour over wine. Cover and chill, turning peaches once. Decorate and serve.

Serves 4.

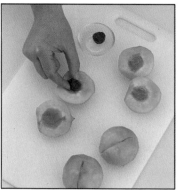

FRESH FRUIT PLATTER

¼ oz/4 teaspoons low fat spread
2 tablespoons all-purpose flour
10 fl oz/1¼ cups semi-skimmed milk
1 oz/5 teaspoons superfine sugar
1 mango, peeled, pitted and puréed
1 melon
4 kiwi fruit
2 peaches
4 red dessert plums
2 bananas
4 oz raspberries
6 oz strawberries
8 oz green grapes, in small bunches

To make mango sauce, melt fat gently in a saucepan. Remove from heat, stir in flour, then gradually stir in milk, blending well. Bring slowly to the boil, stirring continuously, until mixture thickens. Simmer for 3 minutes. Remove from heat and add sugar and mango purée, mixing well. Serve mango sauce hot or cold with fruit. To prepare fruit, peel melon, remove seeds and cut into small slices. Peel kiwi fruit and quarter each fruit.

Peel and pit peaches, then cut each into 8 pieces. Pit and quarter plums. Peel bananas and cut into long thin slices. Arrange selection of fruit decoratively on a large platter or serving dish. Serve immediately with hot or cold mango sauce.

Serves 8.

SPICED HOT FRUIT KABOBS

2¼ lb prepared mixed fresh fruits, such as mango,
  papaya, pineapple, nectarine, plum, banana,
  lychees, cherries
5 oz/⅔ cup unsalted butter
3 tablespoons grated fresh root ginger
1 tablespoon confectioners' sugar
1 tablespoon lime juice

Soak about 20 bamboo skewers in water for
30 minutes. Cut fruit into bite-size chunks.
Thread a selection of fruits on each skewer.

Melt butter and stir in ginger, confectioners'
sugar and lime juice.

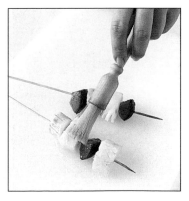

Brush over kabobs. Preheat broiler. Cook
kabobs, turning frequently and brushing
with butter mixture, for about 5 minutes
until beginning to caramelize. Serve warm.

Makes about 20.

AMARETTI-STUFFED PEACHES

4 large peaches
2 oz amaretti biscuits
1 egg yolk
4 teaspoons superfine sugar
1 oz/2 tablespoons softened butter
9 fl oz/1 cup sweet white wine
toasted flaked almonds and vine leaves, to decorate

Preheat the oven to 375F (190C). Butter an
ovenproof dish. Cut the peaches in half and
remove the pits.

Scoop out a little flesh from each peach half
and place in a bowl. Crush the amaretti biscuits and add to the bowl. Stir in the egg
yolk, superfine sugar and butter and mix
well. Put some filling in each peach half,
forming it into a smooth mound.

Put the peaches in the dish and pour in the
wine. Bake in the oven for 30-40 minutes
until the peaches are tender and the filling is
firm. Transfer to serving plates, sprinkle with
toasted almonds and decorate with vine
leaves. Spoon around the baking juices and
serve.

Serves 4.

Note: Be careful not to bake the peaches for
too long – they should retain their shape.

ROAST FIGS

SAFFRON NECTARINES

12 figs
3 tablespoons superfine sugar
1 tablespoon orange juice
2oz/⅔ cup walnut halves
1 tablespoon clear honey
Greek yogurt, to serve

4 ripe nectarines
½ oz/1 tablespoon butter
4 tablespoons clear blossom honey
pinch of saffron strands
1 tablespoons rosewater
toasted flaked almonds, to decorate

Preheat the oven to 400F (200C). Butter a shallow flameproof dish. Put the figs side by side in the dish.

Cut the nectarines in half and remove the pits. Put the nectarine halves in a saucepan with the butter.

Sprinkle with 2 tablespoons of the sugar and the orange juice. Bake for 20 minutes, basting from time to time with the cooking juices. Add the walnuts and sprinkle with the remaining sugar.

Spoon over the honey and scatter with saffron. Add 4 fl oz/½ cup water and the rosewater. Bring slowly to the boil and simmer gently for 8-12 minutes until the nectarines are tender.

Reduce the oven temperature to 300F (150C) and bake for a further 10 minutes. Remove the figs and walnuts with a slotted spoon and arrange on a serving dish. Add the honey to the cooking juices and warm through over a low heat. Spoon the syrup over the figs and serve warm or cold with Greek yogurt.

Serves 4.

Remove with a slotted spoon and arrange on serving plates. Decorate with toasted flaked almonds and serve warm or cold.

Serves 4.

BANANAS WITH RUM & LIME

2oz/¼ cup butter
2oz/¼ cup light brown sugar
½ teaspoon ground cinnamon
4 bananas, peeled and cut diagonally into ½ in. slices
2½ fl oz/⅓ cup light rum
grated rind and juice of 1 lime or lemon
2 tablespoons chopped almonds, toasted
shavings of fresh coconut or toasted shredded
  coconut, to garnish (optional)

Heat the wok until hot. Add the butter and swirl to melt and coat wok. Stir in sugar and cinnamon and cook for 1 minute until sugar melts and mixture bubbles.

Add banana slices and stir-fry gently for 1-2 minutes, tossing to coat all pieces and heat through. Add rum and, with a match, light rum to ignite. Shake wok gently until flames subside.

Add rind and juice of the lime or lemon and toasted almonds, and stir in gently. Spoon into dessert dishes and garnish with fresh or toasted coconut.

Serves 4.

TOFFEE PEARS & PECANS

4 dessert pears, cut lengthwise in half and cored
2 tablespoons lemon juice
2½ oz/5 tablespoons butter
2½ oz/about ½ cup brown sugar
1 teaspoon ground cinnamon
½ teaspoon ground ginger
3 oz/1 cup pecan halves
9 fl oz/1 cup heavy or whipping cream
few drops vanilla extract

Cut pear halves into ¼ in. thick slices. Sprinkle with the lemon juice.

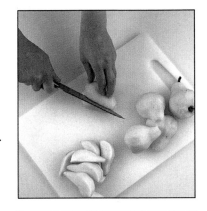

Heat the wok until hot. Add 2 tablespoons butter and 3 tablespoons brown sugar and swirl to melt and coat wok. Stir until sugar melts and bubbles. Add pear slices, cinnamon, ginger and pecans and stir-fry gently for 4-6 minutes until pear slices are tender but still crisp. Remove pear slices and pecans to a shallow serving bowl.

Add remaining butter and sugar and stir for 2 minutes until sugar dissolves and sauce boils and bubbles. Stir in cream and bring to the boil. Simmer for 2-3 minutes until sauce thickens. Remove from heat, stir in vanilla extract and pour over pear slices and pecans. Cool slightly before serving or serve at room temperature.

Serves 4-6.

LYCHEE SORBET

1 lb fresh lychees in their shells or 6 oz canned
  lychees
1 oz/3 tablespoons sugar
4 fl oz/½ cup water
fresh mint sprigs, to decorate

Peel fresh lychees and pit them. Place the
lychees in a food processor or blender.
Dissolve the sugar in the water and add to
the blender of food processor. Process to a
smooth purée.

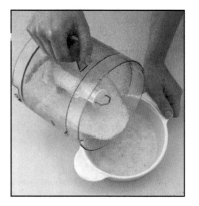

Pour the purée into a freezerproof container
and place in the freezer for about 2 hours
until almost set.

Break up the iced mixture and whip until
smooth. Return mixture to the freezer for 30-
45 minutes to set until solid. Serve the sorbet decorated with mint leaves.

Serves 4-6.

Variation: 2 teaspoons grated root ginger
can be added to the sorbet mixture before
blending, if wished.

POMEGRANATE SORBET

8 oz/1 cup granulated sugar
4-6 large pomegranates
grated rind and juice of ½ orange
grated rind and juice of ½ lemon
1 egg white
pomegranate seeds and mint sprigs, to decorate

Turn the freezer to its coldest setting. Put the
sugar and 10 fl oz/1¼ cups water in a
saucepan. Heat gently until the sugar has
dissolved then bring to the boil and simmer
for 5 minutes. Leave to cool. Cut the pomegranates in half.

Squeeze the pomegranates on a lemon
squeezer to give 14 fl oz/1¾ cups juice. Strain
the pomegranate juice into the cooled syrup.
Stir in the orange and lemon rind and juice.
Pour into a freezerproof container. Put in the
freezer. When the sides are beginning to set,
transfer to a bowl and beat thoroughly or
process in a food processor or blender.
Return to the container and freeze for 30-40
minutes.

When the sorbet is just beginning to solidify,
whisk the egg white until stiff. Beat the sorbet again until smooth. Fold in the egg
white. Return to the freezer until firm.
Transfer the sorbet to the refrigerator 20
minutes before serving. Decorate with pomegranate seeds and mint sprigs and serve.

Serves 4-6.

PISTACHIO ICE CREAM

8 oz/2 cups roasted pistachio nuts
8 oz/1 cup superfine sugar
4 egg yolks
16 fl oz/2 cups full-fat milk
10 fl oz/1¼ cups thick cream
4 fl oz/½ cup Greek yogurt
roughly chopped pistachio nuts, to decorate
quartered figs, to serve

Turn the freezer to its coldest setting. In a food processor finely ground the pistachio nuts with 1 tablespoon of the sugar.

Whisk the egg yolks and remaining sugar in a large bowl until thick and foamy. Put the pistachio nuts, milk and cream in a small saucepan and bring to the boil. Pour on to the egg yolk mixture, whisking constantly. Put the bowl over a pan of simmering water. Heat, stirring, for about 8 minutes, until the mixture is thick enough to coat the back of the spoon. Cover and leave to cool. Stir in the Greek yogurt.

Pour the mixture into a freezerproof container. Put in the freezer. When the sides are beginning to set, transfer to a bowl and beat thoroughly or process in a food processor or blender. Return to the container and freeze for 30-40 minutes. When the ice cream is just beginning to solidify, transfer to a bowl and beat again. Return to the freeze until firm. Transfer to the refrigerator 20 minutes before serving. Decorate with pistachios and serve with figs.

Serves 4-6.

COFFEE GRANITA

1½ oz finely ground espresso coffee
finely grated rind of 1 lemon
5 oz/2½ cup superfine sugar
1 tablespoon lemon juice

Put espresso coffee into a pan with 18 fl oz/ 2¼ cups water. Bring to the boil and remove from the heat. Add the lemon juice and leave to infuse for 5 minutes. Strain through a coffee filter.

Mix 5 fl oz/⅔ cup water with the superfine sugar until dissolved. Stir in infused coffee and lemon juice, leave to cool, then chill in the refrigerator. Pour into a shallow container to a depth of 2¾ in. Cover and freeze for 1 hour until the liquid has formed an ice rim around the edge and is starting to freeze on the base.

Scrape away ice rim with a fork and mash evenly with the remaining liquid. Repeat every 30 seconds until the mixture forms a smooth consistency of ice crystals. Serve in chilled glasses (frosted in freezer, if suitable) with a dollop of whipped cream, if wished.

Serves 8.

LAVENDER HONEY ICE CREAM

**5 sprigs lavender flowers
20 fl oz/2½ cups milk
6 oz lavender honey
4 egg yolks
5 fl oz/⅔ cup thick cream
5 fl oz/⅔ cup crème fraîche
lavender flowers, to decorate**

Turn the freezer to its coldest setting. Put the lavender sprigs and milk in a saucepan and heat almost to boiling point. Remove from the heat and discard the lavender sprigs.

Heat the honey in a small saucepan until just melted. Whisk the egg yolks in a large bowl until thick and foamy. Gradually whisk the melted honey into the egg yolks. Bring the milk back to the boil. Pour the boiling milk on to the egg yolks, whisking constantly. Put the bowl over a pan of simmering water. Heat, stirring, for about 8 minutes until the mixture is thick enough to coat the back of the spoon. Strain into a bowl, cover and leave to cool. Stir in the thick cream and crème fraîche.

Pour the mixture into a freezerproof container. Put in the freezer. When the sides are beginning to set, transfer to a bowl and beat thoroughly or process in a food processor or blender. Return to the container and freeze for 30-40 minutes. When the ice cream is just beginning to solidify, transfer to a bowl and beat again. Return to the freezer until firm. Transfer to the refrigerator 20 minutes before serving. Decorate with lavender flowers and serve.

Serves 4-6.

STRAWBERRY SORBET

**9 oz/1½ cups superfine sugar
1 lb fresh sweet strawberries
1 tablespoon balsamic vinegar**

Pour 8 fl oz/1 cup water into a saucepan and add the sugar. Heat gently to dissolve sugar, then bring to boil and boil for 1 minute. Cool then chill in refrigerator. Meanwhile, wash and hull the strawberries. Purée in a blender or food processor until smooth, and pass through a sieve, if liked. Chill the purée.

Stir the syrup into the chilled strawberry purée and add the balsamic vinegar. Freeze in an ice cream maker for the best results.

Alternatively, pour mixture into a shallow freezer tray and freeze until the sorbet is frozen around the edges. Mash well with a fork, beat and refreeze until almost solid. Repeat this twice more. Serve in chilled glass dishes.

Serves 6.

MOCHA ESPRESSO ICE CREAM

16 fl oz/2 cups milk
5 fl oz/⅔ cup thick cream
1 oz/⅓ cup medium ground espresso coffee
3 oz/3 squares dark chocolate, chopped
6 egg yolks
6 oz/¼ cup superfine sugar
chocolate shavings, to decorate

Place the milk, cream, coffee grains and 2 oz/ 2 squares of the chocolate in a small saucepan and heat slowly until almost boiling. Remove from the heat and set aside for 30 minutes for the flavors to infuse.

Beat the egg yolks and sugar together in a large bowl until thick and pale. Gradually beat in the mocha mixture and transfer to a clean saucepan. Heat gently, stirring, until the mixture thickens, but do not allow to boil. Leave to cool.

Transfer the mixture to a plastic container and freeze. Beat to mix and break up ice crystals after about 1 hour and again at hourly intervals until almost firm. Stir in the remaining chocolate, cover and allow to freeze completely. Remove from the freezer for 20 minutes before serving to allow ice cream to soften. Decorate with chocolate shavings, if wished.

Serves 4.

COFFEE BOMBE

12 fl oz/1⅓ cups light cream
5 fl oz/⅔ cup heavy cream
4 tablespoons Greek yogurt
2 teaspoons instant coffee powder
2oz/⅓ cup confectioners' sugar, sifted

In a large bowl, mix creams and yogurt together.

Dissolve coffee powder in 1 tablespoon warm water. Fold into cream mixture with the confectioners' sugar and mix gently but thoroughly. Pour mixture into a lightly greased 30 fl oz/3¼ cups bombe mold or pudding basin. Freeze until firm.

Transfer bombe to the refrigerator 45 minutes before serving to soften slightly. Turn out on to a serving dish.

Serves 8.

Variation: Decorate with flaked almonds, if wished.

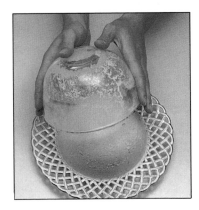

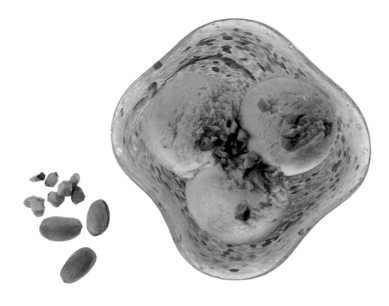

FEATHER-LIGHT TIRAMISU

3 tablespoons very strong cold espresso coffee
few drops of vanilla extract
1 tablespoon brandy or rum
3½ oz/⅓ cup vanilla sugar (see page 203)
2 egg whites
8 oz reduced-fat cream cheese
4 fl oz/½ cup reduced-fat crème fraîche
18 sponge fingers (ladyfingers)
2 oz/2 squares dark chocolate, grated

In a bowl, mix together coffee, vanilla and brandy. In another bowl, beat sugar and cream cheese together. Whisk crème fraîche until just holding its shape and fold into the cream cheese mixture.

In a clean bowl, whisk the egg whites until forming soft peaks, then fold into the cheese and cream mixture.

Break half the ladyfingers into pieces and place on the bottom of 6 glasses. Drizzle with half the coffee mixture. Spoon on half the cream mixture and sprinkle with half the grated chocolate. Repeat with remaining ingredients, finishing with grated chocolate. Chill until firm and serve within 1 day.

Serves 6.

PISTACHIO HALVA ICE CREAM

3 egg yolks
4 oz/½ cup superfine sugar
10 fl oz/1¼ cups light cream
10 fl oz/1¼ cups heavy cream
4 oz pistachio halva
chopped pistachio nuts, to decorate

Turn freezer to its lowest setting. In a bowl, whisk together egg yolks and sugar until thick and pale. In a small saucepan, bring light cream to the boil, pour on to egg yolk mixture and mix well.

Transfer to double boiler or bowl placed over a pan of boiling water. Cook, stirring constantly, until thick enough to coat the back of a spoon. Strain into a bowl and leave to cool. In a bowl, whip heavy cream lightly, then whisk in custard. Crumble halva into mixture and stir in gently.

Pour into a freezerproof container. Cover and freeze for 3 hours or until half set. Stir well, then return to freezer until frozen. Remove from freezer 15 minutes before serving. Decorate with chopped pistachio nuts.

Serves 6.

BAKED MANGO CUSTARDS

2 large ripe mangoes
juice 1 lime
4 egg yolks
3 oz/⅓ cup superfine sugar
1 teaspoon ground ginger
¼ teaspoon ground mixed spice
20 fl oz/2½ cups thick cream
toasted flaked almonds, to decorate

Preheat oven to 325F (170C). Peel the mangoes, cut away and discard the pit and coarsely chop the flesh. Place in a blender or food processor, add the lime juice and purée until smooth.

Beat the egg yolks and spices together until pale and thick and stir in the mango purée. Put 16 fl oz/2 cups thick cream into a pan and heat until gently simmering. Beat into the mango mixture until evenly blended and pour into 8 ramekin dishes. Place in a roasting pan and pour in enough boiling water to come two-thirds of the way up the sides of the dishes. Bake for 30 minutes, remove from the oven and leave to cool, then chill for several hours.

Beat the remaining cream until stiff and spoon or pipe a swirl on to each custard and decorate with the almonds.

Makes 8.

BLACKCURRANT ICED TERRINE

16 fl oz/2 cups skimmed milk
4-5 tablespoons granulated sugar
3 teaspoons cornstarch
pinch of salt
3 egg yolks
5 fl oz/⅔ cup heavy cream
8 fl oz/1 cup light cream
1 teaspoon vanilla extract
8 oz blackcurrants
3 oz/½ cup confectioners' sugar, sifted
mint sprigs, to decorate

Put milk in a saucepan and heat gently until almost boiling.

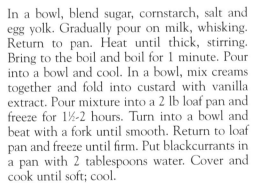

In a bowl, blend sugar, cornstarch, salt and egg yolk. Gradually pour on milk, whisking. Return to pan. Heat until thick, stirring. Bring to the boil and boil for 1 minute. Pour into a bowl and cool. In a bowl, mix creams together and fold into custard with vanilla extract. Pour mixture into a 2 lb loaf pan and freeze for 1½-2 hours. Turn into a bowl and beat with a fork until smooth. Return to loaf pan and freeze until firm. Put blackcurrants in a pan with 2 tablespoons water. Cover and cook until soft; cool.

In a blender or food processor, blend blackberries and confectioners' sugar together until smooth. The sauce may be sieved at this stage to remove pips, if wished. To serve terrine, transfer to the refrigerator for 30 minutes before serving to soften. Turn terrine out on to a serving plate and pour blackcurrant sauce over the top. Decorate with mint.

Serves 8.

PETITS POTS AU CHOCOLAT

20 fl oz/2½ cups light cream or milk
1 vanilla bean
butter for greasing
1 egg
5 egg yolks
3 tablespoons superfine sugar
8 oz bitter chocolate, chopped
1 tablespoon instant coffee granules
whipped cream and chocolate shavings to decorate

Put cream or milk and vanilla bean into a small saucepan and bring to the boil over a low heat. Cover, remove from heat and leave to infuse for 15 minutes.

Preheat oven to 300F (150C). Butter individual custard pots or ramekins and put in a roasting pan. Put egg yolks and sugar in a large bowl and whisk together until thick and pale. Remove vanilla bean from cream or milk and return to the boil.

Remove milk from heat, add chocolate and coffee and stir until dissolved. Stir into egg mixture. Strain into pots. Pour boiling water into roasting pan to come halfway up sides of pots and bake for about 1 hour, until very lightly set. Transfer pots to a wire rack and leave to cool. Chill. Decorate with whipped cream and chocolate shavings and serve.

Serves 6-8.

BRAMBLE JELLY RING

8 oz blackberries
8 oz raspberries
2oz/¼ cup superfine sugar
5 teaspoons powdered gelatine
10 fl oz/1¼ cups unsweetened apple juice
fresh berries and herb sprigs, to decorate

Place blackberries and raspberries in a saucepan with 10 fl oz/1¼ cups water and the sugar. Simmer over a low heat until soft. Allow to cool.

Purée fruit mixture in a blender or food processor, then press through sieve, until all the juice has been extracted. Discard pips. Sprinkle gelatine over 3 tablespoons water in a small bowl and leave for 2-3 minutes to soften. Stand bowl in a saucepan of hot water and stir until gelatine has dissolved. Cool slightly.

Stir gelatine into fruit juice mixture with apple juice. Mix well and pour into a wetted 30 fl oz/3¾ cup ring mold. Chill in the refrigerator until set. To serve, turn out of mold and decorate with fresh berries and herb sprigs.

Serves 4.

COEURS À LA CRÈME

16 fl oz/2 cups fromage frais or curd cheese
8 fl oz/1 cup thick cream
3 egg whites
TO SERVE:
sugar or vanilla sugar
fresh fruit

Line 6 individual coeurs à la crème molds with pieces of cheesecloth.

In a large bowl, beat fromage frais or curd cheese until smooth, then whisk in cream. Whisk egg whites until stiff. Fold into the cheese mixture. Spoon into molds, put molds in a roasting pan or on a tray and leave in the refrigerator for 12-24 hours, to drain; the longer the mixture is left, the firmer it becomes.

Turn molds on to chilled serving plates. Decorate with mint sprigs and serve with sugar or vanilla sugar and fresh fruit.

Serves 6.

Note: To make vanilla sugar, simply store a vanilla bean in a jar of sugar, so that it absorbs the flavor.

OEUFS À LA NEIGE

3 eggs, separated
4 oz/½ cup superfine sugar
2 egg yolks
16 fl oz/2 cups milk
1½-2 tablespoons Cointreau or orange flower water
  or rose water
strips of orange rind and mint sprigs, to decorate

Whisk egg whites until stiff but not dry. Gradually whisk in half the sugar until mixture is stiff and shiny. Meanwhile, bring a large skillet of water to the boil.

Lower heat beneath pan so water is barely simmering. Float dessertspoons of egg white on to water, a few at a time so they are not crowded, and poach for 2-3 minutes, turning halfway through. Remove with a slotted spoon, transfer to a tilted tray and leave to drain. Whisk all 5 egg yolks with remaining sugar until thick and pale. Put milk into a saucepan and bring to the boil.

Stir a little milk into egg yolk mixture then, over a low heat, stir back into milk. Cook gently, stirring, until thickened slightly: do not boil. Leave to cool, stirring occasionally. Just before serving, add Cointreau or flower water and pour custard into shallow serving bowls. Float meringues on top, decorate with orange rind and mint sprigs and serve.

Serves 4-6.

LYCHEES & COCONUT CUSTARD

3 egg yolks
3-4 tablespoons caster sugar
7 fl oz/scant 1 cup coconut milk
3 fl oz/⅓ cup coconut cream
about 1 tablespoon triple distilled rose water
red food coloring
about 16 fresh lychees, peeled, halved and pits
   removed
rose petals, to decorate

In a bowl, whisk together egg yolks and sugar.

In a medium, preferably non-stick, saucepan, heat coconut milk to just below boiling point, then slowly stir into bowl. Return to pan and cook very gently, stirring with a wooden spoon, until custard coats the back of the spoon.

Remove from heat and stir in coconut cream, rose water to taste and sufficient red food coloring to color pale pink. Leave until cold, stirring occasionally. Spoon a thin layer of rose-flavored custard into 4 small serving bowls. Arrange lychees on custard. Decorate with rose petals. Serve remaining custard separately to pour over lychees.

Serves 4.

EXOTIC FRUIT BRÛLÉE

3 egg yolks
2oz/¼ cup vanilla sugar
5 fl oz/⅔ cup crème fraîche
2 teaspoons kirsch or brandy
1 small ripe mango, peeled
1 small ripe pear, peeled, quartered and cored
1 large ripe fig
8 large ripe strawberries, hulled
freshly grated nutmeg
tuille biscuits, to serve

Preheat broiler. Beat the egg yolks and sugar together until pale and thick and stir in the crème fraîche and kirsch or brandy; set aside. Remove the mango pit and cut the flesh into thin slices; slice the pear, fig and strawberries thinly. Arrange all the fruit over the bases of 4 individual gratin dishes or flameproof plates.

Carefully pour a quarter of the sauce over each dish, as evenly as possible, to cover the fruit and grate over a little fresh nutmeg. Place under medium broiler and cook for 3-4 minutes until the sauce is lightly caramelized. Cool slightly and serve with tuille or other sweet cookies.

Serves 4.

RICOTTA & COFFEE DESSERT

CRÈME CARAMEL

12 oz reduced-fat ricotta cheese, at room
  temperature
12 oz reduced-fat cream cheese, at room temperature
1 tablespoon rum
2 tablespoons brandy or Tia Maria
few drops of vanilla essence
2 tablespoons espresso ground Italian roast coffee
3 tablespoons confectioners' sugar
5 fl oz/⅔ cup whipping cream
2 oz chocolate shavings, to decorate

Sieve ricotta and mascarpone together, then
beat with a wooden spoon. Do not attempt
to do this in a food processor.

20 fl oz/2½ cups milk
1 vanilla bean
2 eggs
2 egg yolks
3 oz/⅓ cup sugar
mint sprigs, to decorate
CARAMEL:
4 oz/¾ cup superfine sugar

To make caramel, put superfine sugar in a
small heavy saucepan with 5 tablespoons
water and heat gently until sugar has dissolved. Increase heat and boil until golden
brown.

Beat in the rum, brandy, vanilla and ground
coffee. Taste and add confectioners' sugar.
Carefully spoon mixture into small freezerproof dishes or demi-tasse cups, piling the
mixture high. Place in freezer for 30 minutes
and transfer to the refrigerator to soften
slightly for about 10 minutes before serving
it. The dessert should be only just frozen or
very chilled.

Remove from heat and pour into six 5 fl oz/⅔
cup ramekins, turning dishes to coat sides
with caramel. Put in a roasting pan and leave
to cook. Preheat oven to 325F (170C). Put
milk and vanilla bean into a small saucepan
and bring to the boil. Cover, remove from
the heat and leave to infuse for 20 minutes.
Put eggs, egg yolks and sugar in a large bowl
and whisk together. Remove vanilla bean
from milk and return milk to the boil. Stir
into egg mixture.

Just before serving, whisk the whipping
cream to soft peaks and spoon a blob on top
of each dessert, then sprinkle with chocolate
flakes. Place on saucers and serve at once.

Serves 6.

Strain into ramekins. Pour boiling water into
roasting pan to come halfway up sides of
ramekins and bake for 40-50 minutes, until
lightly set. Remove from pan and leave to
cool. One hour before serving, run knife
around edge of caramels and turn out on to
serving plates. Decorate with mint and serve.

Serves 6.

MANGO WITH STICKY RICE

8 oz/1¼ cups sticky rice, soaked overnight in cold
   water
8 oz/1 cup coconut milk
pinch salt
2-4 tablespoons sugar, to taste
2 large ripe mangoes, peeled and halved
3 tablespoons coconut cream
mint leaves to decorate

Drain and rinse rice thoroughly. Place in a
steaming basket lined with a double thickness of cheesecloth. Steam over simmering
water for 30 minutes. Remove from heat.

In a bowl, stir together coconut milk, salt
and sugar to taste until sugar has dissolved.
Stir in warm rice. Set aside for 30 minutes.

Thinly slice mangoes by cutting lengthwise
through flesh to the pit. Discard the pits.
Spoon rice into a mound in center of serving
plates and arrange mango slices around. Pour
coconut cream over rice. Decorate with mint
leaves.

Serves 4.

ORANGE 'FLAN'

grated rind 1 orange
10 fl oz/1¼ cups fresh orange juice
3 whole eggs
3 egg yolks
2 tablespoons superfine sugar
orange slices and mint, to decorate
CARAMEL:
4 oz/½ cup superfine sugar

Put orange rind and orange juice in a small
bowl; set aside to soak. Preheat oven to 350F
(180C). Warm 4 ramekin dishes.

To make the caramel, gently heat sugar in 1
tablespoon water in a small, heavy-based
saucepan, swirling pan, until sugar has dissolved, then cook until golden brown.
Immediately pour a quarter into each dish
and swirl them around so caramel coats sides
and base. Put in a baking pan. Gently heat
orange juice and orange rind to just below
simmering point.

Meanwhile, whisk whole eggs and egg yolks
with sugar until thick, then slowly pour in
orange juice and rind, whisking constantly.
Divide between dishes then pour boiling
water around them. Cover dishes with baking parchment then bake for about 25
minutes until lightly set. Remove dishes
from baking pan and leave until cold. Just
before serving, unmold puddings on to cold
plates. Decorate with orange and mint.

Serves 4.

LYCHEE & GINGER MOUSSE

COCONUT CUSTARD

12 oz fresh lychees, peeled and pitted
½ teaspoon ground ginger
3 tablespoons ginger wine
2 pieces stem ginger in syrup, chopped
1 oz ground almonds
2 teaspoons powdered gelatine dissolved in 2
**   tablespoons boiling water**
2 egg whites
sliced stem ginger and mint leaves, to decorate

Place lychees in a food processor with the ground ginger, ginger wine and chopped ginger. Blend until smooth. Transfer to a small bowl and stir in ground almonds and gelatine mixture.

Chill for 30-40 minutes, or until beginning to set. In a large, grease-free bowl, whisk the egg whites until very stiff. Using a large metal spoon, carefully fold in the lychee mixture.

Divide mixture between 4 sundae glasses or dishes and chill in the refrigerator for 1 hour or until set. Decorate with stem ginger and mint leaves and serve.

Serves 4.

3 eggs
2 egg yolks
16 fl oz/2 cups coconut milk
3 oz/⅓ cup superfine sugar
few drops rosewater or jasmine extract
toasted coconut, to decorate

Preheat the oven to 350F (180C). Place 4 individual heatproof dishes in a baking pan.

In a bowl, stir together eggs, egg yolks, coconut milk, sugar and rosewater or jasmine essence until sugar dissolves. Pass through a sieve into dishes. Pour boiling water into baking pan to surround dishes.

Cook in oven for about 20 minutes until custards are slightly set in center. Remove from baking pan and allow to cool slightly before unmolding. Serve warm or cold. Decorate with coconut.

Serves 4.

PEARS WITH CHOCOLATE SAUCE

4 oz/½ cup ricotta cheese
2oz/½ cup ground hazelnuts
2 tablespoons clear honey
2 small egg yolks
seeds from 1 cardamom pod, crushed
4 large pears
CHOCOLATE SAUCE:
4 oz plain chocolate
1½ oz/3 tablespoons unsalted butter
2 tablespoons brandy
2 tablespoons thick sour cream

Cream together the ricotta cheese, hazelnuts, honey, egg yolks and crushed cardamom seeds.

Preheat oven to 375F (190C). Cut a thin slice from the base of each pear and using a corer or small spoon, carefully scoop out the core as far up inside the pear as possible, without damaging the flesh. Fill cavities with the ricotta mixture, pressing in well; smooth the bases flat. Peel the pears and place in a small roasting pan. Cover with foil and bake for 45-50 minutes until pears are cooked.

Just before pears are cooked, place the chocolate, butter, brandy and thick sour cream in a small pan and heat gently until melted. Stir well and keep warm. Transfer the cooked pears to serving plates, slice in half to reveal filling and pour over the sauce. Serve immediately.

Serves 4.

COFFEE BRÛLÉE

8 egg yolks
4 oz/½ cup superfine sugar
8 oz/2 cups thick cream
1 teaspoon coffee essence
summer berries, to decorate
TOPPING;
2oz/¼ cup superfine sugar

In a large bowl, beat together the egg yolks and sugar until light and foamy.

Put the milk, cream and coffee essence in a flameproof casserole. Heat gently but do not boil. Remove from the heat and leave to cool. Preheat oven to 300F (150C). Pour the milk mixture on to the egg yolk mixture and stir well. Pour into a large jug and allow the froth to rise to the surface. Skim off the froth. Pour the mixture back into the casserole.

Put a piece of baking parchment in a roasting pan. Put the casserole on top of the paper. Pour enough boiling water into the pan to come halfway up the sides of the casserole. Bake for 45 minutes, until the mixture has set. Leave to cool then chill. To make the topping, preheat the broiler. Sprinkle the top of the custard with the sugar and broil until the sugar melts and turns a deep golden brown. Decorate with summer berries and serve.

Serves 6.

ZABAGLIONE

4 egg yolks
2½ oz vanilla sugar
4 fl oz/½ cup Marsala
ladyfingers, to serve

With an electric whisk, whisk the egg yolks and sugar together in a large heatproof bowl until pale and fluffy. Place the bowl over a pan of gently simmering water. Mix in the Marsala.

Start whisking slowly. Gradually whisk faster until the mixture doubles in volume and becomes very thick and glossy. Take care not to overheat or the mixture will scramble.

Spoon the zabaglione into heatproof glasses or ramekins and serve immediately with ladyfingers.

Serves 6.

Note: To make vanilla sugar, simply store a vanilla pod in a jar of sugar and leave for at least 2-3 weeks for it to flavor the sugar.

SWEET DESSERT COUSCOUS

9 oz couscous
4 oz fresh dates
4 oz ready-to-eat prunes
3 oz/⅓ cup butter, melted
2oz/¼ cup superfine sugar
1 teaspoon ground cinnamon
½ teaspoon ground nutmeg
rose petals, to decorate

Place the couscous in a bowl and cover with 5 fl oz/⅔ cup warm water. Leave for 15 minutes to swell.

Halve each date lengthwise, remove the pit and cut into 4. Roughly chop the prunes. Fluff up the grains of couscous with a fork then place in a couscoussière or in a cheese-cloth-lined colander and steam over simmering water for 15 minutes until hot.

Transfer to a bowl, fluff up again with a fork. Add the melted butter, sugar, dates and prunes. Pile the couscous in a cone shape in a serving dish. Mix the cinnamon and nutmeg together and sprinkle in delicate trails over the couscous. Serve, decorated with rose petals.

Serves 4.

TROPICAL CHOUX RING

2oz/¼ cup butter
2½ oz/½ cup all-purpose flour
2 eggs, beaten
14 fl oz/1¾ cups low fat ready-made cold custard
1 papaya, peeled, seeds removed and chopped
2 kiwi fruit, peeled and chopped
1 starfruit, sliced
2 tablespoons confectioners' sugar

Preheat oven to 400F (200C). Place butter in a saucepan with 5 fl oz/⅔ cup water. Heat gently until fat has melted, then bring mixture to the boil.

Remove saucepan from heat. Add flour to hot mixture and beat thoroughly with a wooden spoon. Beat mixture until it is smooth and forms a ball in the center of the pan. Allow mixture to cool slightly, then gradually add eggs, beating well after each addition, until pastry dough is smooth and shiny. Drop tablespoons of dough on to a greased baking sheet to form a ring. Bake in oven for 40 minutes until risen and golden brown. Remove from oven carefully, transfer to a wire rack and immediately slice ring horizontally in half to release steam inside.

Allow to cool completely. In a bowl, gently mix together custard and prepared fruit. Spoon fruit mixture on to bottom of pastry ring. Replace top of pastry ring. Sprinkle with sifted confectioners' sugar to serve.

Serves 8.

Note: Place the tablespoons of dough so that they are just touching on the baking sheet.

LOGANBERRY LAYER DESSERT

8 oz loganberries
8 fl oz/1 cup heavy cream
20 fl oz/2½ cups low fat fromage frais
2oz/½ cup confectioners' sugar, sifted
fresh loganberries and herb sprigs, to decorate

Place loganberries in a saucepan with 2 tablespoons water. Cook gently until just softened. Cool slightly, then purée in a blender or food processor. Cool completely. In a bowl, whip cream until thick.

In a separate bowl, gently mix together puréed loganberries, half the cream, half the fromage frais and 1 oz/¼ cup confectioners' sugar. In another bowl, gently mix together remaining cream, fromage frais and confectioners' sugar.

Layer loganberry mixture and fromage frais mixture in 6 glasses, finishing with a loganberry layer. Chill in the refrigerator until ready to serve. Decorate desserts with fresh loganberries and herb sprigs before serving.

Serves 6.

CHOC & STRAWBERRY ROULADE

3 eggs
4 oz/½ cup superfine sugar
3 oz/¾ cup all-purpose flour
1 oz/¼ cup cocoa powder
8 oz/1 cup skimmed milk soft cheese
12 teaspoons strawberry jam
6 oz strawberries
1 tablespoon confectioners' sugar

Preheat oven to 400F (200C). Grease a 13 × 9 in. jelly roll pan. Line with baking parchment and grease the paper. In a bowl placed over a pan of hot water, whisk eggs and sugar until creamy.

Remove bowl from heat and whisk until cool. Sift flour and cocoa powder over egg mixture, add 1 tablespoon hot water and fold in gently with a metal spoon. Pour mixture into prepared pan and tilt tin to level the surface. Bake in oven for 12-15 minutes until well risen, golden brown and firm to touch. Turn out on to a sheet of baking parchment, cut off crisp edges and roll up with paper inside. Leave to cool.

Unroll gently and spread with soft cheese and jam. Slice strawberries and place on jam, reserving a few for decoration. Roll up again and place on a serving dish. Dust with sifted confectioners' sugar and decorate with remaining strawberry slices before serving.

Serves 6.

LEMON CUSTARD SLICES

8 oz puff pastry, thawed if frozen
FILLING:
1 oz/3 tablespoons cornstarch
2oz/¼ cup superfine sugar
5 fl oz/⅔ cup milk
juice 1 lemon
grated rind ½ lemon
1 egg yolk
4 fl oz/½ cup thick cream
TO DECORATE:
3 oz/½ cup confectioners' sugar
2 kiwi fruit, peeled and sliced

Preheat oven to 450F (230C). On a floured surface, roll pastry out thinly to a rectangle 12 × 10 in. With a sharp, floured knife, cut pastry into 8 rectangles. Prick all over with a fork. Place pastry slices on a dampened baking sheet. Bake in the oven for 10-15 minutes until well risen and golden brown. Transfer to a wire rack to cool. Split slices in half.

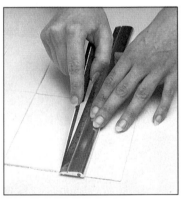

To make filling, smoothly blend cornstarch with sugar and milk in a saucepan; boil, stirring, until mixture thickens. Stir in lemon juice and rind. Beat in egg yolk. Cover and leave to cool. Beat in cream. Mix confectioners' sugar with about 6 teaspoons water to make a smooth paste. Spread over one side of 8 pastry slices. Leave to set. Spread custard over remaining pastry slices. Top with iced slices. Decorate with kiwi fruit.

Makes 8.

DOUBLE CHOCOLATE GÂTEAU

8 oz/1 cup soft butter
8 oz/1¼ cups superfine sugar
4 eggs, beaten
6 oz/1½ cups self-raising flour
2oz/½ cup cocoa
FILLING:
8 fl oz/1 cup whipping cream
5 oz/5 squares white chocolate
FROSTING:
12 oz dark chocolate
4 oz/½ cup butter
3 fl oz/⅓ cup thick cream
TO DECORATE:
4 oz dark chocolate
2 teaspoons confectioners' sugar and cocoa mixed

Preheat oven to 350F (180C). Grease a 8 in. deep round pan and line the base with non-stick paper. In bowl, beat together butter and sugar until light and fluffy. Gradually beat in eggs. Sift together flour and cocoa. Fold into mixture, then spoon into pan. Bake in the oven for 45-50 minutes until springy to the touch and a skewer inserted into the center comes out clean. Leave in pan for 5 minutes, then remove to a wire rack to cool completely.

To make the filling, heat the cream in a saucepan to just below boiling point. In a food processor, chop white chocolate. With motor running, pour hot cream through feed tube and process for 10-15 seconds until smooth. Transfer to a bowl, cover with plastic wrap and chill overnight. The next day whisk the filling until just beginning to hold soft peaks.

To make the frosting, melt chocolate in a bowl over pan of hot water. Stir in butter and cream. Leave to cool, stirring occasionally until mixture is a thick spreading consistency.

To make chocolate curls for decoration, melt chocolate in a bowl over pan of hot water. Spread one-quarter of the chocolate over a baking sheet. Chill sheet for a few minutes until chocolate loses its gloss and is just set, but not hard. Using a palette knife, scrape off large shavings of chocolate, transferring them to a baking sheet lined with non-stick paper. Chill until set. Make 3 more batches of shavings in the same way.

Slice the cake horizontally into 3 layers. Sandwich layers together with white chocolate filling. Cover top and sides of cake with chocolate frosting. Arrange chocolate shavings over top of cake. Sift mixed confectioners' sugar and cocoa over cake.

Makes 10 slices.

HOT CHOCOLATE SOUFFLÉ

BAKED RICOTTA CHEESECAKE

3 oz dark chocolate
5 fl oz/⅔ cup skimmed milk
2oz/¼ cup superfine sugar
2oz/¼ cup all-purpose flour
½ oz/1 tablespoon low fat spread
4 eggs, separated
1 tablespoon confectioners' sugar

Preheat oven to 400F (200C). Grease a 40 fl oz/5 cup soufflé dish. Melt chocolate in a small bowl set over a pan of simmering water.

Place milk and sugar in a saucepan and heat gently until almost boiling. Add chocolate and mix well. In a bowl, blend flour with 2 tablespoons water. Gradually add chocolate mixture, blending well. Return to saucepan, bring gently to the boil, stirring continuously, and cook for 3 minutes. Add low fat spread in small pieces, mix well and leave to cool.

Stir in egg yolks. In a bowl, whisk egg whites until stiff. Using a metal spoon, fold egg whites into chocolate mixture. Pour into soufflé dish and bake in oven for about 35 minutes until well risen and firm to touch. Dust with sifted confectioners' sugar and serve immediately.

Serves 6.

12 oz ricotta cheese
3 eggs, separated
3½ oz superfine sugar
3 tablespoons dark rum
1 teaspoon vanilla extract
finely grated rind of 2 lemons
2 oz ground almonds
2 oz sultanas, soaked in warm water and drained
fresh seasonal fruit, to serve

Preheat oven to 350F (180C). Grease, lightly flour and base-line a 8 in. spring-form pan. Sieve the ricotta into a large bowl and beat in the egg yolks and sugar.

Beat in rum, vanilla and lemon rind. Fold in ground almonds and sultanas. Whisk the egg whites until soft peaks form, then gently fold them into the cheese mixture. Gently spoon into prepared tins and level the surface. Bake in oven for 30-40 minutes until firm and slightly shrunken from the sides of the pan.

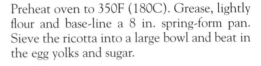

Open the oven door, switch off heat and leave cheesecake inside to cool completely, then chill in refrigerator. To serve, remove cheesecake from pan and top with seasonal fruits. Dust with confectioners' sugar.

Serves 6.

CHERRY CHIMICHANGAS

2 tablespoons arrowroot
10 fl oz/1¼ cups water
2 tablespoons granulated sugar
8 oz ripe red cherries, rinsed, stalks removed, pitted
grated rind of 1 orange
8 wheat tortillas
3 oz/⅓ cup butter
2 oz confectioners' sugar
2 oz toasted slivered almonds to decorate

STRAWBERRY PROFITEROLES

2½ oz/½ cup all-purpose flour
2 oz/¼ cup low fat spread
2 eggs, beaten
5 fl oz/⅔ cup heavy cream
8 oz strawberries
1 oz/2 tablespoons confectioners' sugar

Preheat oven to 400F (200C). Line 2 baking sheets with baking parchment. Sift flour on to a plate. Put low fat spread and 5 fl oz/⅔ cup water into a saucepan, heat gently untl fat has melted, then bring to the boil. Remove from heat, add flour and beat until mixture leaves the sides of the pan.

In a saucepan mix the arrowroot with a little of the water to a smooth paste. Gradually stir in the remaining water, then the granulated sugar. Bring to the boil over a medium heat, stirring. Simmer for 2 minutes. Remove from the heat and stir in the cherries and orange rind. Divide cherry mixture between the tortillas. Fold each tortilla in half, then in half again.

Gradually beat in eggs until mixture is smooth and shiny. Put mixture into a piping bag fitted with a medium plain tip and pipe walnut-sized balls onto prepared baking sheets. Bake in oven for 20-25 minutes until brown and crisp. Make a slit in side of each profiterole to allow steam to escape, then cool on a wire rack. In a bowl, whisk cream until stiff and spoon into a piping bag fitted with a medium plain tip. Pipe some cream into each profiterole.

Heat the butter in a skillet. Add 2 filled tortillas and fry gently for 2½ minutes each side until golden brown. Transfer to a warmed serving plate and keep warm. Repeat with remaining tortillas, adding more butter if necessary. Sieve over confectioners' sugar and decorate with toasted almonds.

Serves 4-8.

Halve strawberries and place some strawberries into each profiteroile. Pile profiteroles into a pyramid on a serving plate and dust with sifted confectioners' sugar. Serve immediately.

Serves 8.

NECTARINE MERINGUE NESTS

3 egg whites
6 oz/¾ cup superfine sugar
4 oz/½ cup soft cheese
5 fl oz/⅔ cup fromage frais
3 nectarines
4 oz blackcurrants
2 tablespoons apricot jam

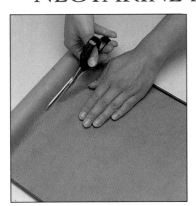

Preheat oven to 300F (150C). Line a large baking sheet with non-stick baking parchment. In a large bowl, whisk egg whites stiffly. Gradually add sugar, beating well after each addition, until mixture is stiff and glossy.

Spoon meringue into a piping bag fitted with a star tip and pipe meringue in six 4 in. rounds on to the lined baking sheet, leaving a gap between them. Pipe remaining meringue in stars around the edge of each round to form an attractive border. Bake meringue nests in oven for 1-1½ hours until crisp on the outside. Cool on a wire rack. In a bowl, stir together soft cheese and fromage frais, mixing well. Peel and pit nectarines and slice thinly. Top and tail blackcurrants, wash and drain well.

In a saucepan, gently heat apricot jam with 1 tablespoon water until warm. To fill each meringue nest, place some cheese mixture in the nest. Top with sliced nectarines and blackcurrants, then brush with warmed jam to glaze. Refrigerate until ready to serve.

Serves 6.

TIA MARIA CHOUX RING

1 quantity Choux Pastry (see page 204)
2 tablespoons all-purpose flour
2 tablespoons cornstarch
2oz/¼ cup superfine sugar
10 fl oz/1¼ cups milk
3 egg yolks
5 fl oz/⅔ cup whipping cream
coffee extract
2 teaspoons Tia Maria
4 oz/½ cup confectioners' sugar

Preheat oven to 425F (220C). Put pastry in a piping bag fitted with a ½ in. plain tip.

Pipe a double 8 in. ring on to a paper-lined baking sheet. Bake ring in the oven for 20 minutes. Lower the temperature to 350F (180C); bake for a further 10-15 minutes until golden brown and hollow. Split horizontally; cool on a wire rack. Sift flour and cornstarch into a bowl. Stir in sugar and 2 tablespoons milk. Stir to form a thick paste. Whisk in egg yolks. In a saucepan, heat remaining milk to just below boiling point. Pour on to egg mixture, stirring occasionally.

Strain mixture back into saucepan and cook gently, stirring constantly, until thickened. Cover closely with cling film and leave until cold. In a bowl, stiffly whip cream and fold into custard. Stir in 2 teaspoons coffee extract and the Tia Maria. Sandwich choux rings together with coffee filling. In a bowl mix together sifted confectioners' sugar, few drops of coffee extract and about 3 teaspoons water. Spoon over cake and leave to set.

Serves 8

CHOC ALMOND MERINGUE

ORIENTAL FRUIT PAVLOVA

MERINGUE:
4 egg whites
8 oz/1¼ cups superfine sugar
4 oz/¼ cup ground almonds
FILLING:
6 oz/6 squares dark chocolate
1½ oz unsalted butter
3 tablespoons black coffee
3 tablespoons brandy
6 fl oz/¼ cup whipping cream
TO DECORATE:
chopped, toasted almonds

Preheat oven to 275F (140C). Line 2 baking sheets with non-stick paper.

To make meringue, whisk egg whites in a bowl until stiff; whisk in half the sugar. In another bowl, mix together remaining sugar and ground almonds. Carefully fold into meringue mixture. Pipe or spread meringue in two 8 in. rounds on the prepared baking sheets. Bake in the oven for about 1½ hours until completely dry. Transfer to wire racks to cool.

To make filling, break chocolate into pieces and put into a bowl with butter, coffee and brandy. Set over a pan of simmering water. When melted, stir and set aside to cool. Whip cream lightly; stir in chocolate mixture. Sandwich meringue rounds together with most of the chocolate cream. Put remaining cream into a piping bag and pipe rosettes on top of cake. Decorate with toasted almonds.

Serves 8.

3 egg whites
6 oz/¾ cup superfine sugar
few drops vanilla extract
½ teaspoon white wine vinegar
1 teaspoon cornstarch
10 fl oz/1¼ cups heavy cream
12 oz prepared fresh fruit, such as starfruit, lychees, mango, lemon and dates

Preheat oven to 300F (150C). Draw a 7 in. circle on a sheet of non-stick baking parchment and place paper, mark-side down, on a baking sheet. In a large bowl, whisk egg whites until stiff.

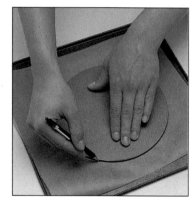

Whisk in half the sugar then, using a metal spoon, gently fold in remaining sugar together with vanilla extract, vinegar and cornstarch. Spread meringue over the circle on the paper, building sides up higher than the center. Bake in oven for 1-1½ hours until meringue is crisp and dry. Cook on a wire rack, then carefully peel off the paper.

In a bowl, whip cream until pale. Place meringue on a serving plate, pile cream into the center and arrange prepared fresh fruit decoratively on top. Serve immediately.

Serves 8.

Note: An electric or hand whisk can be used to make meringue mixtures.

CUSTARD PIES

2 eggs separated
4 oz/½ cup superfine sugar
2oz/⅓ cup semolina
20 fl oz/2½ cups milk
3 oz/⅓ cup butter
8 sheets filo pastry
confectioners' sugar and ground cinnamon, to
  decorate

In a bowl, beat together egg yolks, sugar, semolina and a little of the milk until creamy.

In a saucepan, heat remaining milk until almost boiling. Gradually whisk milk into egg mixture. Return to saucepan. Cook gently, stirring, for 5 minutes until mixture thickens. Stir in a knob of butter. Cover surface closely with plastic wrap. Leave until cold. In a bowl, whisk egg whites until holding peaks. Fold in custard. Preheat oven to 400F (200C). Butter a baking sheet.

In a small pan, melt remaining butter. Brush a sheet of pastry with butter. Place another sheet on top; brush with butter. Repeat with 2 more sheets. Cut pastry into 12 squares. Put a little custard mixture in middle of each square. Draw edges of pastry together to form a pouch. Pinch 'neck' firmly together. Repeat with remaining pastry and filling. Place pies on baking sheets. Bake in the oven for 15 minutes until golden brown. Dust with confectioners' sugar and cinnamon.

Makes 24.

HONEY CHEESECAKES

1 tablespoon raisins
1 tablespoon orange flower water
8 oz/1 cup cream cheese
3 tablespoons orange blossom honey
2 small eggs, beaten
mint leaves, to decorate
PASTRY:
5 oz/2¼ cups all-purpose flour
3 oz/⅓ cup butter
3 tablespoons confectioners' sugar
1 egg yolk
CARAMELIZED ORANGE PEEL:
4 oz/½ cup superfine sugar
1 oz orange peel, cut into julienne strips

Put raisins and orange flower water in a small bowl to soak. Make the pastry. Sift flour into a bowl. Run in butter until mixture resembles breadcrumbs. Stir in confectioners' sugar. Mix in egg yolk and a little water to make a firm dough. Chill for 30 minutes. Make the candied orange peel. Put sugar and 3½ fl oz/⅓ cup water into a saucepan. Heat gently until sugar is dissolved. Bring to the boil and boil for 2 minutes. Blanch orange peel for 2-3 minutes in boiling water. Drain, add to syrup and cook for 20 minutes until peel is transparent.

Preheat oven to 350F (180C). On a floured surface, roll pastry thinly. Use to line 4 deep loose-bottomed 4 in. quiche pans. In a bowl, beat together raisins, cream cheese, honey and eggs. Pour into pastry cases. Bake in the oven for 25-30 minutes until set and golden. Decorate with candied orange peel and mint leaves.

Makes 4.

FIG TARTS

12 oz ready-made puff pastry
confectioners' sugar for dusting
9 oz marzipan
12 fresh figs
1 tablespoon clear honey

Preheat the oven to 400F (200C). On a floured surface, roll out the pastry to a thickness of ¼ in.

Cut out 6 × 5 in. pastry circles and place on a baking tray. Dust a work surface with confectioners' sugar and roll out the marzipan to a rectangle 12 × 8 in. Cut out six 4 in. circles and place one on each pastry circle.

Slice the figs thinly across and arrange overlapping slices on the marzipan circles (2 figs to each tart). Bake in the oven for 25 minutes or until the pastry is risen and golden. Brush the tops of the tarts with honey and serve, warm or cold.

Serves 6.

FOREST FRUITS CHEESECAKE

1½ oz low fat spread
4 oz semi-sweet wheatmeal cookies crushed
8 oz mixed berries, such as raspberries, strawberries, blackberries, black- and redcurrants
3 tablespoons powdered gelatine
4 oz/½ cup skimmed milk soft cheese
1½ oz/3 tablespoons superfine sugar
5 fl oz/⅔ cup low fat fromage frais
5 fl oz/⅔ cup heavy cream
1 tablespoon blackcurrant jam
fresh mixed berries, to decorate

Melt low fat spread in a saucepan over a low heat. Mix in cookie crumbs.

Press mixture into a 8 in. loose-bottomed pan, so that it covers the base. Chill. Place mixed berries in a saucepan with 3 tablespoons water and simmer gently until soft. Cool completely. Sprinkle gelatine over 3 tablespoons water in a small bowl and leave for 2-3 minutes to soften. Place bowl over a saucepan of hot water and stir until dissolved. Leave to cool slightly. Place soft cheese, sugar, fromage frais, cream, cooked fruit, jam and gelatine in a food processor or blender and blend until smooth.

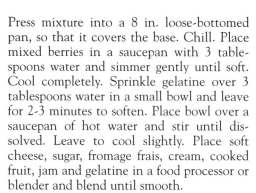

Pour on to cookie base and chill in the refrigerator until set. To serve, remove from the pan, place on a serving plate and decorate with mixed berries.

Serves 8.

Note: To crush cookies easily, place them in a large plastic bag and roll over the bag with a rolling pin until cookies are crushed.

FIG & ORANGE TART

8 oz/1½ cups no-soak dried figs, chopped
juice of 2 lemons
3 oz/⅓ cup butter, diced
2 eggs, beaten
2 tablespoons pine nuts
confectioners' sugar, for dusting
orange slices, to decorate
PASTRY:
5 oz/1¼ cups all-purpose flour
3 oz/⅓ cup butter
2 tablespoons confectioners' sugar
1 egg yolk

To make the pastry, sift the flour into a bowl. Run in the butter until the mixture resembles fine breadcrumbs.

Stir in the icing sugar. Add the egg yolk and 1 teaspoon of water. Stir with a knife to form a smooth dough. Knead lightly, wrap in cling film and chill for 30 minutes. On a lightly floured surface, roll out the dough to fit a 8 in. loose-bottomed flan tin. Line the flan tin with the pastry and chill again for 20-30 minutes. Preheat the oven to 375F (190C). Prick the pastry all over with a fork then line with foil and fill with baking beans. Bake blind for 10-15 minutes until the pastry has set.

Remove the baking beans and foil and bake for a further 10-15 minutes until firm and golden brown. Put the figs and orange juice in a saucepan. Cook for 5-10 minutes, stirring, until thickened. Remove from the heat, add the butter and stir until melted. Beat in the eggs. Pour the mixture into the flan case and scatter with the pine nuts. Bake for 15 minutes until just set. Dust with confectioners' sugar, decorate with orange slices and serve warm or cold.

Serves 6.

APPLE & ALMOND TARTLETS

12 oz prepared shortcrust pastry
3 oz/⅓ cup unsalted butter, softened
3 oz/⅓ cup superfine sugar
2 eggs, beaten
2oz/½ cup ground almonds
1 teaspoon ground cinnamon
3 oz Cheshire or Cheddar cheese
3 small dessert apples
2 tablespoons apricot jam

Divide the pastry into 6 portions. Roll out each portion and use to line six 4 in. tartlet tins. Prick the bases and chill for 30 minutes.

Preheat oven to 375F (190C) and place a baking sheet on the middle shelf. Cream the butter and sugar together until soft and beat in the eggs, almonds and cinnamon. Finely grate the cheese and stir into the mixture. Line pastry cases with foil and baking beans and bake blind on the heated baking sheet for 10 minutes. Remove the beans and foil and bake for a further 8-10 minutes until pastry is crisp and golden. Cool lightly and spread the cheese mixture over the bases.

Quarter and core the apples and cut into thin slices. Arrange the slices over the cheese mixture in circles and bake for 15 minutes. Reduce the oven temperature to 350F (180C) and cook for a further 10-15 minutes until firm to the touch. Heat the jam with 1 teaspoon of water until melted, pass through a fine sieve and carefully brush over the tartlets to glaze. Serve warm with a spoonful of crème fraîche or fromage frais.

Serves 6.

TARTE TATIN

4 oz/½ cup unsalted butter, softened
4 oz/½ cup superfine sugar
about 3 lb firm, well-flavored apples, such as Cox's,
   peeled, cored and cut into wedges
juice of 1 lemon
strips of lemon rind and mint sprigs, to decorate
PASTRY:
8 oz/2 cups all-purpose flour
1 tablespoon superfine sugar
4½ oz/½ cup butter, diced
2-3 tablespoons crème fraîche

Sprinkle with lemon juice and cook over a moderately high heat, shaking tin or pan occasionally, for 20-30 minutes, until apples are lightly caramelized. If a lot of juice is produced, pour it off into a saucepan, boil to a thick syrup and pour back over apples.

To make pastry, combine flour and sugar in a bowl. Add butter and rub in until mixture resembles fine breadcrumbs. Add enough crème fraîche to bind to a dough. Form into a ball, cover and chill for at least 30 minutes.

Preheat oven to 425F (220C). Roll out pastry on a lightly floured surface until slightly larger than tin or pan. Lay pastry on top of apples, tucking edge of pastry down side of pan.

Spread butter over base of a heavy 9½ in. cake pan or ovenproof skillet. Sprinkle over sugar and arrange apples on top, rounded-side down.

Prick pastry lightly with a fork and put pan on a baking sheet. Bake for 20 minutes, until pastry is golden. Turn tart on to a warmed serving plate, decorate with lemon rind and mint sprigs and serve with cream.

Serves 6-8.

Note: Be careful when turning out the tart as the syrup will be very hot and can burn.

RED FRUIT TART

CANDIED FRUIT TARTS

9½ in. loose-bottomed fluted quiche pan, lined with
    pâte sucrée (see page 217)
about 26 each raspberries, halved strawberries and
    pitted cherries
3 tablespoons red fruit jam
1 tablespoon lemon juice
raspberries and raspberry leaves, to decorate
CRÈME PÂTISSIÈRE:
5 fl oz/⅔ cup milk
5 fl oz/⅔ cup light cream
1 vanilla bean
3 egg yolks
2 oz/¼ cup sugar
1 tablespoon all-purpose flour
1½ tablespoons cornstarch
½ oz/1 tablespoon sweet butter

8 oz/1 cup ricotta cheese
3 egg yolks
2oz/¼ cup superfine sugar
1 tablespoon brandy
grated rind of 1 lemon
1 tablespoon lemon juice
4 oz/⅔ cup crystallized fruit, finely chopped
confectioners' sugar for dusting
mint sprigs, to decorate
PASTRY:
6 oz/1½ cups all-purpose flour
3 oz/⅓ cup butter
3 oz/⅓ cup white vegetable fat (shortening)

To make the pastry, sift the flour into a bowl.
Add butter and vegetable fat (shortening).

For crème pâtissière, put milk, cream and
vanilla bean in a saucepan and bring to simmering point. Remove from heat, cover and
leave for 30 minutes. Whisk egg yolks and
sugar until very thick. Stir in flour and cornstarch. Remove vanilla bean from milk and
return to the boil. Pour into egg mixture,
whisking constantly. Return to pan and
bring to boil, whisking. Simmer for 2-3
minutes. Remove from heat, stir in butter
and pour into a bowl. Cool, stirring occasionally. Cover and chill. Preheat oven to
400F (200C).

Run in the butter and vegetable fat (shortening) until mixture resembles fine breadcrumbs. Stir in 2 tablespoons of cold water
and use a knife to mix to a smooth dough.
Knead lightly, wrap in cling film and chill for
30 minutes. Preheat the oven to 350F
(180C). On a lightly floured surface, roll out
the pastry until ⅛ in. thick. Cut out 4 circles
to fit four 4 in. quiche pans.

Prick pastry case with a fork, line with baking parchment or foil and fill with baking
beans. Bake for 10-12 minutes. Lower oven
temperature to 375F (190C). Remove paper
and beans and bake for 8-10 minutes. Cool
on a wire rack. Fill pastry case with crème
pâtissière and arrange fruit on top. Put jam
and lemon juice in a pan and heat gently, to
soften. Pass through a sieve and brush over
fruit. Leave to cool, decorate and serve.

Serves 6.

Put the ricotta cheese, egg yolks, superfine
sugar, brandy, and lemon rind and juice in a
bowl. Beat together until smooth them stir
in the crystallized fruit. Divide the mixture
among the pastry cases. Bake for 30-40
minutes or until the filling is set and golden.
Leave to cool. Dust with confectioners'
sugar, decorate with mint sprigs and serve
cold.

Serves 4.

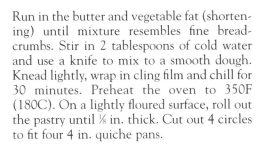

PRUNE & ALMOND TART

8 oz prunes
4 tablespoons brandy
8 oz shortcrust pastry, thawed if frozen
4 oz/½ cup unsalted butter, softened
4 oz/½ cup confectioners' sugar
3 eggs, beaten
2oz/½ cup all-purpose flour
4 oz/½ cup ground almonds
2 oz/½ cup flaked almonds

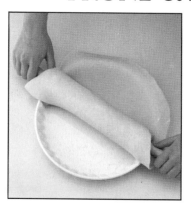

Put the prunes and brandy in a bowl and leave to soak overnight. Roll out the pastry on a lightly floured surface and use to line a 10½ in. quiche pan.

Trim the pastry and prick the base all over with a fork. Drain the prunes and arrange in the pastry case. Preheat oven to 400F (200C). In a bowl, beat together the butter and confectioners' sugar. Beat in the eggs and fold in the flour and ground almonds. Spread the mixture evenly over the prunes.

Sprinkle the flaked almonds over the top. Bake for 40-45 minutes, until the filling is risen and golden brown. Serve warm.

Serves 6-8.

WALNUT PASTRIES

10 oz/2½ cups all-purpose flour
6 oz/¾ cup butter
3 oz/⅓ cup confectioners' sugar
1 egg yolk
3 tablespoons superfine sugar
4 oz/1 cup walnuts, coarsely chopped
3 oz/½ cup chopped mixed citrus peel
¼ teaspoon freshly grated nutmeg
3 tablespoons rosewater
confectioners' sugar for coating

Sift flour into a bowl. Run in butter until mixture resembles breadcrumbs.

Sift in confectioners' sugar and stir. Mix in egg yolk and a little water to make a firm dough. Chill for 30 minutes. Preheat oven to 350F (180C). Butter a baking sheet. To make the syrup, put superfine sugar and 3½ fl oz/⅓ cup water in a saucepan. Heat gently until sugar has dissolved. Bring to the boil and boil for a few minutes until syrup has reduced and thickened slightly.

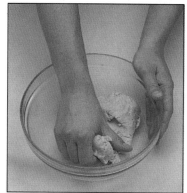

In a bowl, mix together walnuts, chopped mixed citrus peel and nutmeg. Moisten with the syrup. On a floured surface roll out pastry. Cut out 4 in. circles. Place a teaspoon of walnut mixture on each circle. Fold in half, pressing edges together. Bake in the oven for 20-30 minutes until pale golden. Brush with rosewater. Coat liberally with confectioners' sugar.

Makes about 20.

TARTE AU CITRON

3 eggs
1 egg yolk
5 oz/¼ cup superfine sugar
grated rind and juice of 3 lemons
grated rind and juice of 1 orange
2½ oz/½ cup confectioners' sugar
thinly pared rind of 1 lemon
confectioners' sugar for dusting
lemon twists and chervil sprigs, to decorate
PÂTE SUCRÉE:
7 oz/¼ cup all-purpose flour
pinch of salt
4 tablespoons superfine sugar
4 oz/½ cup sweet butter
2 egg yolks

Prick base of pastry case with a fork, line with baking parchment or foil and fill with baking beans. Put quiche pan on a baking sheet and bake for 10-12 minutes. Lower oven temperature to 375F (190C). Remove paper and beans and bake for 5 minutes, until golden. Transfer pan to a wire rack and leave to cool. Leave oven on.

To make pâte sucrée, sift flour and salt on to a marble slab or a work surface and make a well in center. Put sugar, butter and egg yolks into well and pinch them together to form a paste, then lightly draw in the flour, adding about 1 tablespoon cold water to make a soft but firm dough. Cover and chill for 2 hours.

Mix together eggs, egg yolk, superfine sugar and lemon and orange rind and juice. Return quiche pan to baking sheet and ladle in filling. Bake for 25-30 minutes, until set. Transfer tin to a wire rack, cool slightly, then remove outer ring of quiche pan. Leave tart to cool completely.

Roll out pastry on a lightly floured surface and line a 9½ in. loose-bottomed fluted quiche pan, pressing pastry well into sides and base. Run rolling pin over top of pan to cut off excess pastry. Chill for 20 minutes. Preheat oven to 400F (200C).

Put confectioners' sugar and 5 fl oz/⅔ cup water in a small pan and heat gently, stirring, until dissolved. Boil for 2 minutes then add pared lemon rind and simmer until glassy. Remove with a slotted spoon and leave to cool on baking parchment. Just before serving, dust tart thickly with confectioners' sugar and scatter over candied lemon rind. Garnish with lemon twists and chervil sprigs and serve with cream, if liked.

Serves 6-8.

ORANGE & ALMOND CAKE

1 orange
4 oz/½ cup softened butter
4 oz/½ cup superfine sugar
2 eggs, beaten
6 oz/1 cup semolina
3½ oz/1 cup ground almonds
1½ teaspoons baking powder
4 oranges, peeled and sliced
4 oz pitted dates, roughly chopped
confectioners' sugar, to decorate
SYRUP:
10 fl oz/1¼ cups orange juice
4½ oz superfine sugar

Preheat oven to 350F (180C). Butter and base-line a 8 in. cake pan.

Grate the rind from the orange, and squeeze the juice from one half. In a bowl, beat together the butter, orange rind and superfine sugar until light and creamy. Gradually beat in the eggs. Mix together the semolina, ground almonds and baking powder and fold into the creamed mixture with the reserved orange juice. Spoon the mixture into the prepared pan and bake for 30-40 minutes until well risen and a skewer inserted into the center comes out clean. Leave to cool in the pan for a few minutes.

Meanwhile, make the syrup. Put the orange juice and sugar in a pan; heat gently until the sugar dissolves. Bring to the boil and simmer for 4 minutes until syrupy. Turn the cake out on to a deep serving dish. Using a skewer, make holes in the warm cake. Spoon three quarters of the syrup over, and leave for 30 minutes. Place the oranges and dates in the remaining syrup and leave to cool. Dust the cake with confectioners' sugar and cut into slices. Serve with the fruit in syrup.

Serves 8.

VINE FRUITS GÂTEAU

4 eggs
4 oz/½ cup superfine sugar
4 oz/½ cup all-purpose flour
8 fl oz/1 cup heavy cream
4 oz black grapes
½ small cantaloupe melon
2 kiwi fruit
1 tablespoon confectioners' sugar

Preheat oven to 375F (190C). Grease a 8 in. deep cake pan. Place eggs and sugar in a large bowl and whisk until thick, pale and creamy. Sift flour over mixture and fold in gently, using a metal spoon.

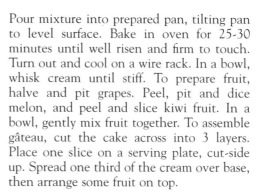

Pour mixture into prepared pan, tilting pan to level surface. Bake in oven for 25-30 minutes until well risen and firm to touch. Turn out and cool on a wire rack. In a bowl, whisk cream until stiff. To prepare fruit, halve and pit grapes. Peel, pit and dice melon, and peel and slice kiwi fruit. In a bowl, gently mix fruit together. To assemble gâteau, cut the cake across into 3 layers. Place one slice on a serving plate, cut-side up. Spread one third of the cream over base, then arrange some fruit on top.

Place a cake layer on top and spread this with another third of cream. Arrange fruit on top. Place remaining cake slice on top, cut-side down. Spread or pipe remaining cream over top and arrange remaining fruit decoratively over cream. Dust fruit with sifted confectioners' sugar and serve immediately.

Serves 10.

LEMON MOUSSE GÂTEAU

CAKE:
3 eggs
4½ oz/½ cup plus 1 tablespoon superfine sugar
few drops vanilla extract
3 oz/¾ cup all-purpose flour
FILLING:
grated rind and juice 2 lemons
2 teaspoons powdered gelatine
3 eggs, separated
4 oz/½ cup superfine sugar
5 fl oz/⅔ cup thick cream
TO DECORATE:
confectioners' sugar
raspberries
lemon geranium or raspberry leaves, if available

To make mousse filling, put juice of 1 lemon and 1 tablespoon water in a bowl. Sprinkle over gelatine, ensuring it is completely covered with liquid. Leave to stand for 10 minutes until spongy. In a bowl, whisk together egg yolks, sugar and lemon rind until thick and mousse-like. Gradually whisk in remaining lemon juice, keeping mixture as thick as possible.

Preheat oven to 350F (180C). Grease a 9 in. spring-release pan and line with non-stick paper. To make cake, whisk eggs and superfine sugar together in a bowl until very thick and light. Stir in vanilla extract, then sift flour over mixture and fold in gently. Spoon into prepared pan and bake in oven for 25 minutes until golden and the cake springs back when pressed. Turn on to a wire rack covered with sugared baking parchment. Peel off lining paper and leave to cool.

Place bowl of gelatine over a pan of simmering water until gelatine has dissolved. Immediately whisk it into egg yolk mixture. In a bowl, whip cream until it just holds its shape. Fold cream into egg mixture. Whisk egg whites until stiff but not dry. Gently fold into mousse. Pour mixture into prepared pan. Level surface. Cover and chill for 45-60 minutes until lightly set. Place second layer of cake on top. Cover and chill overnight.

Slice the cake horizontally into 2 layers. Wash and dry cake pan and line base and sides with non-stick paper. Place one half of cake in base of pan.

To serve, remove sides of pan and carefully peel away paper. Place a flat plate on top of cake and quickly invert cake. Ease off bottom of pan. Dust gâteau with sifted confectioners' sugar and decorate with raspberries and geranium or raspberry leaves, if using.

Serves 8-10.

ARTEMIS CAKE

WALNUT CAKE

14 oz dark chocolate
5 eggs, separated
8 oz/1 cup butter, softened
4 oz/¾ cup confectioners' sugar
2 tablespoons all-purpose flour, sifted
1 teaspoon ground cinnamon
confectioners' sugar, to decorate

12 oz walnut pieces
4 eggs, separated
8 oz/1¼ cups superfine sugar
finely grated rind of 1 lemon
confectioners' sugar, to decorate

Preheat oven to 350F (180C). Butter and line a 8 in. cake pan (preferably a loose-bottomed pan). Break chocolate into a bowl and stand bowl over a pan of hot water until melted. Leave until almost cold.

Preheat oven to 350F (180C). Grease, flour and base-line a 9 in. spring-bottomed pan. Grind the walnuts in a blender or food processor until fine but not greasy.

In a bowl, whisk egg whites until stiff. In a bowl, beat butter and confectioners' sugar until light and creamy. Beat in egg yolks. Add chocolate; stir in lightly. It does not need to be thoroughly mixed.

With an electric beater, whisk the egg yolks and sugar together until pale and creamy. Fold in the lemon rind and nuts. Whisk egg whites until stiff and carefully fold into the nut mixture. Gently pour into prepared pan.

Stir in flour and cinnamon and then fold in whisked egg whites. Pour mixture into prepared pan. Bake in the oven for 45 minutes until well-risen and firm to the touch. Leave in pan until almost cool, then transfer to a wire rack. Sift confectioners' sugar over the top and place on a serving plate.

Serves 8.

Bake in oven for 45-60 minutes until risen and firm. Cool in the pan. It will shrink away from the edges. Remove from the pan and dredge with confectioners' sugar. Serve in thin wedges with vanilla custard, if liked.

Serves 12.

FESTIVAL GÂTEAU

3 egg whites
6 oz/¾ cup superfine sugar
½ teaspoon vanilla extract
½ teaspoon white wine vinegar
1 teaspoon cornstarch
10 fl oz/1¼ cups heavy cream
2 kiwi fruit
4 oz strawberries
4 oz raspberries

BAKLAVA

4 oz/1 cup blanched almonds
4 oz/1 cup walnuts
2oz/⅓ cup shelled pistachio nuts
2oz/⅓ cup soft brown sugar
1 teaspoon ground cinnamon
¼ teaspoon freshly grated nutmeg
2oz/¼ cup butter
8 sheets filo pastry
SYRUP:
8 oz/1 cup granulated sugar
1 tablespoon lemon juice
1 tablespoon orange flower water

Preheat oven to 225F (110C). Draw two 8 in. circles on baking parchment; place on 2 baking sheets. In a large bowl, whisk egg whites until stiff.

Whisk in half the sugar and then gently fold in rest of the sugar, vanilla extract, vinegar and cornstarch with a metal spoon. Spread or pipe meringue over circles on parchment on baking sheets. Bake in oven for 1-1½ hours or until dry. Transfer to a wire rack to cool. Meanwhile, prepare filling. In a bowl, whisk cream until thick. Peel kiwi fruit and slice. Halve strawberries. In a separate bowl, mix fruit together gently. To assemble gâteau, place one meringue circle, flat side down, on a serving plate.

To make syrup, in a saucepan, heat sugar, 5 fl oz/⅔ cup water and the lemon juice until sugar dissolves. Boil gently for 5 minutes until syrupy. Add orange flower water and boil for a further 2 minutes. Leave to cool completely. In a food processor, process one third of all nuts until finely chopped. Coarsely chop the remainder. In a bowl, mix together nuts, brown sugar, cinnamon and nutmeg. Butter a large baking pan. Preheat oven to 350F (180C). In a saucepan, melt butter.

Spread it with most of the cream, reserving a little for piping. Place most of the fruit on top of the cream, reserving some pieces for decoration. Top with second meringue circle, flat side down. Pipe remaining cream decoratively on top of the gâteau and decorate with remaining pieces of fruit. Serve immediately.

Serves 8.

Cut pastry sheets in half. Brush one halved sheet with butter and place on bottom of baking pan. Repeat with 3 more sheets. Spread one third of nut mixture over the top, then repeat the layers twice more, ending with a layer of pastry. With a sharp knife, cut top layer of pastry into diamonds. Bake in oven for 30-40 minutes until crisp and golden. Pour cold syrup over the top. When cold, trim edges and cut into diamond shapes.

Makes about 20.

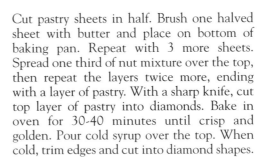

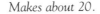

MARRAKESH SERPENT CAKE

12 sheets filo pastry, 16 × 12 in.
2oz/¼ cup unsalted butter, melted
confectioners' sugar, for dusting
ground cinnamon, to decorate
ALMOND FILLING:
8 oz/2 cups ground almonds
4 oz/¾ cup confectioners' sugar
grated rind of 1 orange
2 tablespoons orange juice
½ teaspoon almond essence
2oz/¼ cup softened butter

To make the filling, mix the almonds, sugar, orange rind and juice, almond essence and butter. Cover and chill for 30 minutes.

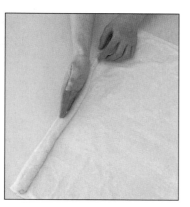

Preheat oven to 350F (180C). Dust a work surface with confectioners' sugar. Divide the almond paste into 3 and roll each piece into a rope 20 in. long. Brush 2 sheets of filo pastry with melted butter and place side by side, with long sides overlapping slightly. Place 2 or more buttered sheets on top. Lay a roll of almond paste along 1 of the long sides and roll up. Place a hand at each end of roll and press in gently so that roll 'concertinas' very slightly. Brush with butter and roll into a tight coil. Place on a baking sheet.

Make 2 more rolls in the same way. Join them to the coil, continuing the shape and sealing the joints with water. Bake for 20-30 minutes until crisp and golden. Invert on to another baking sheet and return to the oven for a further 10 minutes to brown and crisp the other side. Invert on to a serving dish and leave to cool. Thickly sift confectioners' sugar over the cake then sprinkle ground cinnamon from between finger and thumb in thin zig zags across the cake.

Serves 6-8.

CHOCOLATE HONEY SWIRL

12 oz strong white flour
½ teaspoon salt
3 oz/⅓ cup butter
3 tablespoons superfine sugar
6 fl oz/¾ cup milk
3 teaspoons dried yeast
8 oz chocolate dots
3 tablespoons clear honey
2 tablespoons raisins
2 tablespoons chopped candied peel
4 tablespoons chopped nuts (pecans, walnuts, hazelnuts or others)
2 teaspoons ground cinnamon
confectioners' sugar, to sift

Place the flour and salt in a bowl, the rub in the butter. Stir in most of the sugar. Heat the milk until just lukewarm, then stir in the remaining sugar and sprinkle the yeast over the top. Set aside in a warm place, without stirring, for about 15 minutes until frothy. Pour the yeast liquid into the flour mixture and mix to a soft dough. Knead for 10 minutes, then replace in a bowl, cover and leave in a warm place until doubled in size. Meanwhile, mix the remaining ingredients.

Knead the dough briefly, then roll it out into an oval, about ½ in. thick. Spread the chocolate mixture over, leaving a border. Dampen the edge, then roll up the dough. Pinch the edge to seal it well. Place non-stick baking parchment in the soaked pot and put the loaf in it. Cover and leave in a warm place until doubled. Place in the cold oven. Set the oven at 450F (230C). Cook for 45 minutes. Uncover and cook for 10 minutes. Cool on a rack. Sift with confectioners' sugar.

Makes 1 loaf.

MANGO & LYCHEE TURNOVERS

1 tablespoon cornstarch
1 tablespoon sugar
3 tablespoons unsweetened orange juice
1 teaspoon lemon juice
1 teaspoon ground nutmeg
1 mango
10 lychees
8 sheets filo pastry
2oz/¼ cup low fat spread, melted
1 tablespoon confectioners' sugar

Preheat oven to 400F (200C). In a saucepan, blend cornstarch and sugar with 3 table-spoons water. Add orange juice, lemon juice and nutmeg and mix well.

Heat gently over a low heat until mixture thickens, stirring all the time. Simmer sauce for 3 minutes, then allow to cool. Peel, pit and roughly chop mango and lychees. Add fruit to cooled sauce, mixing well. To make turnovers, cut each filo sheet in half cross-wise to make two 4 in. squares (total of 16 squares). Brush 2 squares of pastry lightly with melted fat and place one on top of the other. Place some filling in the center of the pastry, fold diagonally in half and press edges to seal.

Place on a greased baking sheet and brush lightly with melted fat. Repeat with remaining pastry squares and filling to make 8 turnovers. Bake in oven for 30 minutes, until golden brown and crisp. Dust with sifted confectioners' sugar and serve immediately with low fat ice cream.

Makes 8.

PISTACHIO & HAZELNUT ROLLS

2oz/½ cup coarsely ground pistachio nuts
2oz/½ cup ground hazelnuts
2oz/¼ cup granulated sugar
1 tablespoon orange flower water
6 sheets filo pastry, 16 × 12 in.
3 oz/⅓ cup unsalted butter, melted
confectioners' sugar, to decorate

Preheat the oven to 350F (180C). Grease 2 baking sheets. In a bowl, mix together the ground pistachio nuts, ground hazelnuts, granulated sugar and orange flower water.

Cut each sheet of filo pastry across into 4 rectangles. Pile on top of each other and cover with a tea towel to prevent them dry-ing out. Working with 1 filo rectangle at a time, brush the pastry with melted butter; spread a heaped teaspoon of filling along the short end.

Fold the long sides in, slightly over the fill-ing. Roll up from the filled end. Place on a prepared baking sheet with the seam under-neath and brush with melted butter. Repeat with the remaining pastry and filling. Bake in the oven for 20 minutes or until crisp and lightly colored. Transfer to wire racks to cool. Sift confectioners' sugar over.

Makes 24.

APRICOPITTA

2¼ lb fresh apricots
seeds from 5 cardamom pods
4 oz/½ cup superfine sugar
¼ teaspoon vanilla extract
3 oz/⅓ cup butter, melted
12 sheets filo pastry
3 egg whites
1½ oz brown sugar
4 oz/1¼ cup ground almonds
confectioners' sugar

Put apricots in a bowl. Cover with boiling water. Leave for 2 minutes, then drain. Cover with cold water, leave for 2 minutes and drain again.

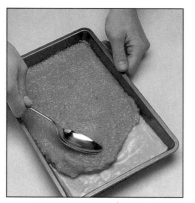

Peel skins off apricots. Cut in half and remove pits. Put apricots in a saucepan with cardamom seeds, superfine sugar and vanilla essence. Cook gently until apricots are soft. In a blender or food processor, purée the apricots. Preheat oven to 375F (190C). Brush a small roasting pan with melted butter. Brush a sheet of pastry with butter and lay in pan. Repeat with 3 more pastry layers. Spread apricot purée on pastry. Cover with 4 more layers of buttered pastry.

In a bowl, whisk egg whites until stiff. Whisk in brown sugar. Fold in ground almonds. Spread meringue on pastry. Cover gently with 4 more sheets buttered pastry. Tuck top layer of pastry down sides. With a sharp knife, cut diamond shapes in pastry, down to meringue layer. Dust with confectioners' sugar, then bake in oven for 40-59 minutes until browned and crisp. Serve warm or cold, cut into diamonds, and dusted with more sugar.

Serves 6-8.

ARAB PANCAKES WITH HONEY

1 lb/4 cups strong white bread flour
6 g sachet easy-blend dried yeast
1 teaspoon superfine sugar
1 egg, beaten
20 fl oz/2½ cups lukewarm water
vegetable oil for shallow frying
3 oz/⅓ cup clear honey
2 teaspoons orange flower water
butter and warm honey, to serve

Sift the flour into a large bowl and stir in the dried yeast and sugar. Mix the egg with half the water and gradually stir into the flour.

Gradually stir in the remaining water, beating well until the batter is smooth and creamy, cover the bowl with a damp tea towel and leave in a warm place for 1 hour or until the batter rises and bubbles. When the batter is ready, lightly oil a heavy based skillet. Heat the pan until it is very hot, then reduce to a medium heat. Drop 3 tablespoons of batter into the pan. It should not spread out too much. Fry until bubbles burst on the surface of the pancake and it comes away easily from the pan.

Turn it over and cook the other side until lightly browned. Place the cooked pancakes in a heatproof dish in overlapping circles and keep warm while cooking more pancakes. In a small saucepan, gently heat the honey. Stir in the orange flower water. Serve the pancakes with a knob of butter and the warm honey.

Serves 4-6.

Variation: These pancakes are often served layered with clotted cream.

RASPBERRY & APPLE STRUDEL

8 oz cooking apples
8 oz raspberries
2oz/¼ cup superfine sugar
2oz/½ cup chopped mixed nuts
1 teaspoon ground cinnamon
8 sheets filo pastry
2oz/¼ cup low fat spread
1 tablespoon icing sugar

Preheat oven to 375F (190C). Peel, core and slice apples. Place in a saucepan with raspberries and 2 tablespoons water. Cover and cook gently until just soft. Stir in sugar and cool. Add nuts and cinnamon and mix well.

Place one sheet of pastry on a sheet of baking parchment and brush lightly with melted fat. Place another sheet of pastry on top and layer all 8 sheets on pastry on top of one another, brushing each one lightly with melted fat. Spoon fruit mixture over pastry leaving a 1 in. border uncovered all around edge. Fold these edges over fruit mixture.

With a long side towards you, using baking parchment, roll up strudel. Carefully place it on a greased baking sheet, seam-side down. Brush it lightly with melted fat. Bake in oven for about 40 minutes until golden brown. Dust with sifted confectioners' sugar.

Serves 8.

KADAIFI

4 oz/1 cup finely chopped walnuts
4 oz/1 cup finely chopped almonds
2oz/¼ cup superfine sugar
½ teaspoon ground cinnamon
14 oz kadaifi pastry (see Note)
2oz/¼ cup butter
SYRUP:
8 oz/1 cup granulated sugar
3 teaspoons lemon juice
3 teaspoons orange flower water

Preheat oven to 350F (180C). Butter a baking tray. In a bowl. Mix together walnuts, almonds, sugar and cinnamon.

Tease pastry out to a rectangle 18 × 15 in. Cut into 18 pieces measuring 5 × 3 in. Place 1 tablespoon of nut mixture on short end of each rectangle of pastry. Roll up, enclosing filling. Place rolls on the baking tray. In a small saucepan, melt butter, then pour it over the rolls. Bake in the oven for 25-30 minutes until golden and crisp. Leave to cool for 15 minutes.

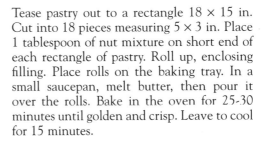

To make the syrup, put sugar, the lemon juice and 10 fl oz/1¼ cups water in a saucepan. Heat gently until sugar has dissolved, then boil for 5 minutes until slightly thickened. Add orange flower water, then pour syrup over pastry rolls.

Makes 18.

Note: Kadaifi is a white shredded raw pastry available from delicatessens and Greek shops. It has to be teased into shape rather than rolled.

FRESH FRUIT SAVARIN

1 oz fresh yeast or 1 tablespoon dried yeast plus 1
   teaspoon sugar
6 tablespoons tepid skimmed milk
8 oz/2 cups strong all-purpose flour
½ teaspoon salt
2 tablespoons superfine sugar
4 eggs, beaten
4 oz/½ cup low fat spread
4 tablespoons clear honey
2 tablespoons brandy
12 oz prepared fresh fruit, such as kiwi fruit,
   strawberries, peaches, raspberries, bananas
1 oz/¼ cup flaked almonds, toasted
mint leaves, to decorate

Grease a 40 fl oz/5 cup savarin or ring mold.
In a bowl, blend together yeast, milk and
2 oz/½ cup flour. If using dried yeast, add the
1 teaspoon sugar and leave in a warm place
until frothy (about 15 minutes). Add
remaining flour to the yeast mixture,
together with salt, sugar, eggs and low fat
spread. Beat well for 5 minutes. Pour into
mold, cover with a clean tea towel and leave
to rise in a warm place for 15 minutes.
Preheat oven to 400F (200C). Bake in oven
for 30 minutes until golden brown.

Turn out savarin on to a plate. Place honey
in a saucepan with 2 tablespoons water and
heat gently until hot. Add brandy and spoon
over savarin while still hot. Cool. Transfer to
a serving plate and pile prepared fresh fruit
into center of savarin. Sprinkle with flaked
almonds and decorate with mint leaves.

Serves 10.

HALVA CAKE

4 oz/½ cup butter
4 oz/½ cup superfine sugar
grated rind 1 orange
juice ½ lemon
2 eggs, beaten
6 oz/1 cup semolina
2 teaspoons baking powder
3½ oz/1 cup ground almonds
1 teaspoon ground cinnamon
SYRUP:
6 oz/¾ cup superfine sugar
juice ½ lemon
juice ½ orange
2 tablespoons orange peel, to decorate

Preheat oven to 425F (220C). Butter a ring
mold. In a blender or food processor, put butter, sugar, orange rind, lemon juice, eggs,
semolina, baking powder, ground almonds
and cinnamon. Process until well mixed.
Turn mixture into prepared pan. Bake in the
oven for 10 minutes, then reduce heat to
350F (180C) and bake for a further 25
minutes or until a cake tester inserted into
the cake comes out clean. Leave to cool in
the pan for a few minutes, then turn out into
a warm, deep plate.

Meanwhile, make the syrup. In a pan, put
sugar, lemon juice, orange juice and 4 fl oz/½
cup water. Heat gently until sugar has dissolved, then bring to the boil and simmer for
4 minutes. Stir in candied peel. As soon as
cake is turned out, bring syrup to the boil;
spoon over cake so that peel is arranged decoratively over the cake.

Serves 8.

BISCOTTI & VIN SANTO

6 oz whole blanched almonds, toasted
4 oz sweet butter, softened
7 oz granulated sugar
2 eggs, beaten
finely grated rind of 1 orange
1½ teaspoons baking powder
½ teaspoon salt
3 oz polenta
about 12 oz all-purpose white flour
Vin Santo, to serve

Coarsely chop one third of the almonds and mix these with the whole almonds. Cream butter with the sugar until just mixed. Beat in eggs, orange rind, baking powder and salt

Stir in polenta, almonds and 10 oz of the flour. Turn onto a floured work surface and knead to a smooth dough, adding the remaining flour little by little, until the dough is soft not sticky. Divide dough into 4 equal pieces and roll each into a sausage 2 in. wide and ¾ in. deep. Place them on 2 greased baking sheets and bake for about 35 minutes until just golden around the edges. Cool for 5 minutes.

Cut rolls diagonally into ½ in. thick slices. Place the slices cut side down on the baking sheets and bake them for another 10 minutes until golden brown. Transfer to a wire rack to cool completely. Serve with small glasses of Vin Santo for dipping.

Makes about 50.

PECAN CANDY

8 oz/1½ cups soft dark brown sugar
5 fl oz/⅔ cup milk
3 tablespoons light maple syrup
salt
4 oz/1¼ cups pecan halves
1 oz/2 tablespoons butter, softened
few drops vanilla extract

Line a baking tray with waxed paper. Put sugar, milk, maple syrup and salt into a large heavy based saucepan. Stir with a wooden spoon over a medium heat, until sugar has dissolved then bring to the boil. Add nuts. Cook until the soft ball stage, 238F (115C). Remove from heat. Cool until lukewarm. Stir in butter and extract and continue to stir for 2 minutes until mixture begins to thicken and become creamy.

Drop teaspoonsfuls of the mixture onto the waxed paper. Leave to set. Store in a plastic bag in refrigerator for 2-3 days.

Makes 18 sweets.

Note: To test for soft ball stage without a sugar thermometer, remove pan from heat, dip bottom in cold water. Drop a small amount of syrup into very cold water, roll it into a ball, and remove. The ball should flatten under slight pressure.

APRICOT & COCONUT BALLS

6 oz/1⅓ cups dried apricots, finely chopped
4 oz/2½ cups flaked coconut
2 oz/1½ cup blanched almonds, finely chopped
few drops vanilla extract
half of 14 oz can condensed milk
confectioners' sugar to coat

NUT & COFFEE MERINGUES

2 egg whites
4 oz/½ cup superfine sugar
2 oz/½ cup ground walnuts
chocolate-coated coffee beans, and pecan halves, to
  decorate
FILLING
7 fl oz/scant 1 cup heavy cream
about 1 tablespoon confectioners' sugar, sifted
about 1 teaspoon expresso coffee powder

Put apricots, coconut, almonds and vanilla extract into a bowl; mix together. Stir in enough condensed milk to bind to a stiff mixture.

Preheat oven to 250F (120C). Cover baking sheets with baking parchment. Whisk egg whites until stiff. Gradually add sugar, whisking constantly, and continue to whisk until mixture is very stiff and shiny. Gently fold in ground walnuts. Spoon into a piping bag fitted with a plain nozzle and pipe about 45 small discs of meringue on the baking sheets. Bake for about 1 hour until dry, very lightly colored and can be lifted easily from baking parchment. Cool on a wire rack.

Shape into balls about the size of a large hazelnut, roll in sieved confectioners' sugar, and place in small paper cases.

Makes 24 sweets.

To make filling, whip cream with sugar and coffee to taste. Just before serving, pipe a small swirl of cream on each base. Decorate some with chocolate-coated coffee beans and some with pecan halves. Serve in small paper cases.

Makes about 45.

CHOCOLATE MINI MUFFINS

5 oz/1¼ cups self-rising flour
2½ tablespoons cocoa powder
1 teaspoon baking powder
pinch of salt
2 oz/¼ cup light brown sugar
1 small egg, lightly beaten
5 fl oz/⅔ cup milk
2 oz/¼ cup butter, melted and cooled slightly
½ teaspoon vanilla extract
chocolate and hazelnut spread or chocolate frosting,
   for filling

Preheat oven to 400F (200C). Grease 20 mini muffin cups, about 1¾ × ¼ in., or put small paper cases in cups.

Sift flour, cocoa powder, baking powder and salt into a shallow bowl. Stir in sugar. Stir egg into milk, butter and vanilla extract. Pour on to dry ingredients and mix briefly using a large metal spoon and a lifting figure-of-eight movement; there should not be any free flour but mixture should still be lumpy.

One third- to half-fill paper cases or muffin tins with mixture. Put ½-1 teaspoon of spread or frosting on each portion of mixture and cover with more mixture so that cases or cups are almost filled. Bake for 20 minutes until risen and tops spring back when lightly touched. Paper cases can be removed immediately, alternatively place cups on a wire rack and leave to cool for 5 minutes, then remove muffins from cups. Serve warm.

Makes about 20.

ORANGE TRUFFLE CUPS

9 oz plain chocolate, grated
1 egg yolk
1 tablespoon sweet butter
1 tablespoon finely grated orange rind
3½ fl oz/scant ½ cup whipping cream, whipped
fine strips peel from marmalade, to decorate

Put half the chocolate into a heatproof bowl over a saucepan of hot water. Stir occasionally until chocolate has melted.

Using a small pastry brush or paint brush, brush melted chocolate over inside of paper petit-four cases. Leave to set then repeat and leave until firm. Make a small tear in paper case then carefully peel off.

Meanwhile, in a heatproof bowl over a pan of hot water, warm remaining chocolate until almost melted. Add egg yolk and stir until thickened. Remove bowl from heat and stir in butter and orange rind. Set aside to cool to room temperature. Fold in cream and spoon into a piping bag fitted with a star tip. Pipe filling neatly into each chocolate case. Decorate with peel from marmalade.

Makes 24.

DRINKS AND COCKTAILS

HORCHTA

8 oz/2 cups tiger nuts
1¾ pints/4½ cups water
finely grated rind ½ lemon
about 3 oz/⅓ cup sugar

Rinse nuts well under cold running water. Soak in clean water overnight. Drain.

In a blender or food processor, process nuts with sufficient of the water to make a fine paste. Return mixture to the bowl and add remaining water, lemon rind and sugar to taste.

Leave in a cold place for 4 hours. Strain the liquid through a cheesecloth-lined sieve. Chill until ice cold.

Serves 4.

Note: Some of the horchta can be poured into a metal tray and frozen until slushy, then added to the drink as it is served.

SPANISH HOT CHOCOLATE

3 oz/3 squares chocolate, broken into pieces
16 fl oz/2 cups milk
cinnamon sticks and orange rind, to decorate

Put chocolate in top of a double boiler or a boiler placed over a saucepan of hot water. Leave chocolate to melt.

Heat milk to boiling point. Using a wooden spoon, slowly stir a little boiling milk into chocolate.

Using a wire whisk, whisk in remaining milk and continue to whisk until mixture is frothy. Pour into heatproof glasses or cups and decorate with cinnamon sticks and orange rind.

Serves 2.

Variation: Rub 2 sugar cubes over a whole orange to extract the zest, then add the sugar to the hot milk. Sprinkle cinnamon on the top of the hot chocolate.

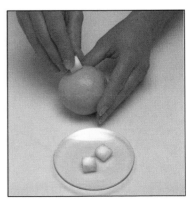

ICED ROSE TEA

SPICED TEA

1½ oz Ceylon breakfast tea
35 fl oz/4½ cups lukewarm water
sugar, to taste
few drops rosewater, to taste
12 ice cubes
6 sprigs of mint
fresh rose petals

Put tea in a bowl, pour over warm water and leave to stand overnight.

small piece of fresh root ginger, peeled
4 whole cloves
1 in. stick cinnamon
1 oz Ceylon tea
2oz/¼ cup sugar
2½ fl oz/⅓ cup orange juice
juice of ½ lemon
TO DECORATE:
4-6 cinnamon sticks

Bruise ginger and put in a saucepan with cloves and cinnamon. Add 35 fl oz/4½ cups cold water and bring to the boil.

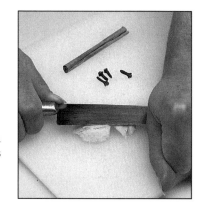

Strain tea into a large jug. Stir in sugar and rosewater to taste and add ice cubes. Place a sprig of mint and a few rose petals in each of 6 glasses and pour the tea on top.

Serves 6.

Put the tea in a bowl, pour on the spiced water and leave to infuse for 5 minutes. Add sugar and stir until dissolved, then stir in orange and lemon juice.

Variations: For Vanilla Iced Tea, omit rosewater. Put a vanilla bean in the bowl with tea to soak overnight. Remove it before serving. For Mint Tea, omit the rosewater and rose petals. Put a sprig of mint in the bowl with tea to soak overnight. Remove it before serving. Place a small sprig of fresh mint in each glass.

Reheat before serving, but do not allow to simmer or boil. Strain spiced tea into heatproof glasses. Serve with a cinnamon stick in each glass.

Serves 4-6.

Note: This drink is also delicious served chilled.

Variation: To make Party Punch, add extra sugar, to taste, then just before serving, add 10 fl oz/1¼ cups rum.

CAFÉ DE OLLA

40 fl oz/9 cups water
1 in. piece cinnamon stick
2 cloves
2oz/¼ cup muscovado sugar
4 tablespoons freshly ground coffee

SUMMER TEA CUP

1 Lapsang Souchong tea bag
20 fl oz/2½ cups boiling water
4 teaspoons soft brown sugar
10 fl oz/1¼ cups pineapple juice
2½ fl oz/⅓ cup white rum
20 fl oz/2½ cups ginger ale
ice cubes
TO DECORATE:
pieces fresh pineapple

Place tea bag in a bowl and pour over the boiling water.

Put the water, cinnamon and cloves into a saucepan and bring to the boil. Lower the heat, add the sugar and stir until dissolved. Stir in the coffee and simmer for 2 minutes.

Leave tea to infuse for 5 minutes, then remove tea bag. Stir in brown sugar and leave until cold. Stir the pineapple juice and rum into the cold tea.

Turn off the heat and allow to stand, covered, for about 5 minutes until all the coffee has settled. Strain into individual mugs.

Serves 4.

Just before serving, pour ginger ale into tea. Add ice cubes. Place a few pieces of pineapple in each glass and pour in the chilled tea.

Makes about 52 fl oz/6¾ cups.

OLD-FASHIONED LEMONADE

3 lemons
4 oz/½ cup sugar
TO FINISH:
ice
sprigs of mint
lemon slices

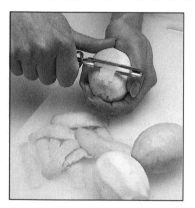

Using a potato peeler, thinly pare the rind from the lemons and put in a bowl or large jug with sugar. Squeeze juice from lemons into a bowl and set aside.

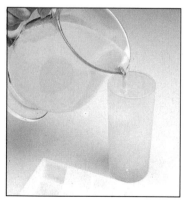

Boil 30 fl oz/3¼ cups cold water and pour over lemon rind and sugar. Stir to dissolve sugar and leave until completely cool. Add lemon juice and strain into a jug. Chill well. Serve in ice-filled tumblers, decorated with mint and lemon slices.

Serves 6.

Variations: To make Pink Lemonade, add just enough pink grenadine syrup to each glass to give lemonade a pale pink colour. Omit the mint and lemon slices and decorate each glass with a cherry.

To make Orangeade, use 3 oranges and 1 lemon instead of 3 lemons. Omit the mint and lemon slices and decorate the glasses with orange slices.

GRAPEFRUIT BARLEY WATER

2 oz pearl barley
2oz/¼ cup sugar
2 pink grapefruit
TO DECORATE:
mint leaves

Put barley into a saucepan. Just cover with cold water and bring to the boil. Tip barley into a colander and rinse thoroughly under cold running water.

Return barley to the saucepan, add 20 fl oz/ 2½ cups cold water and bring to the boil again. Cover and simmer for 1 hour. Strain liquid into a jug, stir in the sugar and leave until completely cold.

Squeeze juice from grapefruit and add to cooled barley water. Chill well. Serve decorated with mint leaves.

Makes about 20 fl oz/2½ cups.

Variation: To make Lemon Barley Water, use 2 lemons instead of grapefruit.

PINA COLADA

crushed ice
16 fl oz/2 cups fresh pineapple juice
8 fl oz/1 cup coconut milk
8 fl oz/1 cup white rum
TO DECORATE:
pineapple slices
cherries with stalks

LIMEADE

6 limes
4 oz/½ cup sugar
24 fl oz/3 cups boiling water
pinch salt
lime slices, to serve

Place crushed ice in 4 tall glasses to three-quarters full.

Cut each lime in half and squeeze juice.

Pour pineapple juice into a cocktail shaker or large screw-topped jar. Add coconut milk and white rum, and shake vigorously to blend. Pour into glasses over the ice.

Place skins in a jug, then stir in sugar followed by boiling water. Cover and leave for 15 minutes.

To decorate, cut each pineapple slice into quarters and cut a slit half-way through each wedge. Place over rims of glasses. Hang cherries over glass rims and serve immediately.

Serves 4.

Stir in salt. Strain into another jug and add lime juice. Leave to cool, then cover and chill. Serve over ice with lime slices.

Makes about 35 fl oz/4¼ cups.

TEQUILA SUNRISE

2 fl oz/¼ cup tequila
5 fl oz/⅔ cup fresh orange juice
1 tablespoon grenadine
1 teaspoon fresh lime juice
crushed ice
cocktail cherry to decorate

MARGARITA

1 lime, halved
salt
crushed ice
2 fl oz/¼ cup tequila
1 tablespoon Triple Sec or Cointreau
wedge of lime to serve

Pour tequila, orange juice, grenadine and lime juice into a blender or food processor; mix well. Put crushed ice into a tall, chilled glass.

Rub the rim of a chilled cocktail glass with one of the lime halves then dip into salt. Add crushed ice to a cocktail shaker or mixing glass. Squeeze the juice from the remaining lime half.

Strain tequila mixture over the ice. Decorate with a cocktail cherry on toothpick.

Serves 1.

Pour into the shaker or glass with the tequila and Triple Sec or Cointreau. Shake or stir well. Strain into the glass. Serve with a wedge of lime to squeeze into drink.

Serves 1.

SCORPION

5 ice cubes, crushed
1 measure brandy
½ measure white rum
½ measure dark rum
2 measures fresh orange juice
2 teaspoons Amaretto di Saronno
2-3 dashes Angostura bitters
TO DECORATE:
½ slice orange
½ slice lemon
twist of orange rind
twist of lemon rind

Put half the ice into a cocktail shaker or screw-top jar.

Pour brandy, rums, orange juice, Amaretto and bitters into shaker or jar. Shake to mix.

Put remaining ice into a goblet. Strain in cocktail. Decorate with orange and lemon slices and rinds.

Serves 1.

FROZEN PEACH DAIQUIRI

1 ripe peach
1¼ measures white rum
¾ measure peach brandy
juice of ½ lime
1 teaspoon sugar syrup OR 1 teaspoon powdered
   sugar
TO DECORATE:
twist of lime rind
1 cocktail cherry

Cut a cross in skin at rounded end of peach. Put into a bowl and pour over boiling water. Leave for about 20 seconds; lift peach and remove skin. Cut in half and discard pit. Chop flesh into a blender.

Add ice, rum, peach brandy, lime juice and sugar syrup to a blender.

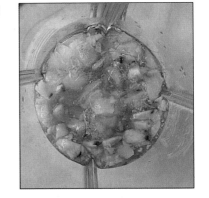

Mix ingredients at high speed for about 30 seconds until mixture is slushy. Pour, unstrained into a tall glass. Decorate with twist of lime rind and a cocktail cherry. Serve with drinking straws.

Serves 1.

HARVEY WALLBANGER

cracked ice
fresh orange juice
1 measure vodka
½ measure Galliano

CHAMPAGNE COCKTAIL

1 sugar cube
3 dashes Angostura Bitters
½ measure Cognac
champagne, chilled for topping up

Put sugar cube into champagne flute.

Fill a tall glass with cracked ice. Pour orange juice over ice until glass is three-quarters full.

Sprinkle Angostura bitters on to sugar cube. Pour in cognac.

Add vodka to glass and stir. Pour Galliano on top of drink so that it floats; do not stir.

Serves 1.

Top up drink with champagne and stir gently.

Serves 1.

BULLDOG

PARADISO

3 ice cubes, cracked
½ measure gin
1 measure cherry brandy
juice ½ lemon

Put ice into a cocktail shaker or screw-top jar.

4 ice cubes, cracked
1½ measures white rum
¼ measure apricot brandy
¼ measure orange liqueur, such as Cointreau or
   curacao
TO DECORATE:
apricot slice
twist of lemon
twist of orange

Put half the ice into a cocktail shaker or screw-top jar.

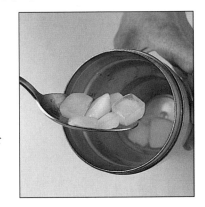

Pour gin and cherry brandy into shaker or jar. Add lemon juice and shake to mix.

Pour rum, apricot brandy and orange liqueur into a shaker or jar. Shake drink to mix.

Strain drink into a cocktail glass.

Serves 1.

Put remaining ice into a glass. Strain cocktail into a glass. Decorate with an apricot slice and slices of lemon and orange twisted together.

Serves 1.

BEHIND THE WALL

1 measure fresh orange juice
1 measure vodka
½ measure Mandarin napoleon liqueur
½ measure Galliano
ginger ale, for topping up

Put ice into a cocktail shaker, or screw-top jar.

Pour orange juice, vodka, Mandarin Napoleon and Galliano into shaker or jar. Shake together to mix.

Strain cocktail into glass and top with ginger ale.

Serves 1.

BRANDY ALEXANDER

3 ice cubes, cracked
½ measure of cream
½ measure of brandy
½ measure crème de cacao or Tia Maria
1 chocolate stick, to serve
TO DECORATE:
beaten egg white
finely grated or chopped plain chocolate or cocoa
    powder mixed with superfine sugar, or coffee. Put
    cracked ice into a cocktail shaker or screw-top jar.

Pour the cream, brandy or crème de cacao into shaker or jar. Shake to mix.

Strain drink into glass. Add the chocolate stick.

Serves 1.

PINEAPPLE MANGO PUNCH

1 ripe pineapple
½ large, ripe mango, peeled and chopped
5 fl oz/⅔ cup traditional ginger beer
sparkling water
lemon or lime juice, to taste

Using a large, sharp knife, slice off top of pineapple. Scoop fruit from center without piercing shell. Reserve shell. Discard tough core. About ½ lb flesh and juice should remain.

Put pineapple flesh and juice, mango and ginger into blender. Mix until smooth. Dilute to drinking consistency with sparkling water.

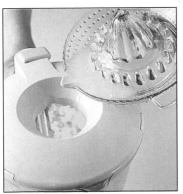

Flavor drink with lemon or lime juice to taste. Pour into reserved pineapple shell. Serve with straws.

Serves 2.

DRIVER'S PINEAPPLE PUNCH

1 ripe pineapple
1 ripe mango
5 fl oz/⅔ cup traditional ginger beer
sparkling mineral water
juice of 1 lime

Cut top off pineapple and scoop out flesh, leaving shell intact. Discard core and reserve any juice.

Peel mango and coarsely chop the flesh. Place pineapple pulp and juice into a blender or food processor. Add mango and ginger beer. Process until smooth.

Add sparkling water to thin to a drinking consistency and add lime juice. Pour punch into pineapple shell to serve.

Serves 2.

TENNIS CUP

8 oz/1 cup granulated sugar
1 lemon
2 oranges
2 bottles red or white wine
20 fl oz/2½ cups soda water
TO DECORATE:
thin slices of cucumber and orange
borage flowers or violets, if available

Put sugar in a saucepan with 5 fl oz/⅔ cup cold water. Heat gently until sugar has dissolved. Bring to the boil until syrup reaches 220F (105C).

With a potato peeler, thinly pare rind from lemon and oranges. Add to syrup and simmer gently for 10 minutes. Set aside until completely cold.

Squeeze juice from lemon and oranges and strain into syrup, then pour in the wine and chill. Just before serving, add soda water. Pour into glasses. Decorate with slices of cucumber and orange and sprigs of borage or violets.

Makes about 70 fl oz/9 cups.

SANGRIA

6-8 ice cubes
1 bottle red wine, chilled
2 strips orange peel
2 strips lemon peel
juice 4 oranges
2 tablespoons superfine sugar
juice 2 lemons
24 fl oz/3 cups soda water, chilled
mint sprigs and orange and lemon slices

Put ice cubes in a large bowl, pour in the wine and add strips of orange and lemon peel.

Put orange juice in a small bowl, add sugar and stir until sugar dissolves. Stir into wine with lemon juice. Top up with soda water. Pour into a large, cold serving jug. Decorate with mint sprigs and orange and lemon slices.

Serves 4.

TROPICAL PARTY PUNCH

RUM PUNCH

14 oz can mango slices
6 oz/¾ cup granulated sugar
juice of 4 limes
juice of 4 lemons
5 fl oz/⅔ cup grenadine
9 fl oz/generous 1 cup white rum
35 fl oz/4½ cups tropical fruit juice
35 fl oz/4½ cups lemonade
ice cubes, to serve
TO DECORATE:
slices of orange
slices of lime

Empty mangoes and their syrup into a food processor and process to a purée.

Put granulated sugar and 6 fl oz/¾ cup water in a saucepan. Bring slowly to the boil, stirring, until sugar has dissolved. Lower heat and simmer for 3 minutes. Remove from heat and set aside to cool.

8 oz/1 cup granulated sugar
4 fl oz/½ cup fresh lime juice
12 fl oz/1½ cups golden rum
12 ice cubes
Angostura bitters
grated nutmeg
TO DECORATE:
fresh mint
slices of lime

Put granulated sugar and 8 fl oz/1 cup water in a saucepan. Bring slowly to the boil, stirring until sugar has dissolved.

Lower heat and simmer for 3 minutes. Remove from heat and set aside to cool. When completely cold, pour syrup into a jug.

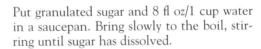

Add lime and lemon juice, mango purée, grenadine and rum. Stir well then chill. Just before serving, stir in tropical fruit juice and lemonade. Put into 2 large jugs filled with ice cubes. Decorate with orange and lime slices.

Makes 16 glasses.

Add lime juice, rum, ice cubes and 16 fl oz/ 2 cups water. Stir well then strain into glasses. Add a dash of Angostura bitters to each glass and sprinkle with nutmeg. Decorate with mint and lime slices and serve.

Serves 4.

SPICY OLIVES

1 lb green or black olives
1 sprig oregano
1 sprig thyme
1 teaspoon finely chopped fresh rosemary
2 bay leaves
1 teaspoon fennel seeds, bruised
1 teaspoon finely crushed cumin seeds
1 fresh chili, seeded and chopped
4 cloves garlic, crushed
olive oil to cover

DUKKAH

4 oz sesame seeds
2 oz shelled, skinned hazelnuts
2 oz coriander seeds
1 oz ground cumin
1 teaspoon dried thyme
1 teaspoon salt
½ teaspoon freshly ground black pepper
bread and olive oil, to serve

Heat a large heavy skillet over a medium heat. Add the sesame seeds and roast, stirring, until they are a light golden brown. Set aside to cool.

Using a small sharp knife, make a lengthways slit through to pit of each olive. Put olives into a bowl. Stir in oregano, thyme, rosemary, bay leaves, fennel seeds, cumin, chili and garlic.

Add the hazelnuts to the pan and roast, stirring until lightly and evenly browned. Set aside to cool. Add the coriander seeds to the pan and roast until they begin to pop. Set aside to cool. Place the sesame seeds, hazelnuts, coriander seeds, cumin, thyme, salt and pepper in a food processor or blender and process to a coarse powder.

Pack olive mixture into a screw-top or preserving jar. Pour over sufficient oil to cover, close the lid and leave for at least 3 days, shaking jar occasionally, before using.

Serves 6.

Transfer the dukkah to a serving bowl. To serve, dip a piece of bread into the olive oil and then into the dukkah mixture.

Serves 6.

Note: Take care not to over-grind the nuts and seeds otherwise they will release their oils and form a paste. Dukkah can be made in large quantities and stored in an airtight container.

SESAME-HERB LABNA BALLS

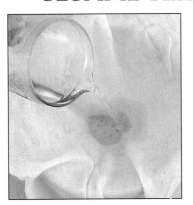

18 fl oz/2¼ cups live cows' or goats' milk yogurt
a little cream or crème fraîche, optional
1 teaspoon salt
2 tablespoons sesame seeds
1 tablespoon chopped fresh parsley
1 tablespoon chopped fresh mint
vine leaves, to garnish

Place a non-reactive colander or sieve over a bowl. Place a large double square of cheesecloth in the colander and pour boiling water through, to scald it. Pour off the water.

Pour the yogurt into the cheesecloth square. Add the cream or crème fraîche, if using. Draw up the sides and corners of the cheesecloth and tie with string. Hang the cheesecloth bag over the bowl and leave in a cool place overnight. Tip the curds into a bowl and stir in the salt. Return to the cheesecloth and hang over the bowl again for several more hours. Roll the cheese into balls and chill for 1 hour.

Heat a skillet and add the sesame seeds. Heat until golden brown, stirring frequently. Transfer to a plate and leave to cool. On a plate, mix together the chopped parsley and mint. Roll half the balls in the sesame seeds and half in the herbs. Garnish with vine leaves and serve with pitta bread.

Serves 4.

Variation: Instead of rolling the mixture into balls, serve with olive oil drizzled over.

STUFFED CELERY

4 large sticks celery, cut diagonally into 5 pieces
celery leaves, to garnish
FILLING:
2oz/½ cup pine nuts
2 oz cilantro leaves
1 plump clove garlic, crushed
2oz/½ cup freshly grated Parmesan cheese
2 tablespoons olive oil
freshly ground black pepper

To make filling, preheat broiler. Spread pine nuts on a baking sheet and toast lightly, stirring frequently. Leave to cool then chop finely. With a pestle and mortar, crushed toasted nuts, cilantro and garlic together to a nubbly texture. Work in Parmesan then oil. Season to taste with pepper.

Divide filling among celery pieces. Garnish with celery leaves and serve.

Makes 20.

STUFFED FRESH DATES

20 fresh dates
4 oz/½ cup cream cheese
1 oz/¼ cup pistachio nuts, finely chopped
1 tablespoon chopped stem ginger
1 tablespoon chopped fresh mint
salt and freshly ground black pepper
small mint leaves, to garnish

ORIENTAL CRACKERS

½ red bell pepper, deseeded and chopped
½ yellow bell pepper, deseeded and chopped
2 teaspoons grated fresh root ginger
2 tablespoons toasted sesame seeds
2 tablespoons sesame oil
2 tablespoons light soy sauce
few drops of chili sauce
40 prawn crackers

With the point of a small sharp knife, cut a slit along length of each date. Ease out the pits.

In a bowl, mix chopped peppers, ginger, sesame seeds, sesame oil and soy sauce together. Season with chili sauce to taste. Cover and keep cool for up to 4 hours.

In a bowl, mix together remaining ingredients, except garnish. Fill dates with a little cheese mixture. Chill for 1 hour. Garnish with mint leaves and serve.

Makes 20.

Transfer pepper mixture to a cool serving bowl. Stand bowl on a serving plate and surround with prawn crackers.

Makes 40.

CAMEMBERT BAKED IN A BOX

1 whole ripe but reasonably firm Camembert, in a box
1 clove garlic, halved
a little fruity white wine
grissini and/or crudités, to serve

TUNA CROSTINI

24 slices from thin French loaf
oil from jar of sun-dried tomatoes in oil or virgin olive oil for brushing
7 oz can tuna in brine, drained
2 tablespoons lemon mayonnaise
4 sun-dried tomatoes in oil, drained and finely chopped
2 tablespoons chopped fresh basil
2 tablespoons chopped fresh flat-leaf parsley
squeeze of lemon juice, to taste
salt and freshly ground black pepper
TO GARNISH:
coarsely chopped capers
sliced black olives

Preheat oven to 400F (200C). Remove cheese from box and discard the wrapping. Return cheese to box. Rub cut sides of garlic over top of cheese. With a sharp knife, slice top off Camembert then replace it on top of cheese.

Preheat oven to 350F (180C). Brush both sides of bread with oil. Place slices on a baking sheet and bake for about 10 minutes until pale golden brown. Cool on a wire rack.

Pierce 6 holes in top of cheese with a skewer and trickle in a few drops of wine. Replace lid of box. Bake cheese for 25-30 minutes, or until hot and bubbling. Remove box lid and top slice of cheese. Place box of cheese on a plate and surround with grissini and/or crudités. Serve immediately while cheese is melted and runny.

Serves 6-8.

In a bowl, mix together tuna, mayonnaise, sun-dried tomatoes, basil and parsley. Add lemon juice, and salt and pepper to taste. Spread tuna mixture over crostini. Garnish some of the crostini with capers and some with black olives.

Makes 24.

SAVOURY PALMIERS

about 12 oz puff pastry, thawed if frozen
4-6 tablespoons anchoiade (anchovy paste)
2 tablespoons chopped fresh basil
freshly ground black pepper
vegetable oil, for greasing

FRUITY SAUSAGE BALLS

1 lb good quality, well-flavored sausages
9 oz/1½ cups pitted prunes
3½ oz/scant 1 cup hazelnuts, chopped
10 fl oz/1¼ cups chicken stock
3½ oz redcurrant jelly
lemon juice, to taste
salt and freshly ground black pepper

On a lightly floured surface, roll out pastry to a 8 × 10 in. rectangle. Chill for at least 30 minutes. Mix two-thirds of anchoiade with basil and pepper. Spread anchoiade mixture over pastry. Fold the 2 long sides over pastry to meet in center. Press flat.

Preheat oven to 350F (180C). Slit sausage skins and remove meat. Chop half prunes and mix with sausage meat and hazelnuts. Form into 20 small balls. Place on a baking sheet. Bake for 40 minutes.

Spread remaining anchoiade on top. Fold in half and press down firmly. Slice thinly. Grease baking sheets, and place slices cut-side up on baking sheets. Chill for 30 minutes. Preheat oven to 425 (220C). Bake palmiers for 10 minutes. Turn them over and bake for a further 4-5 minutes until golden. Cool slightly on a wire rack and serve warm.

Makes about 24.

In a blender, purée remaining prunes, the stock and redcurrant jelly. Add lemon juice, and salt and pepper to taste. Pour into a small saucepan and bring just to the boil. Transfer to a warm serving dish. Put sausage-meat balls on a warm serving plate and stand dish of sauce in center.

Makes 20.

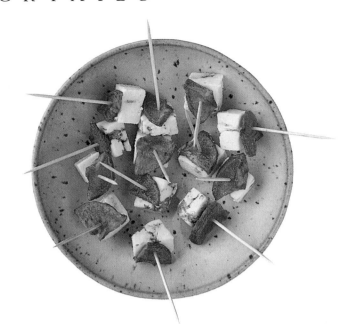

SMOKED SALMON ROLLS

8 oz/1 cup full-fat cream cheese
2½-3 tablespoons finely chopped fresh chives
about 1 tablespoon lemon juice
salt and freshly ground black pepper
about 9 oz sliced smoked salmon
lemon wedges (optional), to serve

Beat cheese, then beat in chives, lemon juice, a little salt and plenty of pepper. Cover and chill for about 4 hours.

Spread cheese mixture over slices of smoked salmon and roll up tightly. Chill. Using a sharp knife, cut rolls into ¼ in. slices. Arrange, cut-side up, on a cold serving platter. Add lemon wedges, if you like, and serve.

Makes about 70.

HOME-DRIED PEARS & CHEESE

2 large, ripe Comice or Williams pears, peeled, halved, cored and thickly sliced
12 oz Stilton or other blue cheese (not Danish or Roquefort), rind removed, cut into bite-size cubes

Preheat oven to 225F (110C). Spread pears on a jelly roll pan. Put in oven for 4-6 hours until flesh feels firm when pressed and, when cut, edges curl and are browned slightly. Cool completely.

Cut pear slices into bite-size pieces. Spear toothpicks with a piece of pear and a piece of cheese.

Makes about 36.

CHEESE & TOMATO KABOBS

8 oz pecorino cheese, cut into about ½ in. cubes
24 small cherry tomatoes
3 tablespoons extra virgin olive oil
1½ tablespoons lemon juice
1 tablespoon chopped fresh parsley
1 tablespoons chopped fresh oregano
freshly ground black pepper

PARMESAN CRISPS

melted butter for greasing
8 oz Parmesan cheese, freshly grated
2 tablespoons very finely chopped fresh chives

Thread cheese and cherry tomatoes alternately on to toothpicks. Put in a shallow, non-metallic dish.

Preheat oven to 400F (200C). Cover baking sheets with non-stick baking parchment. Sprinkle cheese in mounds on baking sheets and flatten slightly with a fork to 2 in. rounds.

Whisk together olive oil, lemon juice, fresh herbs and plenty of coarsely ground black pepper. Pour over kabobs, and turn them to coat in dressing; cover and marinate in the refrigerator for 2 hours.

Makes 24.

Bake for 2½ minutes. Sprinkle Parmesan rounds with chives and bake for a further 30 seconds. Remove Parmesan rounds from oven. Leave for 2 minutes to become crisp. Using a metal palette knife, transfer to a wire rack to cool.

Makes about 16.

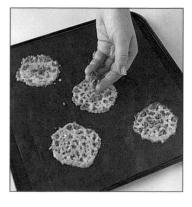

STILTON WITH WALNUT BISCUITS

8 oz Stilton without rind or other blue cheese, crumbled
small bunch of fresh flat-leaf parsley, finely chopped
4 sticks celery, finely chopped
freshly ground black pepper
flat-leaf parsley leaves (optional), to garnish
COOKIES:
1 oz/¼ cup walnut halves
4 oz/½ cup usweet butter, chopped
8 oz/2 cups all-purpose flour

Using a fork, mash cheese with parsley, celery and black pepper. Cover and chill. To make cookies, preheat broiler. Spread walnuts on a baking sheet and toast lightly, stirring nuts frequently. Leave to cool, then chop nuts. Rub butter into flour and black pepper until mixture resembles fine breadcrumbs. Stir in nuts. Form into a dough with 3-4 tablespoons water. Knead lightly on a lightly floured surface. Cover and chill for 30 minutes.

Preheat oven to 350F (180C). Grease baking sheets. On a lightly floured surface, roll out dough until thin. Use a 1½ in. cutter to cut into rounds. Re-roll trimmings as necessary. Transfer to baking sheets and bake for 10-15 minutes, or until browned. Remove to a wire rack to cool. Serve cookies topped with Stilton mixture, and garnished with parsley, if you like.

Makes about 80.

STUFFED CHERRY TOMATOES

30 cherry tomatoes
1 oz/2 tablespoons sweet butter
4 eggs, lightly beaten
2 tablespoons heavy cream
1 tablespoon finely chopped fresh dill
1 tablespoon finely chopped green olives
3 tablespoons freshly grated pecorino or Parmesan cheese
salt and freshly ground black pepper
sprigs of dill, to garnish

Slice off tops of tomatoes. Using a melon baller or small teaspoon, carefully scoop out insides of tomatoes; take care not to pierce skin. (Use tops and tomato flesh in sauces or soups.) Stand tomatoes upside down on paper towels. Melt butter in a non-stick saucepan. Add eggs and stir over a low heat for 1 minute. Add cream and cook, stirring, until only very lightly cooked. Remove from heat and stir in dill, olives and one-third of cheese. Season with salt and pepper.

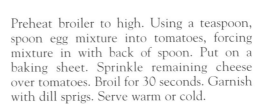

Preheat broiler to high. Using a teaspoon, spoon egg mixture into tomatoes, forcing mixture in with back of spoon. Put on a baking sheet. Sprinkle remaining cheese over tomatoes. Broil for 30 seconds. Garnish with dill sprigs. Serve warm or cold.

Makes 30.

CREAMY CHEESE PUFFS

1 oz/2 tablespoons butter
2 cloves garlic, crushed and finely chopped
4 oz/½ cup mascarpone cheese
2 teaspoons prepared English mustard
salt and freshly ground black pepper
6 tablespoons freshly grated Parmesan cheese
12 oz puff pastry, thawed, if frozen
1 egg, beaten

Melt butter in a small saucepan, add garlic and cook over a medium heat until softened and golden. Leave until cooled but not set. Place mascarpone cheese in a large bowl, add the mustard, salt and pepper, and 4 tablespoons of Parmesan cheese. Strain in melted butter and beat together. On a lightly floured surface, roll out pastry to 14 × 9 in.

Cut pastry into 4 strips lengthwise; cut each strip into 6. Put a heaped teaspoonful of cheese mixture in center of 12 pieces. Brush pastry edges with beaten egg. Put a piece of pastry on top and press edges together firmly to seal. Transfer to a baking sheet. Brush top of puffs with egg and sprinkle with remaining Parmesan. Chill for 30 minutes. Preheat oven to 425F (220C). Bake for 10-15 minutes, or until puffed and golden. Serve straight away.

Makes 12.

PORK NUGGETS

1¼ lb boneless lean pork, cut into 1 in. cubes
1 oz cilantro leaves
3 cloves garlic, peeled
1¼ in. piece fresh root ginger, sliced
1 lemon grass stalk, outer leaves removed
grated rind of 1 lime
large bunch of scallions
2 large fresh red chilies, deseeded
2 tablespoons soy sauce
2 tablespoons clear honey
2 tablespoons white wine vinegar
2 tablespoons Thai fish sauce
2 tablespoons sesame oil
14 fl oz can coconut milk
lime wedges, to serve

Put pork in a shallow non-metallic dish. Place half the cilantro, the garlic, ginger, 1¼ in. lemon grass, lime rind, and remaining ingredients except coconut milk in a blender and process finely. Scrape over pork and stir pork to coat thoroughly. Cover and refrigerate overnight. Remove pork from marinade; thread 2 cubes of pork on each wooden toothpick. Reserve marinade.

Preheat broiler. Broil pork nuggets for 4-5 minutes a side, brushing occasionally with some of the marinade. Meanwhile, scrape remaining marinade into a skillet, add coconut milk and remaining lemon grass. Boil briskly until thick. Discard lemon grass. Chop remaining cilantro and add to sauce with any remaining marinade. Serve hot with pork, accompanied by lime wedges.

Makes about 30.

INDEX

INDEX

INDEX

INDEX